Starting and Operating a Business in Colorado

A Step-by-Step Guide

By Michael D. Jenkins,
Joan D. Ringel and Greg Romberg

The Oasis Press® / PSI Research
Grants Pass, Oregon

92 AA

Published by The Oasis Press®

This publication is designed to provide accurate and authoritative information
in regard to the subject matter covered. It is sold with the understanding that the
publisher is not engaged in rendering legal, accounting, or other professional
service. If legal advice or other expert assistance is required, the services of a
competent professional person should be sought.

> — *from a declaration of principles jointly adopted by a committee of
> the American Bar Association and a committee of publishers.*

The author of chapters 1–10 of the *Starting and Operating a Business* series is
Michael D. Jenkins. The authors of the state chapter of *Starting and Operating
a Business in Colorado* are Joan D. Ringel and Greg Romberg.

Managing Editor: Vickie Reierson
Editorial Assistance: Melody Joachims and Debbie Johnson
Format Design & Typography: Constance C. Dickinson
Assistant Typographer: Jan Olsson
Administrative Editor: Rosanno Alejandro

Please direct any comments, questions, or suggestions regarding this book to
The Oasis Press®/PSI Research:

Editorial Department
300 North Valley Drive
Grants Pass, OR 97526
(503) 479-9464
(800) 228-2275

Library of Congress Catalog Card Number: 80-83053

ISBN 1-55571-114-6 (paperback)
ISBN 0-916378-52-7 (binder)

Printed in the United States of America
Third edition 10 9 8 7 6 5 4 3 2 1 0   Revision Code: 92AA

Printed on recycled paper when available.

Table of Contents

Part IV – State Laws & Related Resources

Forms and Worksheets in this Book

What's New

This new update of chapters 1–10 features a number of major additions, including new sections on emerging trends and issues, environmental laws, and the Americans with Disabilities Act. You will also find changes in current federal tax rates, legislation, and credits. To help you identify the most significant changes and additions to the text, review the list below. This list gives you the chapter–section number where you will find the specific discussions.

- New section on the requirements imposed by the Americans with Disabilities Act – 5.11
- A review of sexual harassment and its definition – 5.8
- A new section and review of environmental laws that affect your business including information on the Comprehensive Environmental Response Compensation and Recovery Act (CERCLA) and the Resource Conservation and Recovery Act (RCRA) – 9.9, 9.14
- A change in how home office expenses are reported – 8.14
- A simplification of the FUTA tax return for small employers – 5.3
- Several types of proposed legislation that will affect many businesses – 9.14
- A new legal form of business organization: the limited liability company – 2.1
- A new exemption from federal wage-hour laws for some small businesses – 5.7
- A new deduction for S corporations regarding medical insurance – 2.4
- A change in requirements for paying estimated corporate taxes – 4.6
- New exemption requirements for outside salespersons – 5.7
- Several fringe benefit plans, including 401(k) plans gain popularity – 8.3
- New information on equal credit opportunity laws – 9.10
- How to avoid having independent contractors treated as employees for tax purposes – 9.11
- More background on the Foreign Direct Investment and International Financial Data Improvements Act of 1990 – 9.13
- A new section on emerging trends and issues that may affect and influence your business – 9.14
- New toll-free hotlines for information and help from federal agencies – 10.3
- Changes in corporate income tax rates limiting some of the tax reasons for incorporating – 2.4

About the Author

The author of chapters 1–10 of the entire *Starting and Operating a Business* series, is Michael D. Jenkins. Mr. Jenkins, an attorney at law and a certified public accountant, is a graduate of Harvard Law School. He has worked in Los Angeles and San Francisco as an accountant and as an attorney with a prominent San Francisco firm well-known in the venture capital arena. He is a member of the State Bar of California, the American Bar Association, the American Institute of Certified Public Accountants, and the California Society of Certified Public Accountants.

How to Use this Book

0.1 Getting the Most Out of this Book

To most effectively use this book, become acquainted with the many helpful features it provides. Remember that each edition is updated annually to provide you with the most current information available. To find the most recent changes made to federal laws in chapters 1–10, refer to the What's New page. For similar state information, refer to the Notes page, which immediately precedes Chapter 11.

0.2 Numbered Section Heads Correspond to Table of Contents and Index

Text

Discussions range from explaining how to start and operate your business to examining such practical issues as insurance, marketing, cashflow management, internal financial controls, and much more. This book also explains federal and state government requirements and tax laws, as well as a number of emerging trends and issues your business may face.

Topics Noted in Margins

To make the information in this workbook easily accessible to busy people, the primary topics discussed within each numbered section are identified by "sideheads" in the margin beside the text.

Smaller Heads for Subtopics

When subsections of primary topics are discussed, the sideheads are slightly smaller.

Lists

- This small bullet helps you easily locate lists of requirements, things to do, and aspects of a particular subject or law.

Checklists

☐ Small boxes encourage you to enter a check, so that you can clearly see those items you've considered and dealt with—and those left to do.

Worksheets

Where the Action Begins

A number of worksheets are provided for you to answer questions and fill in numbers that form the basis for action plans, self-evaluation, budgeting, personnel policies, marketing feasibility studies, and the like.

The worksheets are set apart by boxes to clearly show where your interaction is required, to focus your thoughts, to record information, and to create the plans and reports that will help you establish and guide your business.

Resources

Sources and Data

Resources are set in tabular form to highlight the many agencies and companies listed to assist you.	**Contacts** Addresses Phone Numbers (listed in directory style)

Table of Contents

The detailed Table of Contents will help you quickly find any specific section of the book you wish to refer to. The first digit of the chapter–section number indicates the chapter, followed by a period and the section number.

Footnotes

The footnotes follow each chapter and are provided to assist you in accessing specific statutes, cases, regulations, and publications and to use this book as a starting place for legal research.

Index

The subject-matter index, organized alphabetically with cross-referenced entries, provides an exhaustive list of the topics, indexed not only by the terms actually used in the entries but also by various other terms you might think of instead. The Index is referenced by the chapter–section number, not by page number, to help you find the corresponding discussion in the text.

Related Resources

At the back of this book, you'll find a compendium of additional resources that will save you valuable research time and money.

Appendix

The Appendix features a checklist of tax and various other major requirements for most businesses and a checklist of official government posters and notices required to be displayed by a business.

Forms

Since many business requirements depend on submitting specific forms to various government agencies, some samples of these forms are included for your reference and listed in the Table of Contents.

Post Cards

At the back of this book, you will also find post cards preaddressed to government agencies and other sources so you can request additional information, posters, and forms.

Preface

When I wrote the first edition of *Starting and Operating a Business in California* more than a decade ago, little did I know that its success would spawn a nationwide series. Back then, there was talk of small business declining and big business rising and only a few, if any, small business assistance centers were operating in the United States. There were even fewer "how-to" books available.

Today, however, there are Small Business Development Centers (SBDCs) and "one-stop" business permit offices in almost every state and, while state governments are cutting services left and right, states are expected to maintain or increase services in economic development and assistance to small businesses. Why the turnaround? States recognize how new and existing small businesses can strengthen their economies and provide jobs to their residents, and they are doing as much as possible to encourage business growth, expansion, and relocation.

According to *Time* magazine, an estimated 1.3 million businesses were started in 1991, up nearly 9% from 1980, despite the current recession. Researchers say this increase is mainly due to the fact that most people prefer working for themselves; both white and blue collar workers are being automated out of their jobs with larger companies; and the explosive growth of the "information society" is creating a favorable economic environment for the small, technically oriented firm.

By advising small and large businesses over the years — first as an economic and management consultant, then later as an attorney and more recently as a certified public accountant — I had always been keenly aware of the need for a single authoritative and practical guide that would serve people starting and operating a business in a particular state and their professional advisers.

While most bookstores featured many books that purported to advise the entrepreneur on how to become successful and rich by starting a business, conspicuously absent was a nuts-and-bolts guide that would help an entrepreneur through the maze of red tape at both the federal and state levels of government, as well as provide the basic steps and advice needed to get a business off the ground.

Thus, in 1980, when my friend and publisher, Emmett Ramey, approached me with the idea of writing a starting and operating a business book for the state of California, I was particularly receptive. His idea was to create an operating manual that would draw together — in a readable, usable, and nontechnical format — the practical facts of life a person needed to know when establishing a business in California. Once written, *Starting and Operating a Business in California* accomplished these goals by explaining in layperson's language many of the key financial, tax, and legal pitfalls, as well as planning options, an entrepreneur needed to know before and after embarking on a business venture. The California book's format consisted of chapters 1–10, which focused on general start-up information and federal laws and regulations, and Chapter 11, which focused on the state's laws and regulations.

The success of *Starting and Operating a Business in California* resulted in other state editions, and as of 1991, all 50 state editions, plus the District of Columbia, have been published. Each state chapter is updated annually, and chapters 1–10 are updated every January. These editions make up the 51-volume *Starting and Operating a Business* series.

So, if you want an up-to-date guide to the basic financial, legal, and tax ground rules that apply to most businesses operating in your state, the *Starting and Operating a Business* series has been designed with you in mind as a self-help tool. It is also intended to be a useful reference source to the attorney who has only a limited knowledge of business taxation and the basic regulatory requirements of a large number of federal, state, and local government agencies. Accountants will also find this series a useful resource for understanding the broad scope of government regulations that affect his or her small business clients.

While the *Starting and Operating a Business* books provide an authoritative discussion of many legal and tax matters regarding small business, they are not intended to be a substitute for professional legal or tax advice. On the contrary, they are designed to help you focus on key points to explore in greater depth with your attorney or accountant. By being better informed, you can use your professional advisers' time more efficiently.

Chapter 1 is designed to sharpen the focus of the decision process you typically go through while your new business is still in the idea stage.

Chapter 2 describes the various legal forms in which your business may be operated under — sole proprietorships, partnerships, corporations, and limited liability companies — and outlines the most significant advantages and disadvantages of each. Chapter 3 will prove helpful if you are considering buying an existing business or opening a franchise operation.

Chapters 4–7 describe the various tax authorities and other governmental agencies that most or all businesses must deal with. Chapter 8 describes in nontechnical terms a number of the major income tax benefits that you may be able to enjoy, while chapters 9 and 10 describe miscellaneous business pointers and sources of information that are made available to small businesses by government agencies and private institutions.

Chapter 11 addresses the areas covered in chapters 1–10 by focusing on how the state's laws and regulations deal with those areas. Each Chapter 11 of the series is designed to provide as much state-specific information as possible.

The publisher and I welcome your suggestions or constructive criticisms that may assist us in refining or expanding future editions.

Michael D. Jenkins

January 1992

Dedication

To America's entrepreneurs — tenacious, courageous men and women — whose contribution to the variety, richness, and quality of our lives is immeasurable.

Preliminary Considerations

Chapter 1

Making the Decision to Go into Business

Being boss doesn't make you right; it only makes you boss.

— Milton Metz

1.1 Introduction

Neither this book nor any other book can tell you whether or not you should take the plunge and go into business for yourself. That is a difficult decision that you alone must make.

Before you make this decision, however, there are a number of very basic questions you should first consider very thoroughly. This introductory chapter is designed to alert you to a number of key points you may not have considered yet, as well as assist you in dealing successfully with some of the initial problems you will face.

To get started in most kinds of new businesses, a major financial risk must be taken. Once you have committed yourself, it will not be a simple or easy thing to change your mind and back out.

In evaluating the risks, you should be aware that there is a high failure rate among new businesses. Nearly two out of every three new businesses fail within five years.[1] Year in and year out, statistics show that a very high percentage of those business failures result from poor management.

Poor or ineffective management is usually a lack of balanced experience and competence in three areas:

- Marketing strategies — This means knowing what kind of product or service to sell, how to target and reach your customers, and how to sell your product or service at a price that maximizes your profits.

- Technical ability — You must be able to get the work done and do it right, so you will have satisfied customers. If you are going into the auto repair business, for example, you better know a lot about how to keep autos running right, or you will not be in business very long.
- Financial knowledge — While you do not necessarily have to be a financial wizard, you do need to know how to plan and control your business' cash flow; raise or borrow the money you will need to start your business; and get through tight periods without being caught short of cash. A certain amount of financial sophistication is becoming more and more important in today's increasingly complex financial world, even for the small business owner.

If you are seriously deficient in one or more of these three critical areas, the odds of your business becoming one of the relatively few that succeeds are greatly reduced.

In addition, many other facts will influence the odds of your succeeding or failing in your own business. For example, the magazine *Canadian Business* reported on a survey conducted by Thorne Riddell, a large Canadian accounting firm, of 2,000 sole proprietorships started in Canada. In a follow-up survey three years later, they found four major factors that seemed to separate the winners from the losers. Besides these four factors, the study also determined an interesting fact about these particular businesses; and that is, only 25% of the surveyed firms with male owners survived, while 47% of the ones started by women were still around.

Keeping in mind that the Canadian economy is somewhat different from that of the United States, examine the four main factors below to help you gain an extra insight into successfully starting up your business.

Factor	Successful Firms	Failures
Degree of preparation	Spent 6 to 10 months to research and prepare for their ventures.	Spent less than 4 months to prepare for start up.
Use of advisers	90% utilized professional advisers, such as lawyers and accountants, in starting up.	Only 25% sought professional help at an early stage.
Business education, reading	Almost 70% had taken business-related courses before starting business and regularly read business books and magazines.	Only 10% had attended business courses or now took time to read business material.
Expectations of income	More than half said they started with modest expectations and were prepared to be patient for signs of success.	36% said they fully expected to make barrels of money within 3 years. The anticipated level of annual earnings they most often quoted was more than 3 times the income level typically quoted by those in the successful category.[2]

More recent research, using the much larger U.S. Small Business Data Base, indicates that failure rates are lower than commonly believed and reveals a tie between growing firms — defined as those adding at least one job every two years — and success. In this study of 458,000 firms, of those businesses which did not add at least one job every two years, about 30% failed within two years after start up, and a total of 73% had failed after six years.

Firms that grew by at least one job every 24 months, however, experienced a much greater survival rate; only 8% closed within two years, and only 34% after six years.[3] Although the ability of a firm to generate jobs is not the sole factor in reducing the failure rate, it often increases the firm's flexibility in weathering periods of economic contraction.[4]

This chapter engages you in the process of realistically evaluating your entrepreneurial strengths and weaknesses. It is also intended to cause you to focus on some of the typical start-up problems and choices you are likely to face, as well as assist you in dealing effectively and rationally with those issues.

Where worksheets are provided, feel free to pick up a pencil and write in your responses. Often, the simple process of writing down your thoughts on specific problem areas may provide significant new insights that may suddenly seem terribly obvious to you once you have raised them to the level of conscious thought.

1.2 Advantages and Disadvantages of Owning Your Own Business

Have you realistically considered both the advantages and the disadvantages of owning and operating your own business? If not, the time to do so is before, not after, you have committed yourself.

Advantages

If you are actively considering going into business for yourself, you most likely have already thought about the potential advantages, such as:

- Being your own boss and not having to report to a superior;
- Having the independence and power to make your own business decisions, for better or for worse;
- Direct contact with customers, employees, suppliers, and others;
- The personal satisfaction and sense of achievement that comes with being a success, plus the recognition that goes with it;
- The opportunity to create substantial wealth and job security for yourself;
- The opportunity to be creative, to develop your own idea, product, or service;

- The chance to make a living doing something you truly enjoy; and
- Doing something that contributes to others, whether it be providing an excellent product or service, providing employment, paying dividends to stockholders, or doing something else that is useful or that creates value.

Disadvantages

If you are like most people, you may not have thought much about the downside of going into business; however, awareness of the potential disadvantages should not discourage you from your goal of going into business for yourself, if you have a strong commitment to that goal.

Seriously consider whether you and your family are prepared to handle these disadvantages inherent in being an entrepreneur:

- In a lot of ways, you are still not your own boss. Instead of having one boss, you will now have many — your customers, the government agencies to whom you must report, and, in some cases, your key suppliers.
- There is a large financial risk. The failure rate is high in new businesses, and you may lose not only your own money but also that of your friends and relatives who may have bankrolled you.
- The hours are long and hard. When you start your business, you will no longer be working 9 to 5. Count on working 10- to 12- or even 15-hour days, often six or seven days a week.
- You will not have much spare time for family or social life. And you can forget about taking any long vacations for the first few years, since the business is unlikely to run itself without your presence for any great length of time.
- Your income may not be steady like a salary. You may make more or less than you could working for someone else, but in either case, your income may fluctuate up and down from month to month.
- The buck stops with you. If a problem arises, there is no boss you can take it to and say: "What do we do about this?" You are the boss and all the responsibility is yours. If anything goes wrong, the cost comes out of your pocket.
- You may be stuck for years doing work you do not like. Unlike an employee, you cannot simply quit and look for a better job. It may take you years to sell the business or find some other way to get out of it without a major financial loss.
- As a business grows, the amount of activity not associated with the primary business objective will increase. You will spend more time on personnel, administrative, and legal matters and less doing what you may have wanted most to do in your business.
- Increasing legislation and litigation make owning a business very risky. You can work a lifetime to build a business only to have it lost because of a lawsuit or a new law or regulation.

1.3 Typical Characteristics of the Successful Entrepreneur

A good deal is known about what it takes to be a successful entrepreneur. For the most part, it seems that the one overriding factor is a tremendous need to achieve. In short, attitude seems to have almost everything to do with success in business, while factors, such as intelligence, education, physical appearance, and a pleasing personality, are much less important. Characteristics of typical successful entrepreneurs include:

- An overpowering need to achieve, as opposed to a need to be liked, or to exercise power; the form in which different individuals measure their achievement varies widely, ranging from amassing wealth to building a larger organization to creating a better mousetrap than anyone else;
- The trait of following through on a commitment, not quitting half-way through when the going gets tough: in short, perseverance;
- A positive mental attitude or the ability to remain optimistic in new and unfamiliar situations, which essentially grows out of being self-confident about one's abilities;
- Objectivity — the ability to accurately weigh and assess risks associated with a particular course of action, as well as being realistic about one's own abilities and limitations;
- A respectful attitude toward money, but a tendency to look upon money as a means for accomplishing things, or a way of keeping score in the game of business, rather than as a thing to be sought as an end in itself;
- The tendency to anticipate developments and to make things happen rather than constantly reacting to problems as they arise;
- Resourcefulness — the ability to solve unique problems in unique ways and to be able to handle things that come up for which the entrepreneur has no previous experience to rely on as a guide;
- Good personal relations skills — the characteristics of being cheerful and cooperative, and usually getting along well with, without necessarily being close to, employees and associates;
- Well-developed communication skills, both in oral and written presentations; and
- Well-rounded technical knowledge with emphasis on the knowledge about the physical process of producing goods and services.

How do your personal characteristics stack up against the foregoing profile of the typical successful entrepreneur? If that profile doesn't sound very much like you, maybe you had better give some long, hard thought as to whether you are cut out for making it as a business owner.

Running a business is not like working for someone else. No one is there to tell you what to do when something goes wrong. You are responsible for everything.

Are you capable of handling that kind of total responsibility? Are you a self-starter, capable of planning, organizing, and carrying out projects on your own? If not, you may find that starting and running a successful business is not for you.

Running a business demands a great deal in the way of initiative, hard work, self-discipline, and resourcefulness. On the other hand, solving the problems that arise from day to day and making it all work out can be a source of immense satisfaction, as well as be financially rewarding.

Before reading further, get a pencil and complete Worksheet 1, which is a useful questionnaire that may help you to get a better idea of your suitability for playing the role of entrepreneur in the real world.

Worksheet 1
Self-evaluation Checklist for Going into Business

Under each question, check the answer that says what you feel or comes closest to it. Be honest with yourself.

Are you a self-starter?

☐ I do things on my own. Nobody has to tell me to get going.

☐ If someone gets me started, I keep going all right.

☐ Easy does it. I don't put myself out until I have to.

How do you feel about other people?

☐ I like people. I can get along with just about anybody.

☐ I have plenty of friends; I don't need anyone else.

☐ Most people irritate me.

Can you lead others?

☐ I can get most people to go along when I start something.

☐ I can give the orders if someone tells me what we should do.

☐ I let someone else get things moving; then I go along if I feel like it.

Can you take responsibility?

☐ I like to take charge of things and see them through.

☐ I'll take over if I have to, but I'd rather let someone else be responsible.

☐ There's always some eager beaver around wanting to show how smart she is. I say let her.

How good of an organizer are you?

☐ I like to have a plan before I start. I'm usually the one to get things lined up when the group wants to do something.

☐ I do all right unless things get too confusing; then I quit.

☐ Just when I'm all set, something comes along and presents too many problems, so I just take things as they come.

How good of a worker are you?

☐ I can keep going as long as I need to. I don't mind working hard for something I want.

☐ I'll work hard for a while, but when I've had enough, that's it.

☐ I can't see that hard work gets me anywhere.

Can you make decisions?

☐ I can make up my mind in a hurry if I have to and it usually turns out okay, too.

☐ I can, if I have plenty of time. If I have to make up my mind fast, I think later I should have decided the other way.

☐ I don't like to be the one who has to decide things.

Can people trust what you say?

☐ You bet they can. I don't say things I don't mean.

☐ I try to be on the level most of the time, but sometimes I just say what's easiest.

☐ Why bother if the other fellow doesn't know the difference?

Can you stick with it?

☐ If I make up my mind to do something, I don't let anything stop me.

☐ I usually finish what I start if it goes well.

☐ If it doesn't go right away, I quit. Why beat my brains out?

How good is your health?

☐ I never run down.

☐ I have enough energy for most things I want to do.

☐ I run out of energy sooner than most of my friends seem to.

Count the checks you made.

How many checks are there beside the first answer to each question? _____

How many checks are there beside the second answer to each question? _____

How many checks are there beside the third answer to each question? _____

If most of your checks are beside the first answers, you probably have what it takes to run a business. If not, you're likely to have more trouble than you can handle by yourself. Better find a partner who is strong on the points you're weak on. If many checks are beside the third answer, not even a good partner will be able to shore you up.

Source: U.S. Small Business Administration.

1.4 Knowing Your Market

One of the most important questions you should ask yourself is whether you feel that you know and understand the market for the particular kind of products or services you intend to sell. Do you know who your competition is and whether the particular market you intend to appeal to is large enough for both you and the existing competition? Also, how will your products or services measure up against those of your competitors in terms of quality and price?

If your product or service is something new or unusual, you need to have a sense of whether you will be selling an item that is wanted and needed in the marketplace. Or, even if you intend to sell a product or service that you know there is a need for, you should be satisfied in your own mind that you are going to be making it available at the right place at the right time. Few sights are sadder than the boarded-up mom-and-pop store or restaurant — in which the owners have sunk their life savings — that never got off the ground for some obvious reason, such as lack of visibility from the street, lack of substantial foot traffic by its doors, or some other fatal flaw that the inexperienced owners overlooked.

To succeed, you must find the right business opportunity. If you do not have a clear idea of what business you want to go into and where you want to operate it, you will need to do some intelligent investigation of all possible opportunities that might be suitable for you. If you already have a concept of what you want to do, you will still need to do a great deal of investigating to make sure it is as good an opportunity as it appears to be. In either case, a lot of initial research and footwork is going to be advisable, unless you want to close your eyes and indulge in wishful thinking. As the Canadian study mentioned earlier in this chapter indicated, most of the successful new ventures surveyed had gotten started only after 6 to 10 months of careful investigation and planning.

Determining Market Feasibility

In other words, to quote a well-known brokerage firm: "Investigate before you invest." This often entails doing your own marketing feasibility study before committing yourself to opening a new business. On the other hand, if you have several thousand dollars to spend and a well-defined idea of what it is you want to do, you can hire a professional economist or marketing consultant to do a feasibility study. In every major city, there are several firms that can do a thorough marketing and demographic study for you. Such a feasibility study can be quite valuable, but it will also be fairly expensive. Most people starting a new business probably choose do their own marketing feasibility study.

When choosing a business to go into, keep these thoughts in mind:

- If you see that a particular business is doing quite well and you want to go in and compete head-to-head with it, don't make the mistake of adopting a me-too approach and going in with the assumption that you can take away a lot of their business by competing on a price basis. Other than price, you better have a lot of good reasons why you think another business' customers will switch over to you. Other good reasons could include a distinctly better product, service, or location.

- Keep your eyes open for developing social, economic, and technological trends that will create new markets that you can move into at an early stage. It will help if you are a voracious reader of magazines such as *Time*, *Newsweek* (social trends); *Forbes*, *Business Week* (economic trends); or *Omni* or *Discover* (technological innovations).

An example of how observing social trends can translate into profits — in this instance stock market profits — is the case of an investment analyst in the 60s who noticed the trend toward mini-skirts and correctly anticipated that the spread of mini-skirts among women would create a boom market for panty hose. The analyst made a killing by buying stocks of panty hose makers.

So how do you go about analyzing the market for your product or service once you have focused on a particular business you might want to start? Worksheet 2 will help you in pinpointing the kind of information you need to develop to satisfy yourself that a good market exists for whatever it is you are planning to sell. Before you read any further, take out a pencil and spend some time writing down your responses to each of the items in Worksheet 2.

Worksheet 2
Marketing Feasibility Study Checklist for Your Product or Service

---

Your Product

Describe briefly the nature of the product or service you will offer: _____

_____

_____

Most products or services have a life cycle, beginning with very rapid growth in the introductory stage, which slows down in the maturity stage, flattens out in the saturation stage, and finally begins shrinking in the declining stage. Which stage of its market cycle do you believe your product or service is in?

☐ introductory (high growth)   ☐ saturation (little or no growth)

☐ maturity (slower growth)   ☐ declining (negative growth in demand)

If you believe your product is in one of the earlier, faster growing stages of its life cycle, what edge do you believe your product will have over similar products that may be introduced by new competitors who may come into the field? ____

_____

_____

_____

(Continued)

(Continued)

If you are entering at a fairly late stage of the product marketing cycle, why is it you believe that you can succeed in taking away others' market share with your product? _____

_____

_____

How is your product different in terms of quality and price from what is already on the market? _____

_____

_____

Is there good reason to believe that your customers will recognize the difference? _____ If so, why? _____

_____

_____

What is different about your marketing strategy or distribution strategy that will enable your product or service to succeed in a market where there is little, if any, growth? _____

_____

_____

Your Customers

Not everyone is a potential customer. Certain age groups, income levels, geographic areas, ethnic groups, and educational levels will be more likely than others to be your customers. You need to focus on who will need your product and be most likely to buy it and then where to locate your business or how to structure your marketing approach to reach those segments of the market that you are most interested in reaching. Spell out below, as clearly as you can, who your customers are most likely to be.

The particular area from which I will be able to draw most of my customers is: _____

_____

_____

In addition, I should draw a significant number of customers from the following area or areas: _____

_____

_____

My plan or strategy for reaching potential customers in the above areas can be summarized as follows: _____

_____

_____

The chief market for my product, in terms of age and sex groups, should be among the following persons (describe):

_____

_____

_____

In terms of income groups, my particular product should appeal primarily to people in the following income levels:

☐ Under $25,000 a year household income

☐ $25,000 – $35,000 a year

☐ $35,000 – $50,000 a year

☐ $50,000 – $75,000 a year

☐ $75,000 – $100,000 a year

☐ More than $100,000 a year

My product or service is likely to be more in demand by certain social, cultural, and ethnic groups than others. The groups that are most likely to be customers, if any, are: _____

_____

_____

The groups that are least likely to be customers are: _____

_____

_____

Your Competition

Even though you may have done a great job in pinpointing and studying your market segment, the job isn't done until you have considered your competition.

Main competitors in my market area are (list firms by name):

(1) _____

(2) _____

(3) _____

(4) _____

(5) _____

(6) _____

Based on my market research of statistical data, such as *Sales Marketing and Management Magazine*, the amount of buying power per business represented in my area is $_____.

If I can generate that amount of sales, it: will ☐, will not ☐ be sufficient for me to operate successfully.

Five reasons why customers would buy from me rather than my competitors are:

(1) _____

(2) _____

(3) _____

(4) _____

(5) _____

(Continued)

(Continued)

Five weaknesses my business will have, in comparison to my competitors, are:

(1) _____

(2) _____

(3) _____

(4) _____

(5) _____

To overcome these weaknesses, I will: _____

_____

_____

Market Data Resources

Once you have identified your most likely potential customers, you will need to find out how to locate your business or structure and to direct your advertising and promotional efforts to most efficiently reach them. Fortunately, there is a great deal of published data you can use if you need to do this type of research. One of the best sources is *Sales Marketing and Management Magazine*, which publishes *Survey of Buying Power* each year. This survey provides breakdowns in population, households, retail sales by type of business, and total purchasing dollars for each county in the United States and for cities with a population of more than 10,000. To request information on *Survey of Buying Power*, see Statistical Information in Section 10.4.

Another excellent source is the 1990 U.S. census data, which gives vast amounts of detailed information on the U.S. population and its buying habits by individual census tract. You may want to obtain a couple of useful pamphlets from your nearest U.S. Small Business Administration field office. Ask for the pamphlet entitled *Researching Your Market* for guidance on how to do your own marketing research and the pamphlet entitled *Choosing a Retail Location*.

Finding the Optimum Site

Even more important in your local community may be studies and future projections as to population and income trends that have been done by local groups, such as your local chamber of commerce or, in some areas, the local planning commission. If finding the optimum site to locate is important to your marketing effort, do the following:

- Talk to a knowledgeable person at your local chamber of commerce about business and other trends in the area where you intend to locate.
- Talk to a staff person at your local planning commission about census tract projections of future population growth, income trends, and

economic development in the area you are considering. Also, they (or some other local agency, such as a traffic or streets department) will usually have done traffic counts showing how many cars pass certain points every day. This information can be very useful if you are opening a retail business. Also, consult any trade association, which serves your business and may have available information tailored exactly to your needs.

For a complete guide to specifying, ranking, and evaluating the factors you must consider when choosing an optimum site for your new or relocating business, obtain a copy of *Company Relocation Handbook*. This handbook features a list of related reference publications and economic development organizations. Get your copy through your local book source, or:

The Oasis Press
(800) 228-2275

1.5 Knowing the Business

Do you have any experience in the area of business in which you will be engaged? Of course it is possible to learn while doing, but it helps a great deal to know the business before you start. Often the most successful businesses are started by people who have worked in a particular line of business for years and who finally decide that they know the ropes well enough to leave their employer and start their own similar operation.

It helps to have experience in the particular business you propose to enter, but in most cases, your experience working in some other line of business will also have considerable carryover value. If you have neither type of experience, you may find that you have a lot to learn once you commence.

A major management weakness that causes businesses to fail is the inability to get the job done, and do it right, on time, and efficiently enough to charge a competitive price for your product or service and still make a profit. For example, you may have done a lot of market research and decided that, with the tremendous proliferation of personal computers, a great business to go into is repairing small computers. You may be absolutely right, but unless you have the technical capability to do such repairs, or the ability to properly select and hire employees who can do the job, you had better look for some other kind of business to go into.

In many cases, if you know you lack the technical experience you need to open a particular kind of business, your best approach will be to get a job in that industry and work for someone else for a few years until you learn what you need to know. This may require a lot of patience, but it is definitely preferable to getting into a business you do not know well and losing your shirt in the process.

Worksheet 3
Estimated Cash Inflow from Sales for Year _____

Item: Month:					
Gross Sales for Month					
Less: Credit Sales Made					
Sub-total: Cash Sales					
Plus: Collections on Prior Credit Sales					
Less: Bad Debts*					
Total: Net Cash Flow from Monthly Sales					

* Consider using some percentage, say 1% or 2% of credit sale collections, to estimate your uncollectible debts.

1.6 Money

Can you afford to start a full-time business, if it will mean giving up your current employment and income? Many small businesses never really have a chance to succeed, because the owners run out of money before the business becomes a viable operation. As a result, the owners often wind up having to go back to work for someone else again, disappointed and broke.

You should carefully calculate and schedule out, in as much detail as possible, the income and expenses that you can reasonably expect for at least the first year of operation, as well as your living expenses and a reserve for emergencies.

Be sure that you have enough money to last until the business reaches the point where you expect to make enough profit to live on.

Remember that there are a lot of expenses involved in starting up almost any kind of business and that most businesses start out operating in the red for a time.

Completing worksheets 3 through 5 will help you plan your cash flow for the crucial first year of business. Worksheet 3 will help you to project your monthly sales revenue in terms of actual cash to be received. Worksheet 4 projects your monthly operating expenses for the first year of business, plus one-time, start-up expenses. Worksheet 5 is a schedule of your estimated personal living expenses during the first year.

Once you have completed worksheets 3 through 5, enter the bottom line figures from each on Worksheet 6, which is a summary of your cash needs. This will show you how much cash you will have to put into the business each month — and on a cumulative basis — during the first

							Annual Totals

year of business. Once you have completed Worksheet 6, you will have a pretty good handle on how much money it's going to take you to get the business started and approximately when you will need it.

If, under your most realistic projections, you are still running a deficit in cash flow each month at the end of the first year, you may want to do a similar projection out into the second year of operation.

If it appears that you will need to borrow or raise money to keep the business operating until it gets into the black, find out well in advance whether and how much you will be able to raise. If you plan to borrow, do you know how to put together a strong presentation to demonstrate to the prospective lender how you will be able to repay the loan? If not, see Section 9.7 and Chapter 10 for sources of information and help in obtaining financing for a small business.

For help in putting together an impressive loan application package, you may want to obtain a copy of *The Loan Package*, which will help you identify essential financial information for a loan, analyze your cash needs, and focus on the direction of your company. *The Loan Package* is available through your local book source or the toll-free number below.

Affordable and easy-to-use software programs that are helpful for small businesses have been developed by PSI Successful Business Software. Many of the programs, such as *Financial Templates for Small Business* or *Small Business Expert*, complement this *Starting and Operating a Business* book.

PSI Successful Business Software
(800) 228-2275

Worksheet 4
Estimated Business Cash Outlays for Year _____

Item: Month:					
Monthly Expenses					
Rent					
Salaries and wages (except owner)					
Payroll taxes					
Advertising and promotion					
Insurance					
Federal estimated income tax					
State estimated income tax					
Owner's FICA or SE tax					
Telephone and utilities					
Inventory replacement purchase					
Interest on loans					
Maintenance					
Legal and accounting fees					
Office supplies					
Delivery expense					
Miscellaneous					
One-time Expenses					
Fixtures and equipment					
Decorating and remodeling					
Initial stock of inventory					
Utility and lease deposits					
Licenses and permits					
Other					
Total Expenses for Month					
Plus: Loan principal payment					
Less: Purchases on credit					
Plus: Payment on prior credit					
Net Monthly Cash Outlay					

							Annual Totals

Worksheet 5
Estimated Personal and Living Expenses for Year _____

Item: Month:					
Regular Payments					
Rent or house payment					
Property taxes					
Condo owner's dues					
Car payments					
Furniture and appliance payments					
Loan payments					
Health insurance					
Other insurance					
Household Expenses					
Food – restaurants					
Food – at home					
Telephone and utilities					
Water					
Personal Expenses					
Clothing and laundry					
Medical, dental, and drugs					
Education					
Dues and subscriptions					
Gifts and charity					
Gasoline and auto					
Entertainment and travel					
Miscellaneous spending					
Total Personal Expenses (Draw Required)					

							Annual Totals

Worksheet 6
Summary of Estimated Cash Requirements for Year _____

Item: Month:					
Net cash for month from sales – Worksheet 3					
Less: Net monthly cash outlay – Worksheet 4					
Subtotal: Net operating cash flow (or deficit)					
Less: Owner's draw for living & personal expenses – Worksheet 5					
Add: Money borrowed					
Add (or subtract): Equity capital paid in (or withdrawn) from the business					
Total: Net cash flow (or deficit) for month					
Cumulative* cash flow (or deficit)					

* Add this month's net cash flow to the previous month's cumulative total.

1.7 Signing a Lease

If you will need to lease space for your business location, have you located a suitable place that is available? If so, there are a number of critical points you need to consider before you sign a lease with a landlord.

Remember that a lease is a binding legal contract, and if you agree to pay rent of $1,000 a month for two years, you are on the hook for $24,000, unless you can sublease or assign the lease to someone else, which could be difficult or impossible to do, depending on the terms of the lease. Key points to consider include:

- What are the terms of the lease? Most businesses tend to start off by either growing rapidly or quickly folding. Thus, except in a retail or service business, you will probably be better off initially leasing on a month-to-month basis or for as short a lease term as you can get, such as three or six months, even if the monthly rent is higher than for a longer lease. You will already have enough financial problems if your business fails, without being saddled with a long-term lease obligation.

- Can you put up the kind of sign you must have on the building? A business like a restaurant can be devastated if the landlord doesn't permit a sign that is sufficiently visible to passersby.

- Will the landlord permit you to make necessary improvements and alterations to the leased premises?

							Annual Totals

- Will the local health department, fire and police departments, air pollution control authorities, and zoning rules permit operation of your particular type of business at the location you have chosen?
- Is your location in a high-crime area that will require expensive burglary insurance and security precautions?
- Is there enough parking nearby or good public transit access for customers?
- Is the location appropriate to the kind of business you will conduct? There is usually no need to locate a manufacturing operation in a busy, high-traffic area. On the other hand, retail businesses are usually heavily dependent on the number of people passing nearby on foot or by car.

For example, the Pillsbury Company reportedly selects its sites for Burger King fast food restaurants by looking for locations that have at least 16,000 cars passing by each day at an average speed of about 30 miles per hour.[5]

- Does the lease provide you with an option to renew — and at what rental price — after the initial term expires?
- If the lease is for more than just a few months, do you have the right to sublease or assign the lease? If so, under what conditions or restrictions?

1.8 Will You Hire Employees?

In certain kinds of businesses, during the initial start-up phases — and perhaps even afterwards — you may be able to operate without employees by either doing all your work yourself, with the help of family members, or by contracting out certain functions to independent outside contractors. To the extent you can do so, you will probably find your life is much simpler. Once you hire even one employee, you take on a great many responsibilities as an employer, over and above meeting a payroll every week or two.

This section reviews some of the legal restrictions on your hiring practices and provides you with a working outline of what you will need to consider in the way of personnel policies once your business reaches the point where you will have to hire employees. See Section 5.9 regarding U.S. Immigration Law restrictions on hiring.

Hiring Practices

Hiring personnel can be complicated because of the broad array of state and federal laws designed to prevent an employer from hiring on the basis of discriminatory factors, such as age, sex, race, or religion. Most of these laws affect all but the smallest employers, so you will have to be alert to most of these rules to avoid even the appearance of discrimination in your hiring practices.

While anti-discrimination rules apply to promotions, job assignments, firing, and other aspects of the employment relationship as well as to hiring, the focus here is mainly on hiring practices. This is the area where most small business owners are likely to stumble into trouble, even when they have no intention to discriminate.

Things Not to Do

All questions or information you express should relate to job qualifications only and not to extraneous factors, such as age, race, sex, or physical size or condition.

If there are special occupational requirements — for example, hard physical labor that might preclude hiring certain handicapped individuals — be sure to carefully document such unusual situations or requirements.

Help Wanted Ads

Use the list below to guide you when writing a help wanted advertisement.

- Do not mention race or national origin or any attribute of national origin, such as native language.
- Do not refer to sex classifications, such as "girl wanted."
- Avoid any type of reference to age, such as "young boy" or "recent high school graduate."

Sample Employment Application Form

Employment Application
Personal Data

Name: _____
             (last)   (first)   (middle)

Present address: _____
                     (street address)   (city)   (state)   (zip)

Telephone numbers: _____   _____
                          (home)   (work)

Education

High School: _____ Graduated? Yes ☐ No ☐ Location: _____

College or University: _____ Graduated? Yes ☐ No ☐ Degree(s): _____

Other (specify type): _____ Graduated? Yes ☐ No ☐ Certificate(s): _____

_____ Graduated? Yes ☐ No ☐ Certificate(s): _____

Work Experience

List below all present and previous employment, starting with the most recent.

Company name: _____ From (mo/yr): _____ Type of work: _____

Address: _____ To (mo/yr): _____ Name of Supervisor: _____

_____ Reason you left: _____

Company name: _____ From (mo/yr): _____ Type of work: _____

Address: _____ To (mo/yr): _____ Name of Supervisor: _____

_____ Reason you left: _____

Company name: _____ From (mo/yr): _____ Type of work: _____

Address: _____ To (mo/yr): _____ Name of Supervisor: _____

_____ Reason you left: _____

Company name: _____ From (mo/yr): _____ Type of work: _____

Address: _____ To (mo/yr): _____ Name of Supervisor: _____

_____ Reason you left: _____

May we contact the employers above? Yes ☐ No ☐ If yes, list any employers you do not wish us to contact:

_____

Remarks: _____

_____

_____

Applicant's Signature: _____ Date _____ , 19 __

Job Application Forms

Your employment application forms should avoid any questions or information on these topics:

- Arrest record;
- Whether the applicant has ever filed for unemployment benefits;
- Place of birth or where parents were born;)
- Physical characteristics, such as height or weight;
- Social Security number;
- Marital status;
- Labor union affiliation;
- Request for photograph;
- Religious affiliation;
- Mode of transportation to work;
- Sex;
- Race or national origin;
- Clubs or organizations, unless you instruct the applicant not to list organizations that indicate race or national origin; and
- Native language or how the applicant learned a foreign language.

A sample employment application form is provided for your review on the previous page. If you wish to add additional questions to it, be careful not to indirectly request anything that would reflect on the applicant's race, religion, sex, age, marital status, national origin, or physical condition. Because state laws differ, check with your legal adviser or state employment department before preparing your employment application.

Employment Interviews

During interviews with potential employees, refrain from asking questions, such as:

- Are you a U.S. citizen?
- When did you attend grade school, high school, or college?
- Do you have children, and who will care for them while you are working?
- Do you have any physical or mental handicap?
- What does your spouse do for a living, and are you likely to move elsewhere?
- Would your religion prevent you from working on holidays or certain days of the week?

Federal law generally bans the use of any kind of lie detector tests in most private employment situations, except for drug manufacturers and distributors and certain security firms.[6] Many state laws are even more stringent.

In addition, questions on possible felony convictions, previous military service, and drug or alcohol addiction are not necessarily illegal in all cases, but they may entail difficulties and probably should be avoided.

Checking References

As a general rule, former employers have no legal obligation to give you any information about a former employee. As a practical matter, however, most former employers will at least verify the former employee's employment and the date of employment. Since a former employer can get into trouble for giving you negative information that they cannot substantiate, don't expect them to volunteer much information or to put anything negative in writing. For that reason, you should generally do reference checks by phone. Acceptable questions would include those on:

- Verifying information given by the applicant;
- Asking about the applicant's principal strong points, weak points, and degree of supervision needed;
- Asking about the applicant's attitude;
- Asking how the applicant's performance compared with others; and
- Asking if the applicant would be rehired.

Personnel Policies

Even before you hire your first employee, you will need to outline some basic personnel policies. Better yet, if you write down your policies on matters such as hours, vacation time, and sick leave and can give such a written summary to new employees, it will greatly help to clarify the employment relationship. Perhaps it will even prevent a misunderstanding that could lead to legal action against you by an employee.

Worksheet 7 provides a series of questions that will help you focus on different personnel policies that are typical in a small to medium-sized business. For a more thorough treatment of this area and if you wish to develop a personnel policy manual for your business, you may want to obtain a copy of *A Company Policy and Personnel Workbook* (The Oasis Press, 1991).

Related Information

To supplement the information you have just read in this chapter, you may want to read the following sections which discuss more related information:

- Employee or Independent Contractor? — Section 9.11
- Fair Employment Practices — Section 5.8
- Sexual Harassment — Section 5.8
- Immigration Law Restrictions on Hiring — Section 5.9
- Hiring a Spouse as an Employee — Section 8.12
- Employee Wage-Hour and Child Labor Laws — Section 5.7
- New Civil Rights Act — Section 9.14
- The Americans with Disabilities Act — Section 5.11

In addition, to get an overview of other legal obligations that come with the territory when you have employees, scan through Chapter 5.

Worksheet 7
Defining Your Company's Personnel Policies

Working Hours

Describe briefly the policy you will set for working hours, including:

Starting time? _____

_____

How much time will be allowed for lunch? _____

_____

Quitting time? _____

_____

Which days of the week employees will be expected to work? _____

_____

If, like many companies these days, you want to adopt some kind of "flex-time" system, spell out how that will work.

_____

_____

_____

Overtime

Outline your policy on overtime work. Refer to Section 5.7 of this book for legal requirements for paying overtime premiums. See also Section 11.5 regarding state wage laws. Points to consider here include:

Will you pay exempt employees (administrative or professional) overtime if they work extra hours? _____

_____

Will you require employees to obtain permission to work overtime? _____

_____

Compensation

Make a list of the job positions in the company other than your own and the compensation level for each. On a separate piece of paper, write out a specific job description for each position, outlining duties and responsibilities. Refer to sections 5.7 and 11.5 of this book for a description of hourly minimum wage requirements.

Position	Hourly wage	Salary	Total monthly pay
_____	_____	_____	_____
_____	_____	_____	_____
_____	_____	_____	_____
_____	_____	_____	_____
_____	_____	_____	_____
_____	_____	_____	_____
_____	_____	_____	_____

Vacation Policy

Describe how much paid vacation employees will have and how this may increase after a certain number of years of service. _____

_____

Will vacation time and sick leave time off be combined into a single category for employees (as some companies now do to reward employees who do not abuse sick leave and to discourage others from using sick leave as additional vacation by playing hooky)? _____

_____

Will you pay employees, who terminate, for unused vacation? (The laws of many states require you to do so.) _____

_____

Sick Leave Policy

Outline your policy for both paid sick leave and unpaid sick leave, or whichever you choose to provide, if not both. (Note: Sick pay is no longer exempt from FICA tax, in general.)[7]

Sick leave _____

_____

Unpaid sick leave _____

_____

Leaves of Absence

What will your policy be towards employees who request unpaid leaves of absence? _____

_____

Time Off with Pay

Will you provide other time off with pay for such eventualities as funerals or emergencies in an employee's immediate family?

Funerals or family emergencies? _____

_____

Jury duty? _____

_____

Birth of a child? _____

_____

Promotions and Evaluations

Outline your policy for evaluating employees' performance and determining when promotions will be made. _____

_____   _____

_____

_____

_____

(Continued)

(Continued)

Fringe Benefits

Consider which employee fringe benefits you will provide and specify your policy for each.

Medical Insurance: _____

_____

Long-term Disability Insurance: _____

_____

Life Insurance: _____

_____

Dental Insurance: _____

_____

Medical Expense Reimbursement: _____

_____

Child Care Benefits: _____

_____

Maternity Benefits: _____

_____

Pension or Profit-sharing Plans: _____

_____

Paid Holidays: _____

_____

Automobiles or Allowances: _____

_____

Expense Accounts: _____

_____

Employee Discounts on Purchases: _____

_____

Stock Options (if incorporated): _____

_____

Incentive Bonus Plan: _____

_____

Placement Fees

If you hire employees through a personnel agency or "headhunting" firm, will you pay the placement fee? _____

_____

1.9 Other Questions You Need to Ask

- Will or should you advertise? If you do, you need to decide what kind of advertising will be the most cost-effective for your business, whether it be newspaper ads, direct mail, radio, posters, handbills, or other forms of advertising and promotion.

- Do you understand what will be involved in purchasing, managing, and restocking your inventory of goods?

- How will you go about selling? Will you hire sales clerks or outside salespeople, or will you do most of the selling yourself?

- Will you sell to customers on credit? If so, how will you protect yourself from bad credit risks and outright deadbeats?

- How much of your personal savings are you putting at risk by going into business? Are you willing to risk losing all of it if the business is a failure?

- Can you run the business alone — or with help from family members — or would you do better with one or more partners or business associates to provide additional capital and skills and to divide up some of the responsibilities of running the business?

Again, the questions posed in this chapter are not intended to discourage you from going ahead with starting your business. Chances are you have already considered most of the points raised in this chapter and are reasonably confident that you will be able to do what is necessary to make your business work. If so, many of the questions raised above probably seem rather elementary and obvious to you, as they will to most individuals seriously considering going into business, and you will now want to proceed to the discussions in the remainder of this book.

If you have not previously given serious thought to most of the above points that are relevant to the type of business you are planning to start, now is the time to take a long, hard look at whether you are adequately prepared to embark upon such a venture.

Footnotes

1. McCarroll, *Entrepreneurs: Starting Over,* TIME MAGAZINE (Jan. 6, 1992).

2. Cook, *Women: The Best Entrepreneurs,* CANADIAN BUSINESS (June, 1982). Reproduced with permission.

3. *The State of Small Business, A Report of the President,* Superintendent of Documents, Wash. D.C. (1989).

4. Phillips and Kirchoff, *Analysis of New Firm Survival and Growth,* J. SMALL BUS. ECON. (Winter 1989).

5. San Francisco *Chronicle,* Aug. 3, 1980.

6. The Employee Polygraph Protection Act, 29 U.S.C. 2001.

7. I.R.C. §3121(a)(4).

Chapter 2

Choosing the Legal Form of the Business

The hardest thing in the world to understand is Income Tax.

— Albert Einstein

2.1 General Considerations

There are many ways in which a business venture can be structured; however, the law classifies businesses so that most fall into one of three legal forms — the sole proprietorship, the partnership, or the corporation. There are also certain variations on some of these basic legal forms. For instance, the limited liability company, a relatively new form of business organization, is gaining legal status in a number of states. Limited liability companies are intended to provide the limited liability of corporations and the pass-through taxation of partnerships.

If you are planning to start a business, consider the following questions when deciding your business' legal form:

- Will someone else share in ownership of the business? If so, it will not be a sole proprietorship. Thus, the choice will be between a partnership arrangement and a corporation.

- How important is it to limit personal liability for debts or claims against the business? If this is a major consideration, incorporating the business would generally be the best means of limiting your liability.

- Which form of business organization will result in the least taxes? While there is no universal answer to this question, the rest of this chapter explains when it is and isn't beneficial to incorporate for tax reasons.

Sole Proprietorships

A sole proprietorship is generally the simplest, least regulated form of business and can usually be initiated without any formalities. If you simply start doing business without a partner, the law will classify your business as a sole proprietorship. You do not need a lawyer or approval of any government agency to create a sole proprietorship.

Partnerships

A partnership can also be started with a minimum of formalities. A partnership need not be more than a handshake agreement with your business partner, but it is generally advisable to have a written partnership agreement defining your respective rights and responsibilities, and that usually means incurring fairly significant legal fees. A limited partnership, in which the liability of one or more of the partners is limited, is much more involved, as discussed in Section 2.3 of this chapter.

Corporations

The corporation is the most formalized and regulated business entity; therefore, the costs of establishing and maintaining the legal status of a corporation are generally greater than for a sole proprietorship or partnership.

Limited Liability Companies

In addition to the three traditional forms of business organization discussed above, several states in recent years have created, by statute, a new type of entity called a limited liability company. This entity, which closely resembles and is taxed as a partnership, also offers limited liability like corporations.

In 1988, the IRS's Revenue Ruling 88-76 concluded that a Wyoming limited liability company could be classified as a partnership for federal income tax purposes — which is favorable, from a taxpayer's standpoint, in many cases — based on the following rationale:

- No member has any personal liability for debts of the company; therefore, the company has limited liability.
- The interests of the members are assignable only upon written consent of all the remaining members. This is similar to a partnership; however, the ruling recognized that mere assignees are entitled to receive profits and other compensation.
- Like a partnership, the company is dissolved in situations which are very similar to the dissolution of a limited partnership.
- The company has centralized management.

Because of the absence of continuity of life and free transferability of interests in the entity, the Wyoming limited liability company was held to be a partnership for tax purposes. Florida has also recently adopted a Limited Liability Company Act, which is virtually identical to that of Wyoming. In 1990, Colorado enacted legal provisions that permit the formation of limited liability companies. Colorado's limited liability companies are not subject to income tax and are to be treated as partnerships for state tax purposes. They also have limited liability. The Colorado companies also appear to meet the IRS tests for taxability as a partnership. In addition to these states, several other states have adopted limited liability companies acts. For more information, contact your secretary of state's office.

How difficult is it to change from one legal form to another? As a broad generalization, it is usually a simpler matter to change from a sole proprietorship to a partnership, or to change from a sole proprietorship or partnership to a corporation, than it is to move in the opposite direction.

Changing Legal Forms

For example, converting a business that is operated as a corporation into a sole proprietorship or partnership may result in substantial individual and corporate-level taxes when the corporation is liquidated. This would happen if the value of the business transferred to the owners of the stock of the corporation were greater than their cost or tax basis for such stock or if any corporate assets have values in excess of their tax basis.

While there are almost always some expenses and complications in changing the legal form, such changes are quite routine transactions. Many businesses start off as sole proprietorships, develop into partnerships and later incorporate, if tax and other considerations indicate that it no longer makes good business sense not to be incorporated. Thus, the choice of one legal form when starting a business should not be considered a final choice.

2.2 Advantages and Disadvantages of Sole Proprietorships

The great advantage of operating a new business as a sole proprietorship is that it is simple and does not require any formal action to set it up. You can start your business today as a sole proprietorship — there is no need to wait for an attorney to draft and file documents or for the government to approve them.

Of course, you will need a business license, and a few states require you to register to do business. As a sole proprietor, you are the sole owner of your business. If married, however, your spouse will usually have a one-half interest in the business in a state which has community property laws.

As the owner of the sole proprietorship, you will be personally liable for any debts or taxes of the business or other claims, such as legal damages resulting from a lawsuit. This is one reason why many entrepreneurs prefer to use a corporation rather than a sole proprietorship. Unlimited

Personal Liability

personal liability is perhaps the major disadvantage of operating a business in the form of a sole proprietorship.

All of the profit or loss from your business belongs to you and must be reported on your federal income tax return, *Schedule C, Income (or Loss) from a Business or Profession,* on *Form 1040.* This can either be an advantage or a disadvantage for income tax purposes, depending on the circumstances.

If operating the business results in losses or significant tax credits, you may be able to use the tax losses or tax credits to reduce taxes on income from other sources. Or, if your sole proprietorship generates modest profits — but not more than about $60,000 to $75,000 a year — overall taxes may be less than if incorporated, assuming you need most of the income to live on.

Income Tax Advantage Similar to Corporations

After the Tax Reform Act of 1986 and the Omnibus Budget Reconciliation Act of 1987 (OBRA), a sole proprietorship is now less likely to become disadvantageous in terms of tax rates as compared to a corporation. For one thing, the highest corporate tax rate for 1993 is 34% — 39% on income between $100,000 and $335,000 — which is higher than the maximum nominal individual tax rate of 31%. Thus, corporate tax rates are no longer lower than individual rates, except that the first $50,000 of corporate income is taxed at only a 15% rate and the next $25,000 at 25%.

Unemployment Taxes

As a sole proprietor, you are not considered an employee of your business. As a result, you will avoid having to pay unemployment taxes on your earnings from the business.

Both the state and federal governments impose unemployment taxes on wages or salaries but not on self-employment income. For 1993, the federal unemployment tax rate is effectively 0.8%[1] of the first $7,000[2] of wages paid to each employee, with a $56 maximum per employee. Refer to Section 11.5 regarding the state unemployment taxes you must pay for each employee.

As a sole proprietor, your income would not be subject to either of these taxes. Note that a corporation would normally get an income tax deduction for the unemployment tax it paid on your salary, so that the actual after-tax savings from operating as a sole proprietorship would be somewhat less than the unemployment taxes you would avoid paying.

Another advantage of a sole proprietorship is that you can shift funds in and out of your business account or withdraw assets from the business with few tax, legal, or other limitations. In a partnership, you can generally withdraw funds only by agreement and, in the case of a corporation, a withdrawal of funds or property will usually be taxable as a dividend or capital gain and may violate some states' corporation laws.

A major disadvantage of sole proprietorships and partnerships is that they cannot obtain a number of significant tax benefits regarding group-term life insurance benefits, long-term disability insurance coverage, and medical insurance or medical expense reimbursements. To qualify for favorable tax treatment regarding such fringe benefit plans, it is necessary to incorporate. Note, however, that until July 1, 1992, a self-employed individual was allowed to deduct 25% of his or her health insurance in computing adjusted gross income.[3] Congress has extended this 25% deduction in the past, but if they don't, no deduction will be available after July 1, 1992.

The special advantages of corporate pension and profit-sharing plans have largely been eliminated since 1984. As of now, there are virtually no differences in the tax treatment of self-employed (Keogh) plans of sole proprietorships and partnerships, as compared with corporate retirement plans. See Section 8.3.

See Section 2.4 for further discussion on advantages and disadvantages of sole proprietorships as compared to corporations.

Also, see the table at the end of this chapter which summarizes the key characteristics of sole proprietorships, partnerships, and corporations.

Limited Tax Savings for Fringe Benefits

2.3 Advantages and Disadvantages of Partnerships

A business partnership is much like a sole proprietorship in many respects, except that it has two or more owners. Creating a partnership can be a very simple matter, since the law does not require any formal written documents or other formalities for most partnerships. As a practical matter, however, it is much sounder business practice for partners in a business to have a written partnership agreement that, at a minimum, spells out their agreement on such basic issues as:

General Partnerships

- How much and what kind of property each partner will contribute to the venture;
- What value will be placed on the contributed property;
- How profits and losses will be divided among the partners;
- When and how profits will be withdrawn;
- Whether or how certain partners will be compensated for their services to the partnership or for making capital available to the partnership; and
- How changes in ownership of interests in the partnership will be handled.

A written partnership agreement should be prepared by an attorney and, if possible, should be reviewed by a tax accountant before it is put into effect.

Partnerships are a bit like marriages; they usually start out with a great deal of trust but have a high break-up rate. Be advised that partnerships are easy to get into, require a lot of patience and understanding to live with, and are often costly and painful to get out of.

Liability of Partners

As a partner, you are an agent for the partnership and can do anything necessary to operate the business, such as hire employees, borrow money, or enter into contracts on behalf of the partnership. You and each of your partners (except for a limited partner in a limited partnership) have personal liability for the debts, taxes, and other claims against the partnership.

If the partnership's assets are not sufficient to pay creditors, the creditors can satisfy their claims out of your personal assets. In addition, when any partner fails to pay personal debts, the partnership's business may be disrupted if his or her creditors proceed to satisfy their claims out of his or her interest in the partnership by seeking what is called a charging order against partnership assets.

State and Federal Tax Requirements

While a partnership must file federal and usually state information returns — *Form 1065* is the federal form — it generally pays no income tax. Instead, it reports each partner's share of income or loss on the information return, and each partner reports the income or loss on *Schedule E* of his or her individual tax return, *Form 1040*.

In 1987, tax legislation was passed allowing partnerships and S corporations to elect to retain their fiscal tax year rather than change to a calendar year, as the 1986 Tax Reform Act generally mandated. This election requires the partnership or S corporation to report and pay a tax directly each year under an extremely complex formula — as long as there is a tax-deferral benefit to their partners or shareholders. This complicated extra accounting is the price for retaining a fiscal tax year.[4]

In addition, since 1985, partnerships have been required to file a special report, *Form 8308*, with the IRS each time a sale or exchange of an interest in the partnership occurs.[5]

Like a sole proprietor, a partner is not generally considered an employee of the partnership for income tax and payroll tax purposes. The income tax advantages and disadvantages of a sole proprietorship are equally applicable to a partnership, since a partner's share of income from a partnership is treated essentially the same as income from a sole proprietorship. For example, your income from a partnership may be subject to federal self-employment tax but not to federal and state unemployment taxes as discussed in Section 2.2.

Dissolution

Unless a partnership agreement provides otherwise, a partnership usually terminates when any partner dies or withdraws from the partnership. This is in contrast to a corporation which, theoretically, has perpetual existence.

Under the laws of most states, bankruptcy of a partner or the partnership itself will cause the dissolution of the partnership, regardless of any agreement.

The law provides for a special kind of partnership in which partners have limited personal liability: the limited partnership. The limited partnership is more regulated than the common general partnership discussed above, but it allows investors who will not be actively involved in the partnership's operations to become partners without being exposed to unlimited liability of the business' debts, if it should go out of business.

Limited Partnerships

A limited partner risks only his or her investment but must allow one or more general partners to exercise control over the business. In fact, if the limited partner becomes involved in the partnership's operations, he or she may lose his or her protected status as a limited partner. The general partners in a limited partnership are fully liable for the partnership's debts. Every limited partnership must have one or more general partners as well as one or more limited partners.

State law requires certain formalities in the case of a limited partnership that are not required for other partnerships. To qualify for their special status, limited partnerships must usually file a *Certificate of Limited Partnership* with the secretary of state or other state and county offices. Establishing a limited partnership also requires a written partnership agreement. See Section 11.2 regarding special filing requirements for partnerships under state law.

2.4 Advantages and Disadvantages of Corporations

A corporation is an artificial legal entity that exists separately from the people who own, manage, control, and operate it. It can make contracts, pay taxes, and is liable for debts. Corporations exist only because state statutory laws allow them to be created.

A business corporation issues shares of its stock, as evidence of ownership, to the person or persons who contribute the money or business assets which the corporation will use to conduct its business. Thus, the stockholders or shareholders are the owners of the corporation, and they are entitled to any dividends the corporation pays and to all corporation assets — after all creditors have been paid — if the corporation is liquidated.

The main reason most businesses incorporate is to limit owner liability to the amount invested in the business. Generally, stockholders in a corporation are not personally liable for claims against the corporation and are, therefore, at risk only to the extent of their investment in the corporation.

Limited Personal Liability

Likewise, the officers and directors of a corporation are not normally liable for the corporation's debts, although in some cases an officer whose duty it is to withhold federal income tax from employees' wages may be liable to the IRS if the taxes are not withheld and paid over to the IRS as required.

Potential Loss of Limited Personal Liability

The advantage of limited liability is not always completely available through incorporation. For example, don't start a corporation on a shoestring. If your corporation is capitalized too thinly with equity capital (your money) as compared to debt capital (borrowed money), the courts may determine that your corporation is a thin corporation and hold you and your stockholders directly liable to creditors.

Failure to observe corporate formalities and the separate legal existence of the corporation can have a similar result. This is called "piercing the corporate veil" by the courts, and means if a corporation is not adequately capitalized and properly operated to protect the interests of creditors, the courts can take away the veil of limited liability that normally protects the stockholders.

Piercing the corporate veil is relatively uncommon. A much more frequent problem is that many banks and other lenders will not loan money to a small incorporated business unless someone, usually the stockholders of the corporation, personally guarantees repayment of the loan. Despite this common business practice, the limited liability feature can still be an important protection from personal liability for other debts, such as accounts payable to suppliers and others who sell goods or services to the corporation on credit, typically without requiring any personal guarantee of payment by the owners.

Even this partial protection is a significant advantage of incorporating for most small businesses. Being incorporated can also protect you from personal liability regarding lawsuit damages not covered by your corporation's liability insurance policies; for example, someone slips on a banana peel in your store and sues the corporation for $10 million. To help you avoid personal liability for corporate acts, a partial checklist of do's and dont's is provided at the end of this chapter.

Continuous Existence

Unlike a sole proprietorship or partnership, a corporation has continuous existence and does not terminate upon the death of a stockholder or a change of ownership of some or all of its stock. Creditors, suppliers, and customers, therefore, often prefer to deal with an incorporated business because of this greater continuity.

Naturally, a corporation can be terminated by mutual consent of the owners or even by one stockholder in some instances.

If you would like to learn more about these and other corporate issues, *The Essential Corporation Handbook,* by Carl R.J. Sniffen, is a new, easy-to-understand introduction into the corporate world. This handbook discusses the initial set up of your corporation and explains all the necessary corporate formalities — such as, shareholders' meetings, consent resolutions, and recordkeeping — involved in maintaining your corporation as a successful corporate entity. For more information on *The Essential Corporation Handbook,* contact your book source or:

The Oasis Press
(800) 228-2275

Cost of Incorporating

To set up a corporation, you must file articles of incorporation with the state office that grants and approves corporate charters. See Section 11.2 for more information on state incorporating requirements.

Legal fees usually run between $500 and $1,000, even for a simple incorporation, and if it is necessary to obtain a permit from the state to issue stock or securities, legal fees can be much more.

Thus, it should be apparent that one of the disadvantages of incorporating is the cost involved, which will be substantial even for the simplest incorporation. In addition to the costs of establishing a corporation, there will be recurring costs, often including annual franchise or corporate income taxes.

Federal Corporate Income Taxes

Corporations filing their income tax returns on *Form 1120-A* or *Form 1120* will be taxed at different rates depending on the amount of their taxable income. The corporate tax rates listed on the following table indicate the current federal tax rates. Note that there is a 5% tax on taxable income over $100,000; thus, the 39% rate. The rate drops back to a flat rate of 34% once the taxable income reaches more than $335,000.

Corporate Tax Rate Table

Taxable Income	Tax Rate
Not over $50,000	15%
$50,000 to $75,000	25%
$75,000 to $100,000	34%
$100,000 to $335,000	39%
More than $335,000	34%

As an owner, you will most likely draw a salary from your corporation, which will be subject to FICA (Social Security) taxes and state and federal unemployment taxes. These unemployment taxes are not imposed on your income from a sole proprietorship or partnership. FICA taxes, in 1990 and subsequent years, are generally the same (in total) on the wages of a corporate employee/owner as would be the self-employment tax on the same amount of business income if you were a sole proprietor or a partner in a partnership.

For certain types of unincorporated businesses, however, such as a firm whose income is from interest or real estate rentals, or both, there is no self-employment tax on the income, which could make not incorporating such a firm advantageous for tax purposes.

Personal (Professional) Service Corporations

If you operate a qualified personal (professional) service corporation, you will be taxed at a flat rate of 34%.[6] You cannot use the graduated tax rates listed previously.

According to the *Tax Guide for Small Business, Publication 334,* which is published by the Internal Revenue Service, a qualified personal service corporation is defined by these characteristics:

- At least 95% of the value of its stock is held by employees or their estates or beneficiaries; and
- The employees perform services at least 95% of the time in the following fields: health, law, engineering, architecture, accounting, actuarial science, performing arts, or consulting.

Double Taxation of Dividends Distributed to Shareholders

Another potential disadvantage of a corporation is the double taxation of its income that is distributed to its shareholders. If a corporation has taxable income, pays corporate income taxes on it, and the shareholders withdraw money in the form of a dividend, they will also pay tax on the dividend, as a rule. Thus, the use of a corporation can obviously be disadvantageous if it results in this double taxation of the business' income. Most incorporated small businesses, however, with good tax planning, can avoid double taxation and, instead, often can use the corporation to save taxes.

Since double taxation occurs only if a corporation pays out money or property that is taxable as dividend to its shareholders, most small corporations never, or rarely, pay dividends. Instead, they retain the lightly taxed profits in the business. This is ideal for a business that needs funds to invest in expansion of operations. Many highly profitable businesses could be better off unincorporated or as S corporations since the highest corporate tax rate is now higher than the maximum individual rate.

Accumulated Earnings Tax

Even where the business does not need to retain the profits, the corporation can still safely accumulate up to $150,000 of after-tax profits over a period of years, which can be invested by it in stocks, bonds, real estate, etc., without fear of incurring an accumulated earnings tax.[7] This exemption is $250,000 for most businesses except that only a $150,000 exemption is allowed for professional and certain personal service corporations. Any accumulation of profits, however, in excess of $150,000 or $250,000 that is not needed for use in the business may be hit by the accumulated earnings tax, which is a penalty tax in addition to the regular corporate income tax.

The penalty tax is 28% on these accumulated earnings, which are specially defined and not necessarily the same as net profits for accounting purposes or taxable income.[8] This penalty tax is designed to keep corporations from accumulating large amounts of profits at low corporate tax rates, unless they need to accumulate the profits to reinvest in their business.

You should consult a tax adviser as to what constitutes a legitimate business purpose for your corporation to accumulate profits beyond the $150,000 or $250,000 exemption, since the law in this area is quite complex. The key point to remember is that under present law your corporation can generally accumulate up to $150,000 or $250,000 in profits without incurring an accumulated earnings tax. This can make it an excellent tax shelter.

Income-Splitting

By using a corporation, it may be possible to split your overall profit between two or more taxpayers, so that none of the income gets taxed in the highest tax brackets. For example, with an overall economic profit of $100,000, an incorporated business may be able to reduce its taxable income to $50,000 by paying (and deducting) a $50,000 salary to its owner, as an officer/employee of the corporation. The corporation would pay tax only on the remaining $50,000 profit, at a maximum federal tax rate of only 15%, while the owner would pay tax on the $50,000 salary received.

Because of the progressive tax rate structure under the federal income tax laws, the tax on the $100,000 income divided between the owner and his or her corporation would typically be much less than if the whole $100,000 were taxable to the owner. In 1993, for example, a single individual would pay $26,522 in federal income taxes on $100,000 of taxable income, while if the income were split evenly between the owner and his or her corporation, the corporation's tax would be $7,500 and the owner's $11,127, a saving of $7,895 — assuming the corporation is not a personal services corporation subject to a 34% flat rate of tax.

Another way to split the income of a business between multiple taxpayers is for you to make your children part owners of the business. Ideally, the children should be given an interest in the business when it is started, since the value of the gifts to them will often be minimal for gift tax purposes at that time.

It is frequently more feasible to split corporate income with your children by giving them some of the corporation's stock. This approach, however, will work only if your corporation has filed for an S corporation election on *Form 2553* with the IRS. As discussed later in this chapter, the taxable income of a corporation that qualifies as an S corporation (formerly called a Subchapter S corporation) is taxable to its shareholders — in proportion to the stock they own in the corporation — and is generally not taxed to the corporation.

By giving a number of shares of stock in such an S corporation to one or more of your children, part of the taxable income of the business can often be shifted to the children[9] and taxed at their low tax brackets — assuming, as is usually the case, that the children do not have a lot of taxable income from other sources. If, however, the parents attempt to shift too much income to the children by drawing no salary or too little salary from the corporation, the IRS has the power to reallocate the corporation's income to the parents to reflect the value of services rendered to the corporation. Under the Tax Reform Act of 1986, shifting significant income to your children will not work if the children are under 14 years of age.[10]

Retirement Plans

For many years, corporations — except for S corporations — have had very significant tax advantages over unincorporated businesses with respect to pension and profit-sharing plans; however, this is no longer the case.

Perhaps the most significant remaining difference is that an owner/ employee who participates in a Keogh plan, or a shareholder/employee in the retirement plan of an S corporation, cannot borrow money from the plan without incurring a prohibited-transactions excise tax on such a loan.[11] On the other hand, a participant in a regular corporate retirement plan may be able to borrow as much as $50,000 from the plan, if various tax requirements are met. In addition to covering yourself under a corporate or Keogh retirement plan — or even if you are not covered under either type of plan — it is also possible for you to create your own individual retirement account (IRA) whether or not incorporated. Since only a $2,000-a-year deduction[12] — $2,250 if you have a nonworking spouse — can be taken for contributions to an IRA, it will not be possible to build up a very large retirement fund or to shelter much income from tax with an IRA. Although, it is better than having no tax-qualified retirement plan at all and it can be a useful supplement to a corporate or Keogh plan.

Since 1986, federal law no longer allows deductions for contributions to IRA plans if you or your spouse is also an active participant in a corporate or Keogh qualified retirement plan and if adjusted gross income exceeds $35,000 for a single person or $50,000 for a married couple filing jointly.[13] The maximum $2,000 or $2,250 deduction phases out between income levels of $25,000 and $35,000 for single taxpayers and between $40,000 and $50,000 for married couples.[14]

Tax Advantages

The primary tax advantages of the three types of tax-qualified retirement plans — corporate, self-employed (Keogh), and IRA — are these:

- Amounts contributed, up to certain limits, are deductible from the income of the corporation or individual taxpayer.[15] This deduction can be as much as 25% of the individual's compensation for the year (not counting the plan contribution) or $30,000, whichever is less. Even larger contributions can be made by so-called defined benefit plans.
- Contributed funds can be invested by pension or profit-sharing plans on a tax-free basis.[16] The qualified retirement trust that is usually set up to hold the retirement funds is exempt from state and federal income taxes on its income or capital gains from investments in stocks, bonds, savings accounts, gold, silver, real estate, and other passive investments.

- When trust funds are paid out to you at retirement, you may be in a lower tax bracket than when you made the contributions to the plan. Thus, not only do you get to defer payment of any tax on amounts contributed to the plan until you retire, but the tax you finally pay at retirement is apt to be at a lower rate than you would have paid when you were working.
- Receipt of all your retirement plan funds in a lump sum at retirement, or in certain other circumstances, may often qualify for special low tax rates if the distribution is from a corporate or Keogh plan but not from an IRA.[17]

Exemptions from Estate Tax

Except for the unlimited estate tax marital deduction, there are no longer any exemptions from the federal estate tax.

Before 1983, pension plan benefits left to a beneficiary other than the estate of the deceased employee were exempted from the federal estate tax. For 1983 and 1984, this unlimited exemption was scaled down to a $100,000 exemption for such benefits, and that limited exclusion was finally repealed after 1984.

The Tax Reform Act of 1986, however, retroactively amended certain exclusions from estate tax for pension plan benefits. Under these amendments, an individual who separated from service before January 1, 1983 and was receiving benefits on December 31, 1982 is considered as having made an irrevocable election as to the type of benefits to be received and the value of such benefits may be completely exempt from estate tax, if the form of benefits is not changed before his or her death. A similar rule applies to any person who separated from service before January 1, 1985 and was receiving benefits on December 31, 1984, if the form of benefits is not changed. Such individuals will still qualify for the $100,000 estate tax exclusion for pension benefits.

If you are receiving pension benefits and come within either of the above categories, don't change the form in which your benefits are being paid!

See Section 8.10, under the sidehead of Unlimited Estate Tax Marital Deduction, for a further discussion on estate tax.

Insurance Benefit Plans

The tax law permits you, as a corporate employer, to provide a number of different fringe benefits to employees on a tax-favored basis. Generally, you can deduct the insurance premiums or other payments you make on behalf of the employee, while the employee is not taxed on the value of the benefit provided. This is much more favorable than payments of salary to an employee, which are fully taxable.

In an unincorporated business, the payments made on behalf of the sole proprietor or partners for such benefits are generally not deductible as expenses of the business, in contrast to fringe benefits paid for by a corporation for its stockholder/employees. So the tax benefits of employee fringe benefits, such as those described below, are another reason for incorporating your business and becoming an employee of the corporation.

Note, however, that if your corporation is an S corporation, it will be treated much like a partnership for fringe benefit purposes.[18] Until 1991, that meant it was not allowed a deduction for any of the fringe benefits described below for any 2% or greater shareholder.

Then, in 1991, the IRS ruled that an S corporation may deduct the cost of medical insurance paid on behalf of more-than-2% shareholders. These shareholders must include such amounts in W-2 income — of which they may be able to deduct 25% in computing adjusted gross income, plus possibly deduct part of the remainder as itemized deductions.[19]

Presumably, similar treatment will also apply to disability and group-term life insurance premiums, except that neither will be deductible by the individual, unlike medical insurance. The major types of fringe benefit plans, other than retirement plans, that allow for tax deductions to the corporation and no taxable income to the employee are described below.

Medical Insurance Plans

The corporation that maintains a medical insurance plan, such as Blue Cross or a prepaid health care plan, is permitted to deduct the premiums it pays to the insurer. In addition, the employee is not required to include either the cost of the premiums or the benefits provided by the insurer in his or her taxable income,[20] as a general rule.

Self-Insured Medical Reimbursement Plans

A corporation can set up a plan under which the corporation directly reimburses employees for medical expenses or even for such expenses as dental care, orthodontic work, and prescription eyeglasses or contact lenses.[21] If the plan satisfies tax law requirements prohibiting discrimination in favor of highly paid employees,[22] the reimbursements paid can be deducted by the corporation and are not taxable to the recipients.

Such plans are often set up in addition to medical insurance plans, either to cover deductibles that the insurance does not pay or to cover particular types of medical or dental costs that the insurance plan does not provide for. Note that costs of cosmetic surgery are no longer deductible as medical expenses after 1990.

In the past, it was possible to set up a self-insured medical reimbursement plan so that it covered only the officers of the corporation. As the tax law now stands, such a plan would probably be considered discriminatory in most cases, and the reimbursements paid to the officers would, therefore, be taxable to them. Under present law, it will usually be necessary for a self-insured medical plan to cover most of the corporation's employees to qualify for favorable tax treatment.

Payment by a corporation of disability insurance premiums is deductible by the corporation and is not taxed to the employees covered by the insurance — except in the case of an S corporation.[23] Sole proprietorships and partnerships may not deduct premiums on disability coverage for the sole proprietor or partners.[24]

Disability Insurance

If an employee becomes disabled and receives disability benefits under a policy that the employer has paid the premiums for, the benefits will be included in the employee's income for tax purposes. Note that if an individual, such as a sole proprietor or partner, has paid his or her own premiums for disability insurance, any disability benefits received are tax-free.[25]

You may set up a group-term life insurance plan and deduct the insurance premiums you pay on behalf of your employees. To the extent the life insurance coverage on an employee does not exceed $50,000 under the plan during the taxable year, the premiums paid by you are not taxable income to the employee.[26]

Group-Term Life Insurance

Even to the extent an employee's coverage exceeds $50,000, the amount the employee must include in taxable income from the additional insurance premiums paid by you for the excess coverage is sometimes considerably less than the premium actually paid and deducted.

You cannot deduct the premiums for your own coverage under a group life insurance plan, since you are not considered an employee of the business for tax purposes. See Section 8.3 for a discussion of numerous other kinds of fringe benefit plans.

Another important tax advantage of a corporation (other than for an S corporation, discussed in the next section of this chapter) is that, in general, it can deduct 70% of the dividends it receives from stock investments from its federal taxable income.[27] Thus, if you use your corporation to accumulate profits at low corporate tax rates, as was suggested previously in this chapter, you may want to consider investing some of those accumulated funds in common stock or preferred stock of publicly traded U.S. corporations, since the dividends received by your corporation will be 70% tax-free, in most cases, or 80% if your corporation owns 20% or more of the stock of the company paying the dividend. For example, if your corporation receives $1,000 in dividends from an investment in General Motors stock, only $300 would be taxable for federal income tax purposes. Even if your corporation were in the 34% corporate tax bracket, the federal tax on those dividends would be 34% of $300, or $102, which is a maximum effective tax rate of only 10.2% on the dividends received.

Tax Break for Dividends Received by a Corporation

Note, however, that this deduction will be reduced if your corporation borrows money, on which it pays interest, to purchase dividend-paying stocks.[28]

Many states' corporation tax laws also permit a deduction for dividends received by a corporation.

Corporate Income Tax Disadvantages

While this chapter has outlined a number of important tax advantages of incorporating a business, the picture is not all that one-sided. There are also a number of significant potential tax problems that corporations may face. The potential disadvantages include:

- A maximum corporate tax rate that is now generally higher than the individual tax rate;
- Difficulties in withdrawing profits from the business without incurring double taxation;
- The accumulated earnings tax that may apply if profits are not withdrawn from the corporation or plowed back into the business; and
- The personal holding company tax, a 28% tax that may apply to the undistributed income of certain corporations that have too much passive income.[29]

Each of these potential tax disadvantages of corporations is discussed in more detail in Section 8.9. Note that most of the above disadvantages are not applicable if you elect S corporation status. Deciding whether to incorporate in this state or elsewhere is discussed in Section 9.12.

2.5 S Corporations

The first thing to understand clearly about S corporations (formerly referred to as Subchapter S corporations) is that they are no different than any other corporation under state law in terms of corporate law requirements, limited liability of shareholders, or any other aspect except tax treatment. In fact, some states do not even recognize S corporation elections for tax purposes. An S corporation is simply a regular corporation that meets certain requirements and which has to be treated somewhat like a partnership for federal tax purposes. See Section 11.2 for a discussion of how S corporations are taxed in this state, if at all.

Once a corporation has made an election with the IRS to be treated as an S corporation, its shareholders will generally report their share of the corporation's taxable income or loss on their individual tax returns. That is, the corporation "passes through" its income, or loss, and tax credits to the shareholders in proportion to their stock holdings in the corporation, much like a partnership.

The S corporation does not usually pay tax on any of its income.[30] Any domestic S corporation, however, must file *Form 1120S, U.S. Income Tax Return for an S Corporation*, regardless of any tax due. *Form 1120S* must be filed by March 15 if filing under a calendar year basis; or, the 15th day of the third month following the close of a fiscal year.

An S corporation must furnish a copy of *Schedule K, Shareholder's Share of Income, Credits, Deductions* to each shareholder. By not providing *Schedule K-1* before filing *Form 1120S*, the S corporation could incur penalties.

In certain instances, an S corporation may be subject to tax on "built-in gains." Built-in gains are untaxed gains on the assets of a corporation that would have been recognized as taxable if the assets had been sold at fair market value on the day a corporation became an S corporation. Profits are deemed to be distributed to the shareholders on the last day of the corporation's tax year, whether or not the profits are actually distributed.[31] Thus, if profits of an S corporation are distributed as dividends, the distribution itself is ordinarily not taxable, so that there is no double taxation of distributed profits.

The Tax Reform Act of 1986 has made S corporations a much more attractive form of doing business than before, due primarily to the fact that, for the first time within memory, the top corporate tax rate of 34% (or 39%) is higher than the top individual tax rate of 31% — top rates vary, see sections 2.4 and 2.6. Accordingly, an S corporation election is advisable for many more corporations now than in previous years.

To qualify for S corporation treatment, your corporation must meet the following requirements:

S Corporation Requirements

- It must be a domestic corporation, that is, incorporated in the United States.[32]
- No shareholder can be a nonresident alien individual.[33]
- All of its shareholders must generally be individuals, although certain trusts, called Qualified Subchapter S Trusts .and Grantor Trusts, may hold stock under certain circumstances. No shareholder can be a corporation or a partnership.[34]
- The corporation can have only one class of common stock and no preferred stock.[35]
- There cannot be more than 35 shareholders.[36] For this purpose, a husband and wife who are both stockholders will be counted as only one stockholder, whether or not they hold the stock in joint ownership.[37]
- The corporation cannot be a member of an affiliated group of corporations.[38] If it owns stock in a subsidiary that is considered an affiliate, it may not be able to qualify under the S corporation provisions.
- Less than 25% of the corporation's gross receipts during three successive tax years must be from passive sources, such as interest income, dividends, rent, royalties, or proceeds from the sale of securities.[39] The passive income limit does not apply at all for a brand new corporation or an existing corporation that has no accumulated earnings and profits when it elects S corporation status.[40]

Electing S Corporation Status

To become an S corporation, your company must meet the above requirements and file an election on *Form 2553* with the IRS. The election must be signed by all of the corporation's shareholders,[41] including your spouse, who may have a community property interest in stock that is in your name. The S corporation election must be filed during the first two months and 15 days of the corporation's tax year for which the election is to go into effect or at any time during the preceding tax year.[42]

Since a newly formed corporation that wants to start out as an S corporation does not have a preceding tax year, it has to file an election in the two-month and 15-day period after it is considered to have begun its first tax year. Its first tax year is considered to start when it issues stock to shareholders, acquires assets, or begins to do business, whichever occurs first. Filing of articles of incorporation with the secretary of state usually does not begin the first taxable year.

Care must be taken to file the election at the right time, which can be tricky, since it is sometimes difficult to determine when a corporation first begins to do business. There can be some horrendous tax consequences if you operate the corporation as though it were an S corporation, and the election is later determined to have been filed too early or too late.

Extreme care must also be taken if a regular C corporation elects to change over to S corporation status; this should not be done without consulting a competent tax adviser. A regular corporation that elects to become an S corporation will generally be subject to an eventual corporate-level tax on any built-in gains on its assets — assets with a value greater than their tax basis — if assets are sold for a gain within 10 years.

Terminating an S Corporation Election

If it becomes desirable to revoke or terminate S corporation status after a few years, as is often the case, this can be done if shareholders owning more than half the stock sign and file a revocation form.[43] A revocation is effective for the tax year it is filed, if it is filed during the first two months and 15 days of that tax year.[44] If it is filed later in the year, it does not become effective until the next tax year.[45]

Doing anything, however, that causes the corporation to cease to qualify as an S corporation — such as selling stock to a corporate shareholder — will also terminate the election, effective on the first day after the corporation ceases to qualify as an S corporation. In that case, the company must file two short-period tax returns for the year, the first — up to the date it ceased to qualify — as an S corporation, the second as a regular taxable corporation. Once a corporation terminates an S corporation election, it cannot re-elect S corporation status for five years, unless it obtains the consent of the IRS.[46]

Reasons for Electing S Corporation Status

For a corporation, electing S corporation status can be very advantageous in some instances, and less so, or even disadvantageous in other situations.

An S corporation election should not be made without the advice and assistance of a tax professional, since it is a very complex and technical area of the tax law.

Electing S corporation treatment for a corporation is usually most favorable in these types of situations:

- Where it is expected that the corporation will experience losses for the initial year or years of doing business and where the shareholders will have income from other sources that the "passed through" losses can shelter from tax. Note that if S corporation losses are passive losses — such as losses from real estate investments — they can only be used to offset other passive activity income.

- Where, because of the low tax brackets the shareholders are in, there will be tax savings if the anticipated profits of the corporation are passed through to them, rather than being taxed at higher corporate tax rates.

- Where the nature of the corporation's business is such that the corporation does not need to retain a major portion of profits in the business. In this case, all or most of the profits can be distributed as dividends without the double taxation that would occur if no S corporation election were in effect.

- Where a corporation is in danger of incurring an accumulated earnings penalty tax for failure to pay out its profits as dividends.

It will often be advantageous for your corporation to operate as an S corporation in its early years, when losses can be passed through to shareholders, or when income is not so great as to push the shareholders into higher tax brackets. Also, the nontax advantage of being incorporated and protected from personal liability if the business fails is generally most important during the early years of operation, when the risk of failure is highest.

Thus, many businesses initially start off as S corporations, obtaining the advantage of limited liability while being taxed much like an unincorporated business. Later, when or if the profit from the business becomes very substantial, the S corporation election can be terminated, and the C corporation can be used to split income between the corporation and its stockholder/employees.

Disadvantages of S Corporation Election

While there are some significant advantages to operating as an S corporation, the S corporation election is frequently not advisable under some circumstances. Some of the possible disadvantages of operating your business in the form of an S corporation are:

- The change to S corporation status may eventually result in a large corporate-level tax on built-in gains or an immediate LIFO recapture tax.

- The tax law regarding S corporations is very complex and you should expect to pay fairly substantial additional legal or accounting fees to your tax adviser, compared to what would be necessary with a regular corporation.

- S corporations are now treated almost exactly like regular corporations with respect to pension and profit-sharing plans. One important difference remains; any employee who owns 5% or more of the stock and participates in the S corporation's pension or profit-sharing plan is prohibited from borrowing from the plan, unlike a participant in a regular corporation's retirement plan.[47]

- Certain built-in gains of an S corporation may be taxed to the corporation and the shareholder for federal tax purposes.[48]

- Fringe benefit payments for medical, disability, and group-term life insurance for 2% shareholders are deductible, to the corporation, but are taxable to the shareholder/employee.[49]

- Unlike many regular corporations, very few newly electing S corporations may now have a fiscal tax year that ends earlier than September.[50]

For your convenience, a sample of *Form 2553, Election by a Small Business Corporation,* and a summary of key characteristics regarding business organization forms are provided on the following pages.

Recent Tax Changes for S Corporations

In *Publication 589, Tax Information on S Corporations*, the IRS points out two important recent changes that all S corporations should know. These changes include:

- An increase in corporate estimated tax percentage. For tax years beginning in 1992, the annual estimated tax percentage for S corporations increases from 90%, wherever indicated, to 93%.

- An extension of certain credit provisions. Under the Tax Extension Act of 1991, the research credit, jobs credit, energy credit, and low-income housing credit expired on June 30, 1992, but may be retroactively extended in 1993.

Corporate Do's and Don'ts Checklist

Do:

☐ Maintain capital reserves sufficient to meet reasonably foreseeable needs of the corporation, including liability insurance coverage.

☐ Maintain an active and independent board of directors.

☐ If asked to serve on a board of directors, be active and use your best independent business judgment even if that requires you to disagree with management.

☐ Use business cards and letterhead which reflect the corporate name.

☐ Make certain that corporate letters and agreements are signed by the corporation.

☐ Distinguish preincorporation activities by a promoter from post-incorporation activities by officers or directors.

☐ Use formal loan documents, including notes and security agreements, for corporate loans, especially to officers and directors and be sure to have a board resolution authorizing the transaction.

☐ Use written leases, purchase and sale agreements, and bills of sale in transactions involving shareholders, officers, and directors and be sure to have a board resolution authorizing the transaction.

☐ Use separate offices for activities of separate businesses.

☐ Use separate telephone lines for each business.

☐ Use separate employees for each business.

☐ Allow each corporation to own its own assets or equipment or lease them pursuant to written lease agreements.

☐ Apply for all required permits, licenses, and identification numbers in the corporate name.

☐ Obtain necessary business insurance in the corporate name.

Don't:

☐ Commingle personal and corporate assets or assets among related corporations.

☐ Divert corporate assets for personal use.

☐ Engage in any act for an illegal or improper purpose such as to defraud creditors or oppress minority shareholders.

☐ Hold yourself out as the owner of the business; you may be a shareholder, officer, or director, but the corporation should be held out as the legal entity for the action.

☐ Engage in transactions between corporations and their shareholders, officers, and directors on any basis other than on an arm's length basis.

☐ If several corporations are involved, don't use the same people as officers and directors of each corporation.

For more information on protecting your personal limited liability, plus maintaining corporate formalities, see *The Essential Corporation Handbook*, by Carl R.J. Sniffen, from The Oasis Press® (800) 288-2275.

2.6 Summary of the Key Characteristics of the Various Legal Forms of

	Proprietorship	General Partnership
Simplicity in Operation and Formation	Simplest to establish and operate.	Relatively simple, informal, but is usually desirable to have formal written agreement between partners.
Liability for Debts, Taxes, and Other Claims	Owner has unlimited personal liability.	Partners all have unlimited personal liability.
Federal Income Taxation of Business Profits	Taxed to the owner at individual tax rates of up to 31% or more, depending on exemptions and deductions which may phase out.	Taxed to partners at their individual tax rates.
Double Taxation if Profits Withdrawn from Business	No.	No.
Deduction of Losses by Owners	Yes. May be subject to "passive loss" restrictions.	Yes.
Social Security Tax on Earnings of Owner from Business	15.3% of owner's self-employment earnings in 1992 on first $55,500 of income, plus 2.9% on earnings between $55,500 and $130,200, half of which is now deductible for income tax purposes.	15.3% of each partner's share of self-employment earnings from the business in 1992 on up to $55,500 in earnings, plus 2.9% on earnings between $55,500 and $130,200, half of which is now deductible for income tax purposes on the partner's individual income tax return.
Unemployment Taxes on Earnings of Owner from Business	None.	None.
Retirement Plans	Keogh plan. Deductions, other features now generally the same as for corporate pension and profit-sharing plans. But proprietor cannot borrow from Keogh Plan.	Keogh plan. Same as for proprietorships. A 10% partner cannot borrow from Keogh Plan.
Tax Treatment of Medical, Disability, and Group-Term Life Insurance on Owners	Not deductible, except part of medical expenses may be an itemized deduction on owner's tax return, including medical insurance premiums. But 25% of medical insurance on owner now allowed as a deduction from adjusted gross income — at least until June 30, 1992.[51]	Not deductible, except part of medical expenses may be an itemized deduction on owner's tax return, including medical insurance premiums. But 25% of medical insurance on owner now allowed as a deduction from adjusted gross income — at least until June 30, 1992.[52]
Taxation of Dividends Received on Investments	Dividends received on stock investments are fully taxable to owner.	Dividends taxable to individual partners. See proprietorship.

Business Organization

Limited Partnership	Regular Corporation	S Corporation
More complex and expensive to establish than other unincorporated forms of business. Requires written agreement and filing of certificate. Managed by general partners only.	Requires most formality in establishment and operation.	Same as a regular corporation but requires close oversight by a tax adviser (an additional cost).
General partners are personally liable; limited partners are liable only to the extent of their investment.	Stockholders are not generally liable for corporate debts, but often have to guarantee loans, as a practical matter, if the corporation borrows money. Also, corporate officers may be liable to the IRS for failure to withhold and pay withholding taxes on employees' wages.	Stockholders are not generally liable for corporate debts, but often have to guarantee loans, as a practical matter, if the corporation borrows money. Also, corporate officers may be liable to the IRS for failure to withhold and pay withholding taxes on employees' wages.
Taxed to partners at their individual tax rates.	Taxed to the corporation, at rates higher than those of individuals — maximum of 34% or 39% in 1992.	Taxed to individual owners at their individual rates — certain gains are taxable to the corporation as well.
No.	Yes, but not on reasonable compensation paid to owners who are employees of the corporation.	No, in general.
Yes. Limited partner's deductions generally cannot exceed the amount he or she has invested in a limited partnership interest — except for real estate, in some instances. Losses generally restricted by "passive loss" rules.	No. Corporation must carry over initial losses to offset future profits, if any.	Yes, in general, for federal tax purposes. But not for state tax purposes in all states. Loss for a shareholder limited to investment in stock plus amount loaned to the corporation. Losses may be subject to "passive loss" restrictions.
15.3% of each partner's share of self-employment earnings from the business in 1992 on up to $55,500 in earnings, plus 2.9% on earnings between $55,500 and $130,200, half of which is now deductible for income tax purposes on the partner's individual income tax return.	Owner/employee of corporation pays 7.65% on his or her salary and corporation pays 7.65%. Total Social Security (FICA) tax on employer and employee is 15.3% of employee's first $55,500 of wages (in 1992). Employee and corporation each pay 1.45% on wages above $55,500, up to limit of $130,200.	Owner/employee of corporation pays 7.65% on his or her salary and corporation pays 7.65%. Total Social Security (FICA) tax on employer and employee is 15.3% of employee's first $55,500 of wages (in 1992). Employee and corporation each pay 1.45% on wages above $55,500, up to limit of $130,200.
None.	Yes. State and federal unemployment taxes apply to salaries paid to owners.	Yes. State and federal unemployment taxes apply to salaries paid to owners.
Keogh plan. Same as for proprietorships. A 10% partner cannot borrow from Keogh Plan.	Corporate retirement plans are no longer significantly better than Keogh plans. Deduction limits are same now as for Keogh, but participants can borrow from plan.	Plans now essentially identical to regular corporate retirement plans, except that shareholder/employee (5% shareholder) of S corporation cannot borrow from plan.
Not deductible, except part of medical expenses may be an itemized deduction on owner's tax return, including medical insurance premiums. But 25% of medical insurance on owner now allowed as a deduction from adjusted gross income — at least until June 30, 1992.[53]	Corporations may be allowed to deduct corporation medical insurance premium or reimbursements paid under medical reimbursement plan. Generally not taxable to the employee, even if employee is an owner. Similar treatment for disability and group-term life insurance plans.	Fringe benefits for 2% shareholders are deductible by corporation, but must be included in income of the shareholder who may be allowed to deduct 25% of medical insurance from adjusted gross income.
Dividends taxable to individual partners. See proprietorship.	Dividends are taxable to the corporation. However, 70% of the dividends received are generally free of federal income tax (unless stock is purchased with borrowed money), an important tax advantage.	Dividends taxable to individual shareholders of the S corporation, as in the case of a partnership.

Footnotes

1. I.R.C. §§3301(1) and 3302(b).
2. I.R.C. §3306(b)(1).
3. I.R.C. §162(l).
4. I.R.C. §§444 and 7519.
5. I.R.C. §6050K.
6. I.R.C. §11(b)(2).
7. I.R.C. §535(c)(2).
8. I.R.C. §531.
9. I.R.C. §1366(e).
10. I.R.C. §1(g).
11. I.R.C. §4975(d) (last paragraph).
12. I.R.C. §219.
13. I.R.C. §219(g).
14. I.R.C. §219(g)(3).
15. I.R.C. §§219 and 404(a).
16. I.R.C. §501(a).
17. I.R.C. §402(e).
18. I.R.C. §1372(a).
19. Rev. Rul. 91-26, 1991-15 I.R.B.
20. I.R.C. §§105–106.
21. I.R.C. §105(b).
22. I.R.C. §105.
23. I.R.C. §106.
24. I.R.C. §105(g).
25. I.R.C. §104(a)(3).
26. I.R.C. §79(a).
27. I.R.C. §243(a).
28. I.R.C. §246A.
29. I.R.C. §541.
30. I.R.C. §1374.
31. I.R.C. §1366.
32. I.R.C. §1361(b).
33. I.R.C. §1361(b)(1)(C).
34. I.R.C. §1361(b)(1)(B).
35. I.R.C. §1361(b)(1)(D).
36. I.R.C. §1361(b)(1)(A).
37. I.R.C. §1361(c).
38. I.R.C. §1361(b)(2)(A).
39. I.R.C. §1362(d)(3).
40. I.R.C. §1362(d)(3)(B).
41. I.R.C. §1362(a)(2).
42. I.R.C. §1362(b).
43. I.R.C. §1362(d)(1)(B).
44. I.R.C. §1362(d)(1)(C)(i).
45. I.R.C. §1362(d)(i)(C)(ii).
46. I.R.C. §1362(g).
47. I.R.C. §4975(d).
48. I.R.C. §1374(a).
49. Rev. Rul. 91-26, 1991-15 I.R.B.
50. I.R.C. §1378(a).
51. I.R.C. §162(l).
52. Id.
53. Id.

Department of the Treasury
Internal Revenue Service

Instructions for Form 2553
(Revised December 1990)
Election by a Small Business Corporation
(Section references are to the Internal Revenue Code unless otherwise noted.)

SAMPLE

Paperwork Reduction Act Notice.—We ask for the information on this form to carry out the Internal Revenue laws of the United States. You are required to give us the information. We need it to ensure that you are complying with these laws and to allow us to figure and collect the right amount of tax.

The time needed to complete and file this form will vary depending on individual circumstances. The estimated average time is:

Recordkeeping . . . . .6 hrs., 28 min.
Learning about the law or the form . . . . .3 hrs., 16 min.
Preparing, copying, assembling, and sending the form to IRS . . . .3 hrs., 31 min.

If you have comments concerning the accuracy of these time estimates or suggestions for making this form more simple, we would be happy to hear from you. You can write to both the **Internal Revenue Service,** Washington, DC 20224, Attention: IRS Reports Clearance Officer, T:FP, and the **Office of Management and Budget,** Paperwork Reduction Project (1545-0146), Washington, DC 20503. **DO NOT** send the tax form to either of these offices. Instead, see the instructions below for information on where to file.

General Instructions

A. Purpose.—To elect to be treated as an "S Corporation," a corporation must file Form 2553. The election permits the income of the S corporation to be taxed to the shareholders of the corporation rather than to the corporation itself, except as provided in Subchapter S of the Code. For more information, see **Publication 589,** Tax Information on S Corporations.

B. Who May Elect.—Your corporation may make the election to be treated as an S corporation only if it meets **all** of the following tests:

1. It is a domestic corporation.

2. It has no more than 35 shareholders. A husband and wife (and their estates) are treated as one shareholder for this requirement. All other persons are treated as separate shareholders.

3. It has only individuals, estates, or certain trusts as shareholders. See the instructions for Part III regarding qualified subchapter S trusts.

4. It has no nonresident alien shareholders.

5. It has only one class of stock. See sections 1361(c)(4) and (5) for additional details.

6. It is not one of the following ineligible corporations:

(a) a corporation that owns 80% or more of the stock of another corporation, unless the other corporation has not begun business and has no gross income;

(b) a bank or thrift institution;

(c) an insurance company subject to tax under the special rules of Subchapter L of the Code;

(d) a corporation that has elected to be treated as a possessions corporation under section 936; or

(e) a domestic international sales corporation (DISC) or former DISC.

See section 1361(b)(2) for details.

7. It has a permitted tax year as required by section 1378 or makes a section 444 election to have a tax year other than a permitted tax year. Section 1378 defines a permitted tax year as a tax year ending December 31, or any other tax year for which the corporation establishes a business purpose to the satisfaction of the IRS. See Part II for details on requesting a fiscal tax year based on a business purpose or on making a section 444 election.

8. Each shareholder consents as explained in the instructions for Column K.

See sections 1361, 1362, and 1378 for additional information on the above tests.

C. Where To File.—File this election with the Internal Revenue Service Center listed below.

If the corporation's principal business, office, or agency is located in	Use the following Internal Revenue Service Center address
New Jersey, New York (New York City and counties of Nassau, Rockland, Suffolk, and Westchester)	Holtsville, NY 00501
New York (all other counties), Connecticut, Maine, Massachusetts, New Hampshire, Rhode Island, Vermont	Andover, MA 05501
Florida, Georgia, South Carolina	Atlanta, GA 39901
Indiana, Kentucky, Michigan, Ohio, West Virginia	Cincinnati, OH 45999
Kansas, New Mexico, Oklahoma, Texas	Austin, TX 73301
Alaska, Arizona, California (counties of Alpine, Amador, Butte, Calaveras, Colusa, Contra Costa, Del Norte, El Dorado, Glenn, Humboldt, Lake, Lassen, Marin, Mendocino, Modoc, Napa, Nevada, Placer, Plumas, Sacramento, San Joaquin, Shasta, Sierra, Siskiyou, Solano, Sonoma, Sutter, Tehama, Trinity, Yolo, and Yuba), Colorado, Idaho, Montana, Nebraska, Nevada, North Dakota, Oregon, South Dakota, Utah, Washington, Wyoming	Ogden, UT 84201
California (all other counties), Hawaii	Fresno, CA 93888
Illinois, Iowa, Minnesota, Missouri, Wisconsin	Kansas City, MO 64999
Alabama, Arkansas, Louisiana, Mississippi, North Carolina, Tennessee	Memphis, TN 37501
Delaware, District of Columbia, Maryland, Pennsylvania, Virginia	Philadelphia, PA 19255

D. When To Make the Election.—Complete Form 2553 and file it either: (1) at any time during that portion of the first tax year the election is to take effect which occurs before the 16th day of the third month of that tax year (if the tax year has 2½ months or less, and the election is made not later than 2 months and 15 days after the first day of the tax year, it shall be treated as timely made during such year), or (2) in the tax year before the first tax year it is to take effect. An election made by a small business corporation after the 15th day of the third month but before the end of the tax year is treated as made for the next year. For example, if a calendar tax year corporation makes the election in April 1991, it is effective for the corporation's 1992 calendar tax year. See section 1362(b) for more information.

E. Acceptance or Non-Acceptance of Election.—The Service Center will notify you if your election is accepted and when it will take effect. You will also be notified if your election is not accepted. You should generally receive a determination on your election within 60 days after you have filed Form 2553. If the Q1 box in Part II is checked on page 2, the corporation will receive a ruling letter from IRS in Washington, DC, which approves or denies the selected tax year. When Item Q1 is checked, it will generally take an additional 90 days for the Form 2553 to be accepted.

Do not file Form 1120S until you are notified that your election is accepted. If you are now required to file **Form 1120,** U.S. Corporation Income Tax Return, or any other applicable tax return, continue filing it until your election takes effect.

Care should be exercised to ensure that the election is received by the Internal Revenue Service. If you are not notified of acceptance or nonacceptance of your election within 3 months of date of filing (date mailed), or within 6 months if Part II, Item Q1, is checked, you should take follow-up action by corresponding with the Service Center where the election was filed. If filing of Form 2553 is questioned by IRS, an acceptable proof of filing is: (1) certified receipt (timely filed); (2) Form 2553 with accepted stamp; (3) Form 2553 with stamped IRS received date; or (4) IRS letter stating that Form 2553 had been accepted.

F. End of Election.—Once the election is made, it stays in effect for all years until it is terminated. During the 5 years after the election is terminated under section 1362(d), the corporation can make another election on Form 2553 only with IRS consent.

Specific Instructions

Part I

Part I must be completed by all corporations.

Name and Address of Corporation.— Enter the true corporate name as set forth in the corporate charter or other legal document creating it. If the corporation's mailing address is the same as someone else's, such as a shareholder's, please enter this person's name below the name of the corporation. Include the suite, room, or other unit number after the street address. If the Post Office does not deliver to the street address and the corporation has a P.O. box, show the P.O. box number instead of the street address. If the corporation has changed its name or address since applying for its EIN (filing Form SS-4), be sure to check the box in item F of Part I.

A. Employer Identification Number.— If you have applied for an employer identification number (EIN) but have not received it, enter "applied for." If the corporation does not have an EIN, you should apply for one on **Form SS-4**, Application for Employer Identification Number, available from most IRS and Social Security Administration offices.

C. Effective Date of Election.— Enter the beginning effective date (month, day, year) of the tax year that you have requested for the S corporation. Generally, this will be the beginning date of the tax year for which the ending effective date is required to be shown in item I, Part I. For a new corporation (first year the corporation exists) it will generally be the date required to be shown in item H, Part I. The tax year of a new corporation starts on the date that it has shareholders, acquires assets, or begins doing business, whichever happens first. If the effective date for item C for a newly formed corporation is later than the date in item H, the corporation should file Form 1120 or Form 1120-A, for the tax period between these dates.

Column K. Shareholders' Consent Statement.— Each shareholder who owns (or is deemed to own) stock at the time the election is made must consent to the election. If the election is made during the corporation's first tax year for which it is effective, any person who held stock at any time during the portion of that year which occurs before the time the election is made, must consent to the election although the person may have sold or transferred his or her stock before the election is made. Each shareholder consents by signing and dating in column K or signing and dating a separate consent statement described below. If stock is owned by a trust that is a qualified shareholder, the deemed owner of the trust must consent. See section 1361(c)(2) for details regarding qualified trusts that may be shareholders and rules on determining who is the deemed owner of the trust.

An election made during the first 2½ months of the tax year is considered made for the following tax year if one or more of the persons who held stock in the corporation during such tax year and before the election was made did not consent to the election. See section 1362(b)(2).

If a husband and wife have a community interest in the stock or in the income from it, both must consent. Each tenant in common, joint tenant, and tenant by the entirety also must consent.

A minor's consent is made by the minor or the legal representative of the minor, or by a natural or adoptive parent of the minor if no legal representative has been appointed. The consent of an estate is made by an executor or administrator.

Continuation sheet or separate consent statement.— If you need a continuation sheet or use a separate consent statement, attach it to Form 2553. The separate consent statement must contain the name, address, and employer identification number of the corporation and the shareholder information requested in columns J through N of Part I.

If you want, you may combine all the shareholders' consents in one statement.

Column L.— Enter the number of shares of stock each shareholder owns and the dates the stock was acquired. If the election is made during the corporation's first tax year for which it is effective, do not list the shares of stock for those shareholders who sold or transferred all of their stock before the election was made. However, these shareholders must still consent to the election for it to be effective for the tax year.

Column M.— Enter the social security number of each shareholder who is an individual. Enter the employer identification number of each shareholder that is an estate or a qualified trust.

Column N.— Enter the month and day that each shareholder's tax year ends. If a shareholder is changing his or her tax year, enter the tax year the shareholder is changing to, and attach an explanation indicating the present tax year and the basis for the change (e.g., automatic revenue procedure or letter ruling request).

If the election is made during the corporation's first tax year for which it is effective, you do not have to enter the tax year of any shareholder who sold or transferred all of his or her stock before the election was made.

Signature.— Form 2553 must be signed by the president, treasurer, assistant treasurer, chief accounting officer, or other corporate officer (such as tax officer) authorized to sign.

Part II

Complete Part II if you selected a tax year ending on any date other than December 31 (other than a 52-53-week tax year ending with reference to the month of December).

Box P1.— Attach a statement showing separately for each month the amount of gross receipts for the most recent 47 months as required by section 4.03(3) of

Revenue Procedure 87-32, 1987-2 C.B. 396. A corporation that does not have a 47-month period of gross receipts cannot establish a natural business year under section 4.01(1).

Box Q1.— For examples of an acceptable business purpose for requesting a fiscal tax year, see Revenue Ruling 87-57, 1987-2 C.B. 117.

In addition to a statement showing the business purpose for the requested fiscal year, you must attach the other information necessary to meet the ruling request requirements of Revenue Procedure 90-1, 1990-1 C.B. 356 (updated annually). Also attach a statement that shows separately the amount of gross receipts from sales or services (and inventory costs, if applicable) for each of the 36 months preceding the effective date of the election to be an S corporation. If the corporation has been in existence for fewer than 36 months, submit figures for the period of existence.

If you check box Q1, you must also pay a user fee of $200 (subject to change). Do not pay the fee when filing Form 2553. The Service Center will send Form 2553 to the IRS in Washington, DC, who, in turn, will notify the corporation that the fee is due. See Revenue Procedure 90-17, 1990-1 C.B. 479.

Box Q2.— If the corporation makes a back-up section 444 election for which it is qualified, then the election must be exercised in the event the business purpose request is not approved. Under certain circumstances, the tax year requested under the back-up section 444 election may be different than the tax year requested under business purpose. See **Form 8716**, Election To Have a Tax Year Other Than a Required Tax Year, for details on making a back-up section 444 election.

Boxes Q2 and R2.— If the corporation is not qualified to make the section 444 election after making the item Q2 back-up section 444 election or indicating its intention to make the election in item R1, and therefore it later files a calendar year return, it should write "Section 444 Election Not Made" in the top left corner of the 1st calendar year Form 1120S it files.

Part III

Certain Qualified Subchapter S Trusts (QSSTs) may make the QSST election required by section 1361(d)(2) in Part III. Part III may be used to make the QSST election only if corporate stock has been transferred to the trust on or before the date on which the corporation makes its election to be an S corporation. However, a statement can be used in lieu of Part III to make the election.

Note: *Part III may be used only in conjunction with making the Part I election (i.e., Form 2553 cannot be filed with only Part III completed).*

The deemed owner of the QSST must also consent to the S corporation election in column K, page 1, of Form 2553. See section 1361(c)(2).

*U.S. GPO:1991-518-941/20363

Form **2553**

(Rev. December 1990)

Department of the Treasury
Internal Revenue Service

Election by a Small Business Corporation

(Under section 1362 of the Internal Revenue Code)

▶ For Paperwork Reduction Act Notice, see page 1 of instructions.
▶ See separate instructions.

OMB No. 1545-0146

Expires 11-30-93

Notes:
1. This election, to be treated as an "S corporation," can be accepted only if all the tests in General Instruction B are met; all signatures in Parts I and III are originals (no photocopies); and the exact name and address of the corporation and other required form information are provided.
2. Do not file Form 1120S until you are notified that your election is accepted. See General Instruction E.

Part I Election Information

Please Type or Print

Name of corporation (see instructions)	**A** Employer identification number (see instructions)
Number, street, and room or suite no. (If a P.O. box, see instructions.)	**B** Name and telephone number (including area code) of corporate officer or legal representative who may be called for information
City or town, state, and ZIP code	**C** Election is to be effective for tax year beginning (month, day, year)

D Is the corporation the outgrowth or continuation of any form of predecessor? . . . ☐ Yes ☐ No

If "Yes," state name of predecessor, type of organization, and period of its existence ▶ ....

E Date of incorporation

F Check here ▶ ☐ if the corporation has changed its name or address since applying for the employer identification number shown in item A above.

G State of incorporation

H If this election takes effect for the first tax year the corporation exists, enter month, day, and year of the **earliest** of the following: (1) date the corporation first had shareholders, (2) date the corporation first had assets, or (3) date the corporation began doing business. ▶

I Selected tax year: Annual return will be filed for tax year ending (month and day) ▶ ....

If the tax year ends on any date other than December 31, except for an automatic 52-53-week tax year ending with reference to the month of December, you **must** complete Part II on the back. If the date you enter is the ending date of an automatic 52-53-week tax year, write "52-53-week year" to the right of the date. See Temporary Regulations section 1.441-2T(e)(3).

J Name of each shareholder, person having a community property interest in the corporation's stock, and each tenant in common, joint tenant, and tenant by the entirety. (A husband and wife (and their estates) are counted as one shareholder in determining the number of shareholders without regard to the manner in which the stock is owned.)	**K** Shareholders' Consent Statement. We, the undersigned shareholders, consent to the corporation's election to be treated as an "S corporation" under section 1362(a). (Shareholders sign and date below.)*		**L** Stock owned		**M** Social security number or employer identification number (see instructions)	**N** Shareholder's tax year ends (month and day)
	Signature	Date	Number of shares	Dates acquired		

*For this election to be valid, the consent of each shareholder, person having a community property interest in the corporation's stock, and each tenant in common, joint tenant, and tenant by the entirety must either appear above or be attached to this form. (See instructions for Column K if continuation sheet or a separate consent statement is needed.)

Under penalties of perjury, I declare that I have examined this election, including accompanying schedules and statements, and to the best of my knowledge and belief, it is true, correct, and complete.

Signature of officer ▶ 　　　　　　　　Title ▶ 　　　　　　　　Date ▶

See Parts II and III on back.

Form **2553** (Rev. 12-90)

Part II Selection of Fiscal Tax Year (All corporations using this Part must complete item O and one of items P, Q, or R.)

O Check the applicable box below to indicate whether the corporation is:

1. ☐ A new corporation adopting the tax year entered in item I, Part I.

2. ☐ An existing corporation retaining the tax year entered in item I, Part I.

3. ☐ An existing corporation changing to the tax year entered in item I, Part I.

P Complete item P if the corporation is using the expeditious approval provisions of Revenue Procedure 87-32, 1987-2 C.B. 396, to request: **(1)** a natural business year (as defined in section 4.01(1) of Rev. Proc. 87-32), or **(2)** a year that satisfies the ownership tax year test in section 4.01(2) of Rev. Proc. 87-32. Check the applicable box below to indicate the representation statement the corporation is making as required under section 4 of Rev. Proc. 87-32.

1. Natural Business Year ▶ ☐ I represent that the corporation is retaining or changing to a tax year that coincides with its natural business year as defined in section 4.01(1) of Rev. Proc. 87-32 and as verified by its satisfaction of the requirements of section 4.02(1) of Rev. Proc. 87-32. In addition, if the corporation is changing to a natural business year as defined in section 4.01(1), I further represent that such tax year results in less deferral of income to the owners than the corporation's present tax year. I also represent that the corporation is not described in section 3.01(2) of Rev. Proc. 87-32. (See instructions for additional information that must be attached.)

2. Ownership Tax Year ▶ ☐ I represent that shareholders holding more than half of the shares of the stock (as of the first day of the tax year to which the request relates) of the corporation have the same tax year or are concurrently changing to the tax year that the corporation adopts, retains, or changes to per item I, Part I. I also represent that the corporation is not described in section 3.01(2) of Rev. Proc. 87-32.

Note: If you do not use item P and the corporation wants a fiscal tax year, complete either item Q or R below. Item Q is used to request a fiscal tax year based on a business purpose and to make a back-up section 444 election. Item R is used to make a regular section 444 election.

Q Business Purpose—To request a fiscal tax year based on a business purpose, you must check box Q1 and pay a user fee. See instructions for details. You may also check box Q2 and/or box Q3.

1. Check here ▶ ☐ if the fiscal year entered in item I, Part I, is requested under the provisions of section 6.03 of Rev. Proc. 87-32. Attach to Form 2553 a statement showing the business purpose for the requested fiscal year. See instructions for additional information that must be attached.

2. Check here ▶ ☐ to show that the corporation intends to make a back-up section 444 election in the event the corporation's business purpose request is not approved by the IRS. (See instructions for more information.)

3. Check here ▶ ☐ to show that the corporation agrees to adopt or change to a tax year ending December 31 if necessary for the IRS to accept this election for S corporation status in the event: (1) the corporation's business purpose request is not approved and the corporation makes a back-up section 444 election, but is ultimately not qualified to make a section 444 election, or (2) the corporation's business purpose request is not approved and the corporation did not make a back-up section 444 election.

R Section 444 Election—To make a section 444 election, you must check box R1 and you may also check box R2.

1. Check here ▶ ☐ to show the corporation will make, if qualified, a section 444 election to have the fiscal tax year shown in item I, Part I. To make the election, you must complete **Form 8716,** Election To Have a Tax Year Other Than a Required Tax Year, and either attach it to Form 2553 or file it separately.

2. Check here ▶ ☐ to show that the corporation agrees to adopt or change to a tax year ending December 31 if necessary for the IRS to accept this election for S corporation status in the event the corporation is ultimately not qualified to make a section 444 election.

Part III Qualified Subchapter S Trust (QSST) Election Under Section 1361(d)(2)**

Income beneficiary's name and address	Social security number
Trust's name and address	Employer identification number

Date on which stock of the corporation was transferred to the trust (month, day, year) ▶

In order for the trust named above to be a QSST and thus a qualifying shareholder of the S corporation for which this Form 2553 is filed, I hereby make the election under section 1361(d)(2). Under penalties of perjury, I certify that the trust meets the definition requirements of section 1361(d)(3) and that all other information provided in Part III is true, correct, and complete.

Signature of income beneficiary or signature and title of legal representative or other qualified person making the election   Date

**Use of Part III to make the QSST election may be made only if stock of the corporation has been transferred to the trust on or before the date on which the corporation makes its election to be an S corporation. The QSST election must be made and filed separately if stock of the corporation is transferred to the trust after the date on which the corporation makes the S election.

*U.S. GPO:1991-518-943/20365

SAMPLE

Chapter 3

Buying an Existing Business

Trust in Allah. But always tie your camel.

— Arab proverb

3.1 General Considerations

Obviously, it may not be necessary for you to build your business from the ground up. If you wish to go into a particular type of business, you may find an appropriate existing business that is for sale. Buying an existing business can have considerable advantages over starting one from scratch, and one of the most important of these is the chance to start out with an established customer base. It is also sometimes possible to have the seller stay on as an employee or consultant for a transitional period to help you become familiar with the operation of the business.

Other advantages of purchasing a going business include:

- You may be able to take a regular draw or salary right from the start, if it is a profitable operation. This is usually not the case in a start-up operation, which typically starts off losing money.

- Your risk is frequently less when you buy an established, profitable business. You know that it has a viable market if it is already profitable. Your main risks are that something will change, such as new competition or product obsolescence, that will adversely affect the business after you acquire it. Another risk is that you will mismanage it.

- Getting started is simpler. By buying an established business, you can focus your attention on giving good service and operating profitably. Since most facilities, operating systems, and employees will already be in place, your efforts will not be diluted by remodeling the premises, trying to hire employees, setting up accounting systems, acquiring initial inventory, and the like. With an existing business, in most cases, you should be able to step right into an operation that has already been established by someone else.

While there are some definite advantages to buying an established business, as compared to starting a new business from nothing, it can also be a lot more complicated and involves many potential pitfalls that you must avoid. The watchword in buying any kind of business should be *caveat emptor* — let the buyer beware.

Because the process of buying and selling businesses is very complicated even for experts, do not attempt it without retaining the services of a reliable attorney and, usually, a good accountant. Even skilled professionals, however, can generally only protect you from certain legal, financial, or tax pitfalls that arise in connection with the purchase of a business. Many of the potential problems that would not become obvious until it is too late can only be spotted in advance, if at all, by the exercise of your good judgment and as a result of your doing the necessary homework. Important pitfalls you should look out for in connection with buying an existing business are discussed in Section 3.3.

3.2 Finding a Business for Sale

How do you go about finding a business that is for sale? There are a number of ways to approach the problem, none of which are ideal, so you will probably want to use two or more of the approaches discussed below to find and buy an existing business.

Advertisements

The business opportunities section of your local newspaper, regional magazine, or trade association journal can be a major source of leads to businesses that are for sale. Such ads often do not tell you very much about the nature of the business, but at least they can be a starting point in your search. In many cases, the ads will have been placed by a business broker rather than the owner. The business broker will often be representing people who are seeking to sell their business.

Business Brokers and Realtors

Business brokers and realtors can be excellent sources to contact in your search for a business that is for sale. The main drawback of going through a business broker or realtor is that their fee (paid by the seller) is usually a percentage, often 10%, of the sales price of the business; so they, like the seller, are trying to get the highest possible price for the business. At the same time, the seller will usually want more than he or she would if the sale were made without a broker, since he or she knows that the broker will take a healthy commission out of the negotiated sales price.

Your local chamber of commerce can usually tell you a great deal about the local business community and also provide you with leads to firms that are for sale.

Local Chambers of Commerce

Often professionals, such as accountants, attorneys, and bankers, can provide leads regarding good businesses even before they are on the market. Frequently, a business client will tell his or her accountant, attorney, or banker that he or she is planning to sell out or retire, long before making any formal attempt to put the business up for sale. So, if you have friends who are accountants, attorneys, or bankers, take them to lunch and tell them what you have in mind. Typically, they will have a vested interest in finding a friendly buyer for a retiring client's business, since they may loose that account if the firm is sold to buyers who have their own professional advisers.

Accountants, Attorneys, and Bankers

Certified public accountants (CPAs) can be excellent sources of leads. Not only will they usually not charge you any kind of finder's fee, but they usually know which of their clients' businesses are little gold mines. In some cases, a CPA who has a very profitable client who wishes to sell out may even want to go into the business with you as a financial partner, leaving the day-to-day operations to you. In those cases, you can generally be sure that if the CPA is putting up his or her money, he or she has studied the client's business carefully and feels that it is a real money-maker. In short, the CPA will have already done much of the prescreening for you.

Often, if you see a small business that you think you might like to buy, the simplest approach will be to talk to the owner and see if he or she is interested in selling. While an owner may have had no serious thoughts about selling the business before, the appearance of an interested potential buyer is not only somewhat flattering, but it may even cause him or her to decide to sell out to you. Many businesses are bought and sold this way.

The Direct Approach

3.3 What to Look for Before You Leap

One of the first questions you may want to ask is: "Why are you selling your business?" Often the response will be that the owner wants to retire or is in poor health. While such an explanation may be true in many cases, it is also quite likely to be a well-rehearsed cover story. The real reason may be that the business is in a declining neighborhood, and the owner has been robbed several times recently and wants out. Or, the owners of a profitable little corner grocery store may be anxious to sell out while they can because they have learned that a major chain-store

Why Is the Business for Sale?

supermarket will be opening in the neighborhood in a few months. Another common reason behind a planned sale is that the business is either losing money or is not sufficiently profitable to make continuing worthwhile.

Whatever the real reason behind the owner's attempt to sell the business, you are unlikely to discover it without rolling up your sleeves and doing some independent and in-depth investigation.

Perhaps the best way to find that needle in the haystack is to talk to a number of other business people in the vicinity of the business you are investigating, particularly competitors in the same business. The firm's suppliers can also be a source of important information.

Even if you are very diligent and thorough, you may not be able to discover the hidden reason — if there is one — underlying the owner's desire to sell out. You may simply have to rely on your intuition in deciding whether the seller's reason for getting out of the business is the real reason. Just remember that in most cases a good and profitable small business is not something that most people walk away from, unless there is a very good reason to do so or the price offered is too good to turn down.

What Kind of Reputation Does the Firm Have?

One of the great advantages of taking over an existing business can be the opportunity to enjoy the reputation and goodwill that the existing owner has built up with customers and suppliers over the years. On the other hand, you may be much better off starting your own business from scratch than acquiring a business that has a poor reputation because of inferior work or merchandise or inferior service. It could take you years of hard work and reduced profits to overcome a former owner's poor reputation.

Even if the present owner has an excellent business reputation, you will want to know whether or not that goodwill is based on personal relationships built up between the owner and customers. These types of relationships aren't easily transferable. If the business relies heavily on a few key customers with whom the owner has very favorable business arrangements based on personal relationships, you may find that those business arrangements could be lost when you attempt to take the owner's place. In short, satisfy yourself that the goodwill you are buying is not based solely on personal relationships.

How Profitable Is the Business Now?

Unless you have some very good reasons to believe that you can operate the business more profitably than the current owner, you should not purchase a going business that does not produce a satisfactory profit under its current ownership. Thus, it is extremely important to find out how the business has fared financially for the last few years. This is where the services of a good accountant, who has knowledge of the particular type of business, will be invaluable.

You should insist on having the seller make available the business' financial and business records to your accountant. Be particularly wary of a business that keeps poor records. Often the most reliable sources of financial information can be the owner's income tax and sales tax returns, since it is not very likely that a business owner will report more income than actually earned for tax purposes.

If the owner is not willing to make financial records available, make it clear that you are not willing to negotiate any further. Buying a business is a lot like buying a used car; you want to make sure it runs before you pay for it.

Assets and Liabilities

You will need to review both the tangible and intangible assets of the business to see if they are worth the price you will be paying and also to determine just what assets you will be acquiring under the sales agreement. Personally inspect the business premises, and look for things like obsolete or unsalable inventory, out-of-date or rundown equipment, or furniture or fixtures that you may have to repair or replace. Also, determine whether the business is able to expand at its present location or if it is already too cramped. What you determine might require you to buy or lease additional facilities, if you wish to expand.

Review the terms of any leases. Some businesses close because of the imminent expiration of a favorable long-term lease or because the landlord plans to either raise the rent drastically or not renew the lease at all when the current lease expires.

If you will be acquiring the accounts receivable of the business, review them in detail. An aging of the accounts should be performed to determine how long various receivables have been outstanding. As a general rule, the longer a given receivable has been outstanding, the more likely it will prove to be uncollectible.

If a few large accounts of credit customers make up a significant portion of the receivables, you will want to particularly focus on those accounts and perhaps even have credit checks run on those customers. The bankruptcy of a major credit customer can ruin an otherwise successful business.

Part of your job in investigating a business that you want to buy is to find out what makes it tick — and make sure you will be getting whatever it is. For example, a business that has well-developed customer or mailing lists should ordinarily include those lists in the sales agreement. If there is a favorable lease, make sure it can and will be assigned to you. If patents, trademarks, trade names, or certain skilled employees are vital to the business, be sure that you will get them as part of the package. Also, you need to be aware of potential problems with the government that the seller is experiencing or expects to experience in the near future, such as zoning problems or new environmental restrictions that may hamper the business' profitability.

Hidden Liabilities

Liabilities of the business may not always show up on its accounting records. There may be any number of hidden claims against the business, such as security agreements encumbering the accounts receivable, inventory, or equipment, unpaid back taxes of various kinds, undisclosed lawsuits or potential lawsuits, or simply unpaid bills. If you are going to assume the liabilities of the business, the written agreement of sale should specify exactly which liabilities are being assumed and the dollar amount of each.

Other examples of hidden liabilities to look out for are:

- Pension liabilities — You may be taking on significant termination liability as a successor employer if the seller maintains or contributes to a pension fund and has unfunded pension fund liabilities.

- Vacation liability — If you are a successor employer, you may be liable for accrued but unpaid vacation leave of employees, which can be a significant hidden liability in some cases.

- Environmental problems — In many instances, current trend in the law is to impose liability for past environmental abuses on current land owners or lessors. Many banks and savings and loans have recently learned about this the hard way, after foreclosing on land which had been contaminated over the years by toxic substances and being held liable for clean-up costs as the contamination problems came to light. Many companies, when buying land or other companies that own land, now require the sellers to make detailed representations and warranties concerning environmental matters and to undertake extensive and costly environmental audits as a condition to buying a business. See Section 9.9 for a more detailed discussion of these issues.

If you intend to buy a corporation, you will be well-advised to buy the business assets from the corporation rather than purchase the stock of the corporation itself. The latter approach will subject the business to all hidden or contingent liabilities of the old corporation, whether or not you have agreed to pay for any liabilities of the corporation that predated the sale.

One exception to this general rule would be a corporation that had substantial tax loss or tax credit carryovers that you might be able to utilize if you bought the stock of the corporation rather than the assets. Be aware, however, that the tax law is a mine field when it comes to taking over someone else's tax loss or credit carryovers, so be certain before you do so that you seek good tax advice from a tax attorney or tax accountant, or you may find that the carryovers you thought you were acquiring have evaporated like a mirage.

Note that under the provisions of the Tax Reform Act of 1986, a change in ownership of more than 50% of the stock of a corporation in a three-year period will generally result in a severe restriction on the amount of its prior net operating losses that can be deducted in any subsequent taxable year.

3.4 Should You Consider a Franchise Operation?

Many small businesses, particularly fast food restaurants and print shops, are operated under franchises from a large national company. There can be substantial advantages to operating a franchised business, such as the benefits of national advertising, training programs, and assistance in setting up and running the business. If you are investigating a franchise, determine whether the franchise can be transferred to you, and if so, provide for the transfer as part of the sale in the sales agreement.

Carefully review the franchise agreement with the help of your attorney to determine whether the franchisor must approve the transfer, what the costs of operating are under the franchise and the other terms of the agreement.

If the franchisor is not a well-known and respected company, you should contact your local Better Business Bureau or an appropriate state agency to see if they have any information regarding the history, ethics, and reputation of the franchisor. You do not want to sign on with one of the less-than-reputable franchising operations that charge substantial franchising fees for very little in the way of useful services.

The Federal Trade Commission and a number of states provide franchising laws and regulations that offer you protection. These laws and regulations mandate the timing and content of the various disclosures which the franchisor must make to you, as the potential franchisee. You or your attorney should make sure that you ask for all of these disclosures on a timely basis, and you should be wary of any franchisor who does not provide these disclosures to you unless you ask for them.

A number of excellent publications, including *Franchise Bible: A Comprehensive Guide*, by Erwin J. Keup, can be obtained to help you evaluate various franchise opportunities. *Franchise Bible* explains what the franchise system entails and presents how both the franchisor and the franchisee should approach a franchising venture or opportunity. For more information on *Franchise Bible* and additional franchise publications, refer to Section 10.10.

If you acquire a franchise, either from the franchising company or as a transfer from another franchisee, you may be able to amortize (write off) the cost of acquiring the franchise, under certain circumstances, for federal income tax purposes. Consult your tax adviser as to whether or not this will be possible in your case.

If it is amortizable, you may want to allocate a significant part of the purchase price for the business to the cost of the franchise, which could save you major tax dollars in the long run; however, 1989 tax law changes have somewhat limited these benefits.

Once you've focused on a particular franchise opportunity, you will find the following checklist useful for evaluating the operation.

Checklist for Evaluating a Franchise

The Franchise

YES NO

☐ ☐ After studying it paragraph by paragraph, did your lawyer approve the franchise contract you are considering?

☐ ☐ Does the franchise call upon you to take any steps which are, according to your lawyer, unwise or illegal in your state, county, or city? _____

_____

_____

☐ ☐ Does the franchise give you an exclusive territory for the length of the franchise? or

☐ ☐ Can the franchisor sell a second or third franchise in your territory?

☐ ☐ Is the franchisor connected in any way with another franchise company handling similar merchandise or services?

If the answer to the last question is "yes," what is your protection against this second franchisor organization?

_____

_____

Under what circumstances can you terminate the franchise contract and at what cost to you, if you decide for any reason at all that you wish to cancel it? _____

_____

_____

☐ ☐ If you sell your franchise, will you be compensated for the goodwill you have built into the business?

The Franchisor

How many years has the firm offering you a franchise been in operation? _____

☐ ☐ Does the firm have a reputation for honesty and fair dealing among the local firms holding its franchise?

☐ ☐ Has the franchisor shown you any certified figures indicating exact net profits of one or more going firms?

☐ ☐ Have you personally checked these certified figures with the franchisor?

Will the firm assist you with:

☐ ☐ A management training program?

☐ ☐ An employee training program?

☐ ☐ A public relations program?

☐ ☐ Capital?

☐ ☐ Credit?

☐ ☐ Merchandising ideas?

☐ ☐ Will the firm help you find a good location for your new business?

☐ ☐ Is the franchising firm adequately financed so it can carry out its stated plan of financial assistance and expansion?

YES NO

☐ ☐ Is the franchisor a one-person company? or

☐ ☐ Is the franchisor a corporation with an experienced management trained in depth (so that there would always be an experienced person at its head)?

Exactly what can the franchisor do for you which you cannot do for yourself? _____
_____
_____

☐ ☐ Has the franchisor investigated you carefully enough to assure itself that you can successfully operate one of their franchises at a profit both to them and to you?

☐ ☐ Does your state have a law regulating the sale of franchises? and

☐ ☐ Has the franchisor complied with that law?

You – The Franchisee

How much equity capital will you have to have to purchase the franchise and operate it until your income equals your expenses? _____

Where are you going to get the capital? _____
_____

☐ ☐ Are you prepared to give up some independence of action to secure the advantages offered by the franchise?

☐ ☐ Do you really believe you have the innate ability, training, and experience to work smoothly and profitably with the franchisor, your employees, and your customers? _____
_____
_____
_____

☐ ☐ Are you ready to spend much or all of the remainder of your business life with this franchisor, offering its product or service to your public?

Your Market

☐ ☐ Have you made any study to determine whether the product or service which you propose to sell under franchise has a market in your territory at the prices you will have to charge?

Will the population in the territory given you increase ☐, remain static ☐, or decrease ☐ over the next five years?

Will the product or service you are considering be in greater demand ☐, about the same ☐, or less demand ☐ five years from now than today?

What competition exists in your territory already for the product or service you contemplate selling:
From nonfranchise firms? _____
From franchise firms? _____

Source: *Franchise Opportunities Handbook*, U.S. Department of Commerce, Washington, D.C., 1982.

3.5 Negotiating the Purchase

The Purchase Price

Neither this book nor any other can tell you how much you should pay for the business you are planning to buy. You are on your own on that one. If, however, you have done your homework thoroughly in investigating the business in question and have talked to bankers and other business people about what the normal purchase price for a business of that type and size should be, you should have a fairly good basis for determining whether the purchase price is a reasonable one. For example, you may find that small businesses of the type you are considering generally sell for about one and one-half times their annual gross sales. That could be very important to know if the seller is asking three times last year's gross sales.

Even if you conclude that the purchase price is a fair one, or even a bargain, you still must decide whether the price is one you can afford. Assuming that you can get the purchase price together, will it so deplete your liquid resources that you will not have enough working capital to make the business go or put you in a bind if income from the business drops off while you are at the learning stage? Or, if you are financing a substantial part of the purchase price, will your operating budget be able to stand the cost of making the payments on the debt and still leave enough for you to live on?

Remember, just because you can get the purchase price or down payment together does not necessarily mean that you can afford to buy a particular business even when the price is right.

Disclosure of Financial Information

At an early stage in the negotiations, specify that you want access to tax returns, books of account, and other financial records of the business, and make it clear that you have no interest in continuing the negotiations unless the seller cooperates fully in this respect. Also, be sure that this condition is expressed in any informal "memorandum of understanding" or letter of agreement between you and the seller that is written up prior to the final contract of sale.

Allocation of Purchase Price

One very important item that is often omitted in business sales agreements, perhaps because it is not absolutely necessary, is a provision in the agreement that shows how the parties agree to allocate the purchase price between the various assets that are being acquired. For tax purposes, however, it is often very important to both you, as the purchaser, and the seller to have a written allocation agreement.

Since you and the seller usually have opposing interests in making an agreed allocation, the courts and IRS have generally been willing to abide by any allocation agreement between the parties.

Allocation Formula

The Tax Reform Act of 1986, however, has clamped down rather severely on sale price allocations for businesses sold after May 6, 1986.[1] The 1986 law requires that both you and the seller abide by an allocation formula that works as follows:

- First, reduce the purchase price by the amount of any cash or cash equivalents.
- Next, allocate part of the purchase price to assets like certificates of deposit, government securities, readily marketable stocks or securities, and foreign currencies, up to the fair market value of each such asset.
- Then, any remaining unallocated portion of the purchase price is then allocated to tangible and intangible assets (land, improvements, equipment, inventories, patents, etc.), but not to exceed the fair market value of such assets.
- Finally, if there is still any portion of the purchase price left to be allocated, it must then be allocated to goodwill and "going concern" value, which you cannot deduct, depreciate, or amortize.

Allocation Agreements

Despite the Tax Reform Act of 1986's four-step formula for allocating the purchase price upon sale of a business, there are still some good reasons for having a purchase price allocation agreement when you buy an existing business.

The main advantage for doing so is to create a rationale for allocating at least some part of the purchase price to intangible assets that can be amortized or otherwise written off over some period of time. For example, you may purchase a business for a price well in excess of the value of its specific, easily identifiable assets. This is particularly likely to be the case in some service businesses where the value of the receivables and a few tangible assets, such as office equipment, furniture, and supplies, may be only a small fraction of the price paid for the business. In those cases, it clearly will not be possible to allocate $50,000 of the purchase price to a $5 supply of paper clips.

Instead, consider provisions in your sales agreement that allocate part of the purchase price to some of the following types of assets: customer lists, intangible assets, and a covenant not to compete.

Customer Lists

For some types of businesses, it may be appropriate to create a list of customer accounts that you are buying and an agreed value for each. In recent years, the courts have frequently allowed purchasers of businesses to deduct the price paid for customer accounts on some rational basis, such as writing off the amount agreed to be the value of a particular customer account in the year that customer is lost,[2] or on some other basis.

Other Intangible Assets

Similar advantageous tax treatment for you as the purchaser may be gained from allocating part of the purchase price to items, such as a very favorable lease with several remaining years, or to items like blueprints or technical knowhow that have a limited useful life.[3]

Note that legislation is pending in Congress that would provide for a uniform, 14-year amortization of the cost of all intangible assets, including goodwill.

Covenant Not to Compete

If the agreement includes a covenant by the seller not to compete with you for some period of time, you should seek an allocation in the agreement of a substantial part of the excess purchase price to the covenant, which, if the value assigned is reasonable, you should be able to amortize — deduct in part each year over the term of the covenant. In the past, a seller would have fiercely resisted such an allocation, since the covenant payments would have all been taxable to him or her as ordinary income; this is less of an issue now that capital gains are taxed at ordinary income rates.

Remember that if there is no agreement as to the value of the covenant not to compete, you lose taxwise, since the IRS generally treats the value of such a covenant as zero unless the parties have agreed that it has a particular value.[4]

Please note that tax regulations require both you and the seller to file *Form 8594* with the IRS any time a business is bought or sold. *Form 8594* reports certain information about the purchase price allocation.[5] Penalties for failure to file this form can be extremely large. Needless to say, the information on your *Form 8594* and that of the seller's should be identical, or you will both be inviting IRS audits.

In addition, legislation passed in 1990 now makes any agreement as to the value of an asset binding upon both parties for tax purposes, in most cases. Thus, it is very important from a tax standpoint to negotiate the best possible allocation of the purchase price among the assets you acquire and have that allocation reflected in the contract of sale.[6]

3.6 Closing the Deal

Legal Steps in Buying a Business

The legal procedures involved in buying an existing business are rather complex. To ensure you are protected as fully as possible from liabilities you have not agreed to assume, have your attorney take the steps described below.

File Transfer Notice

In most states, the purchaser of a retail or wholesale establishment or certain other types of businesses must prepare a notice to creditors of bulk transfer and file it in counties where the business operates and publish it in a general circulation newspaper prior to the purchase of the business. If this is not properly done, the seller's unsecured creditors may be able to attach the property that you thought you were buying free and clear. See Section 11.3 for specific state requirements regarding bulk sales law.

Check Security Interests

Before closing the purchase, your attorney should check with the secretary of state's office to determine whether anyone has recorded a security interest — a lien or chattel mortgage — against the personal property of the seller's business. Naturally, if the transaction involves a purchase of real property, you will also have a title search performed to see if the seller has good title and if there are any recorded mortgages or other claims against the property that the seller has not disclosed to you.

For a fee, the secretary of state's office will provide a listing of any security interests that have been recorded as a lien against the assets of the business you are buying.

As the purchaser of the business, you should require that, as a condition of the sale, the seller obtain the required form or certificate from the state agency that collects payroll taxes, certifying that all employment taxes due the state have been paid by the seller. Otherwise, if you fail to withhold enough of the purchase price to cover any of the seller's unpaid employment taxes, you may be liable to the state for those taxes. See Section 11.3 for specifics on state requirements.

Get Tax Releases

Similarly, you should insist that the seller obtain and provide you with a sales and use tax certification showing that all outstanding sales and use tax payments due have been made by the seller, so that you do not unwittingly subject yourself to exposure for paying the seller's unpaid sales or use taxes.

File *Form 8594* with the IRS regarding the purchase price allocation and other information in connection with the transaction. The penalty for intentional disregard of this filing requirement is 10% of the amount that was not correctly reported, which could mean up to 10% of the entire purchase price. Don't forget to file *Form 8594*.

File with IRS

If there is any one thing discussed in this book that you should not attempt to do, it is buying or selling a business without the assistance of an attorney in reviewing and structuring the deal. Preferably, the attorney should be one who specializes in business law practice rather than a litigation specialist or general practitioner. You will also need competent tax advice, either from your attorney or from an accountant, in negotiating and structuring aspects of the deal such as the allocation of the purchase price and the disposition of any employee benefit plans carried on by the seller for the employees of the business.

Retain a Lawyer

In general, both you and the seller will be protected — from the time the sales agreement is signed until the deal closes — if an escrow is used to handle the sale of the business. The escrow holder, which is usually an escrow company or escrow department of a financial institution, will hold the agreement, escrow instructions, funds, and important documents until all conditions for closing the deal or releasing the funds or documents are fulfilled. At that time, it will disburse the funds to the seller

Use an Escrow

and deliver the documents of title to you, if the deal closes; or, if the deal falls through, make such other disposition as is called for by the escrow instructions. Your attorney or the seller's attorney may also act as escrow holder, but you probably will not want the seller's attorney to act in that role in most cases, for obvious reasons.

Build in Holdbacks

If the seller has made misrepresentations to you in the contract of sale regarding assets that do not exist, or the like, you may always seek satisfaction by suing for damages. In view of the cost, delay, and uncertainty in bringing a lawsuit, however, you would generally be far better off if there were some simple way you could merely offset any such overstated asset or understated liability against the purchase price, retroactively.

To make this possible, you should seek to structure the deal so that part of the purchase price is held back for some period, say a year, just in case such a contingency arises. Then, if you discover false representations as to assets or liabilities, it will be relatively simple — compared to bringing a lawsuit against a seller who may have skipped town — to have your claim deducted from the amount held back. Discuss with your attorney the possibilities of structuring the transaction so that you either:

- Give the seller a note as part of the purchase price, with a right to reduce the principal amount of the note if certain contingencies occur; or
- Have part of the cash payment price held in escrow for six months or more after the sale occurs.

3.7 Summary Checklist for Buying an Existing Business

Investigation

- ☐ Why does the present owner want to sell the business?
- ☐ Will the reputation of the business be helpful or harmful if you take it over?
- ☐ Obtain tax returns, bank deposit records, and other financial records.
- ☐ If the business is not currently very profitable, why do you think you can run it more profitably than the present owner?
- ☐ Thoroughly investigate the business' financial records and history, its reputation, and any factors that might unfavorably impact on its future. You may need the help of an accountant or other experts.
- ☐ Review or have reviewed the provisions of key contracts, leases, franchise agreements, or any other legal arrangements which have a significant effect on the business. Be sure you are not assuming an unfavorable lease or contract or losing the benefits of a favorable one.

☐ Make sure that the purchase price is fair. Even if it is, can you afford it? Will you have enough working capital to run the business properly after you pay the purchase price?

☐ Insist on getting accurate financial information and access to the supporting data, early in the negotiations.

☐ Push for an allocation of the purchase price to specific assets in the sales agreement. Seek to maximize the amounts allocable to depreciable assets and any noncompetition covenant. Seek to minimize allocations to goodwill or land purchased.

☐ Look for hidden liabilities, such as pending lawsuits, accrued vacation liabilities, unfunded pension plan liabilities, or potential exposure to environmental clean-up costs.

Negotiations

☐ Retain an attorney to participate in drawing up the sales agreement.

☐ Comply with the requirements of the Bulk Transfer Act if it applies to the particular type of business being acquired.

☐ Be sure that acquired property is not subject to any recorded security interests or other liens beyond those disclosed by the seller.

☐ Have the seller obtain and furnish a certification that all employment taxes due have been paid.

☐ Have the seller obtain and furnish a certification that all sales and use taxes due have been paid.

☐ Seek to hold back part of the purchase price as security to reimburse you for any misrepresentations as to assets or liabilities by the seller.

☐ Prepare *Form 8594* and file it with the IRS.

☐ See Section 11.3 for state law considerations.

Closing the Transaction

☐ Determine whether the sale of the business will result in a sales tax liability with respect to part or all of the purchase price. If so, is there a way to reshape the transaction to reduce or avoid sales tax? For example, allocate more of the purchase price to assets not subject to sales tax and less to assets that are.

☐ If you are buying a corporation that has not been paying income taxes because it has carryovers of net operating losses or investment tax credits, be aware that you may be able to use only a small portion of those carryovers to shelter the income of the business once you become the owner. After 1985, in general, if there is more than a 50% change in the ownership of the stock of a corporation that has net operating loss carryovers, only a certain amount of those carryovers, equal to the yield on long-term, tax-exempt bonds multiplied by the value of the "loss" corporation, may be used each year to offset taxable income for all tax years ending after the change in ownership.[7]

Other Tax Considerations

☐ If the seller has a favorable experience rating for unemployment tax purposes, make sure you act promptly so that you can succeed to that rating as a successor employer.

☐ If you are acquiring a franchise, trademark, or trade name as part of the purchase, be aware that you may be able to amortize the cost of such franchise, etc. over a period of years;[8] despite the 1989 tax legislation limiting such deductions.

Footnotes

1. I.R.C. § 1060(a).

2. *Holden Fuel Oil Co. v. Commissioner*, 479 F.2d 613 (6th Cir. 1973); Rev. Rul. 74-456, 1974-2 CB 65; Computing and Software, Inc., 64 T.C. 223 (1975).

3. U.S. Mineral Products, 52 T.C. 177 (1969) (Acq.). (Sale of technical know-how eligible for capital gain.)

4. George Bacon, 36 T.C. Memo 1977-52.

5. Temp. Treas. Reg. 1.1060-1T.

6. I.R.C. § 1060(a).

7. I.R.C. § 382.

8. I.R.C. § 1253.

Starting the Business

Part II

Chapter 4

A Trip through the Red Tape Jungle: Requirements that Apply to Nearly All New Businesses

The difference between a taxidermist and a tax collector is that the taxidermist leaves the skin.

— Old American proverb

4.1 General Considerations

The purpose of this chapter is to outline the most common governmental requirements and other red tape that virtually everyone starting a new business must attend to. The requirements discussed will also generally apply if you have bought an existing business, unless you have acquired the stock of an incorporated business.

This chapter assumes that your business has no employees. If you expect to have one or more employees, a large number of additional legal requirements will affect your business immediately. Chapter 5 covers the additional requirements that apply to new businesses that have employees. This chapter does not discuss the special licenses that many types of businesses are required to have. If you do not know whether the type of business you are considering going into requires a special license or licenses from federal, state, or local government agencies, refer to Chapter 6.

4.2 Choosing a Name for the Business

The name you choose for your business can be important from a business image standpoint and also in communicating to the public what you have to offer. Most small businesses should select a name that, at least in part, clearly describes the product or service provided. If you ignore this basic common-sense rule, you run the risk of losing many potential customers for the simple reason that they will pass right by without realizing what you do. A fanciful or whimsical name is fine from an image standpoint, but it should also give the public a clear idea of what it is your business provides in the way of goods or services. For example, if you call your restaurant "The Comestible Emporium," a lot of hungry people will probably drive right by without realizing that you serve food.

It is advisable, however, from the standpoint of protecting your business' name as a trademark or service mark under federal or state law, to adopt a name that is also partially arbitrary or nondescriptive, in conjunction with a name that is descriptive of the services or goods provided. An example would be the "21 Club Restaurant." The reason for selecting a name that is partially whimsical or arbitrary is that trademarks or service marks that are merely descriptive of the goods or services cannot be legally protected from use by others unless it can be proven that the name has acquired a secondary meaning, which is very difficult to establish for a new small business.[1]

You also need to think of the possible consequences of putting your name out before the public. You may want to consider using some sort of fictitious name (see Section 4.10) for your business, rather than your name. There is nothing illegal or shady about using a fictitious business name. If you put your name on the business and the venture goes belly up, as so many new businesses do, many people in the community will automatically associate your name with the defunct or bankrupt business, which may make it very difficult if you try to start another business or to obtain credit in the same community in the future.

Once you have settled on a name for your business, you or preferably your attorney, should find out whether the same name, or a confusingly similar name, has already been preempted by someone else. This involves making an inquiry with the state's secretary of state's office to find out whether the name is already being used in the state. Inquiry should also be made of the county clerk, in each county where you will do business, to see if another business is already using the same or a confusingly similar name in the county and has filed a fictitious business name statement. If so, you may have to choose a different name. See Section 9.5 for more information on trademark protection.

4.3 Local Business Licenses

Almost every business will need city or county business licenses, or both. These licenses can be obtained at the local city hall or county offices. Failure to obtain a license when you start business will usually result in a penalty when the local government eventually catches up with you; therefore, obtaining the necessary licenses should be among the first steps taken when you start a business.

Some cities and counties impose a gross receipts, income, or payroll tax on most businesses. Certain types of businesses, such as restaurants, may also be required to obtain special permits from local health authorities and fire or police departments.

If your business will construct its own building, it will be necessary to consult your local city or county zoning ordinances. A building permit must be obtained for both new construction and remodeling in most areas.

In addition, whether or not you plan to carry on any construction activity or do any remodeling, you will need to make certain that the business activity you intend to carry on does not violate any zoning regulations or any ordinances regarding hazardous activities. You may also be required to obtain a use permit from the city or county planning commission.

4.4 State Licenses

Most states impose license fees or taxes on a wide range of businesses, occupations, and professions. The fees often vary widely among the different types of businesses and occupations, ranging from relatively nominal to substantial amounts or rates, depending upon the activity. The many different types of licenses and permits are usually granted based on some combination of requirements such as registration, bonding, education, experience, and passage of licensing examinations. Since you may not legally operate any of these regulated businesses or professions without being licensed, you should find out whether there is a state licensing requirement for the business you plan to start. If so, determine whether and how you will be able to comply with the licensing requirements. See Section 11.6 for a partial listing of businesses, occupations, and professions that must be licensed under the laws of this state.

4.5 Federal Licenses

Most new small businesses are unlikely to require any type of federal permit or license to operate, unless they are engaged in rendering investment advice, making alcohol or tobacco products, preparing meat products, or making or dealing in firearms. Federal permits or licenses would also be necessary to commence certain large-scale operations such as a radio or television station or a common carrier and the production of drugs or biological products. If you wish to engage in any of the foregoing activities, all of which are heavily regulated, you should consult an attorney regarding regulatory requirements well in advance.

4.6 Estimated Taxes

Individual

As a sole proprietor or partner in a partnership, you will have to make advance payments of estimated federal — and possibly state — income taxes and federal self-employment tax once your business begins to turn a taxable profit. Individual estimated tax payments are due in four annual installments on April 15, June 15, September 15, and January 15 of the following year for an individual whose tax year is the calendar year. Any remaining unpaid federal tax is due with your tax return on April 15 of the following year — which is also the date when the first estimated tax installment is due for that year. An individual files *Form 1040-ES* with his or her federal estimated tax payments. Note that you must now pay 90% of your estimated tax during the year rather than the 80% previously required — before 1988.[2]

Corporate

If your business is incorporated, the corporation will generally have to make corporate estimated tax payments, if it has taxable income, as early as the fourth month of its first tax year. In 1992, the percentage your corporation must pay as estimated tax, to avoid underpayment penalties, increased from 90% to 93%. From 1993 through 1996, the tax rate will increase to 95%. Federal estimated tax payments should be computed on *Form 1120-W* — which can be obtained, along with other federal tax forms, from any IRS office — and must be deposited in a bank that is authorized to accept federal tax deposits. The corporate estimated tax deposits must be accompanied by federal tax deposit coupons. Your corporation will be issued one coupon book which contains 23 coupons per book, preprinted with your corporate tax identification number. These coupons can be used for deposits of all types of federal taxes.

On each coupon you must indicate, by checking the applicable box, the kind of tax being deposited and the quarter to which payroll tax deposits are to be applied. The boxes on the coupon indicate the form name for the type of tax being paid.

Federal Tax Deposits

Type of Tax	Box to Check on Coupon
Payroll tax deposits	941
Federal unemployment tax	940 (or 940-EZ)
Corporate income tax estimates (and year-end payments)	1120

For deposits of corporate estimated income tax you must indicate the quarter which most closely corresponds to your fiscal year end, not the calendar quarter to which the payment relates. Example: If your corporate year end is May 31, you would check the "1120" box and darken the box which indicates 2nd quarter. For each of the four quarterly estimates, 2nd quarter would be indicated on each deposit coupon.

Fiscal Year Ends	Applicable Quarter	Tax Periods
January, February, March	1st quarter	
April, May, June	2nd quarter	
July, August, September	3rd quarter	
October, November, December	4th quarter	

The coupon books will be sent to you automatically when you file *Form SS-4*, requesting a tax identification number for the corporation. When you receive your coupon book, a reorder form, *Form 8109A*, will be provided, so you can request additional coupon books for the current year, if needed.

A penalty may be imposed for failure to make deposits directly to an authorized government depository bank. In the recent past, when tax deposit cards were unavailable, it was common practice to mail payments to the Internal Revenue Service accompanied by a letter indicating the nature of the tax payment and requesting additional tax deposit cards. This method of paying business taxes is no longer acceptable. Thus, it is important to mail the reorder form in time to receive additional coupon books before you run out; however, the IRS will sometimes send you blank coupons for temporary use.

Refer to Section 11.4 regarding state filing requirements for individual and corporate estimated income taxes.

4.7 Miscellaneous Tax Information Returns

Reporting Payments to Individuals

As a general rule, every person engaged in a trade or business must report to the IRS any payments of $600 or more made to any person during the calendar year, for items such as rent, compensation for services, commissions, interest, and annuities, plus other items of fixed or determinable income.[3] There are a number of additional new tax reporting requirements listed below you need to be aware of because there are stiff new penalties for failure to comply.

Obtaining Social Security Numbers

Recently enacted laws make it necessary to obtain the name and Social Security number or other tax identification number of any person to whom you make payments of $600 or more. There is a $50 penalty for failure to obtain their tax identification number — unless you have a reasonable excuse, such as their refusal to give you the number.[4] If they do refuse to give you the number, you must withhold 31% of whatever amount you owe them and deposit it with the IRS, or you will be subject to a penalty for failure to withhold.[5]

Reporting Sales to Direct Sellers

You must now report sales of $5,000 or more of consumer products to any individual who is engaged in direct selling — that is, selling in any way other than through a permanent retail establishment.[6] This will mainly apply to sales made to people in direct sales organizations, such as Tupperware, Amway, or Shaklee. It would also apply in many other situations, such as where the person you sell to sells the goods by mail order. Use *Form 1099-MISC* to report these sales.

1099 Forms

These types of payments are usually reportable for each payee on *Form 1099-MISC* (information return) or *Form 1099-INT* (for interest); a duplicate must be sent to the payee. In addition, you must prepare and file a *Form 1096* return summarizing all the information on the 1099-MISC forms and on the other forms in the 1099 series. Each of these forms is due by February 28 each year, for the prior calendar year, and a copy must also be sent to the recipient of the payment by January 31.

Be aware that instructions for *Form 1099* say you should use your personal Social Security number rather than your business' employer identification number on the form. Putting down the wrong taxpayer identification number in such a case will subject you to a penalty.

Payments of compensation to nonemployees — independent contractors — are also reportable on *Form 1099-MISC*.

Penalties

There are stiff IRS penalties for not filing the above 1099 forms. The penalty for not filing or not giving a 1099 to a payee is $50 per failure. Since there is a separate penalty for not giving a copy of the 1099 to the payee as well as for not filing a copy with the IRS, it can cost you $100 for each person for whom you fail to prepare 1099s.[7] Tax law changes in 1989 have reduced the $50 penalty for late-filed 1099s and certain other information returns to $30, if filed more than 30 days late but before August 1 of the year due, or to only $15, if filed within 30 days after the due date.

Independent Contractors

In addition, if you erroneously, but in good faith, treat a person as an independent contractor, and it is later shown that the person was actually an employee, you will only be liable as an employer for 20% of the employee's Social Security tax that should have been withheld, and for income tax withholding equal to 1.5% of what you paid the individual provided that you properly filed *Form 1099-MISC* with the IRS.[8] If you failed to file *Form 1099-MISC* for that person, the amount of withholding tax you are liable for is doubled.[9]

Fortunately, a number of important exemptions from the 1099 filing requirements will eliminate most of the people or companies to whom you are likely to make payments of $600 or more. You do not have to report:

- Payments to corporations — except certain corporations in the medical field;[10]
- Payments of compensation to employees that are already reported on their W-2s;[11]
- Payments of bills for merchandise, telegrams, telephone, freight, storage, and similar charges;[12]
- Payments of rent made to real estate agents;[13]
- Expense advances or reimbursements to employees that the employees must account to you (the employer) for;[14] and
- Payments to a governmental unit.[15]

Businesses must report royalty payments of $10 or more to any person.

Reporting Dividends and Interest

If your business is incorporated, your corporation will have to file a *Form 1099-DIV* for each person to whom it pays dividends of $10 or more each year.[16] You must also file *Form 1099-INT* for each person to whom you pay $10 or more in interest on bonds, debentures, or notes issued by the corporation in registered form.[17] *Form 1099-DIV* or *Form 1099-INT* is also required for any other payment of dividends or interest on which you are required to withhold tax. Payments reported on *Form 1099-DIV* and *Form 1099-INT* must also be reported on the *Form 1096* summary. *Form 1099-S* must be given to recipients of the proceeds from the sales of real estate, in general.

Reporting Large Cash Transactions

Any business that receives a payment of more than $10,000 in cash, in cash equivalents — such as cashier's checks or traveler's checks — or in foreign currency in one transaction, or in two or more related transactions, is required to report the details of the transactions within 15 days to the IRS[18] and to furnish a similar statement to the payor by January 31 of the following year.[19] The form for reporting such "suitcase" transactions is *Form 8300*. The penalties for noncompliance are generally the same as for not filing 1099s, except that in cases of intentional failure to file, there is an additional penalty equal to the higher of $25,000 or the amount of the cash or cash equivalent received in the transaction, up to $100,000.[20]

In addition to the requirement that you file 1099s with the IRS, you may have to file similar forms with the state.

Reporting Mortgage Interest Received

Federal law requires that you give *Form 1098* to any individual from whom you receive $600 or more in mortgage interest during the year, in the course of your trade or business. *Form 1098* has the same filing requirements as *Form 1099*.[21]

**Reporting on
Magnetic Media**

Note that the IRS permits you to file *Form 1098* and *Form 1099*, as well as certain other information returns, on magnetic media (computer tapes or disks) rather than the actual paper forms, if very specific formats for the computer tape or disk are met. The IRS requires that certain information returns be filed on magnetic media, if your business files 250 or more such returns for a calendar year.[22] These include *Form 1098*, all of the 1099 series and W-2 series of information returns, and various others, such as *Form 5498* and *Form 8027*.

A "hardship waiver" to excuse you from having to file in magnetic media format may be granted under certain circumstances, if you file a request on *Form 8508* at least 90 days in advance of the due date.

Failure of a taxpayer to file an information return on magnetic media — or on a machine-readable form where magnetic media filing is not required — when required to do so is treated as a failure-to-file and can result in the imposition of applicable penalties for failure to file, as noted above.

If your firm finds that it will be required to file information returns on magnetic media, there are many data processing firms and computer programs you can buy that will encode the data for you, at a relatively small cost, in a way that meets the IRS' highly technical specifications.

4.8 Sales and Use Tax Permits

With a limited number of exceptions, every business that sells tangible personal property, such as merchandise, to customers must obtain a seller's permit from the state sales tax agency. Usually, a separate permit must be obtained for each place of business where property subject to tax is sold.

See Section 11.4 for a discussion of the state's sales and use tax laws and permit requirements. Some states have a gross income or a gross receipts tax rather than a sales tax.

In general, as a wholesaler or manufacturer, you will not have to collect sales tax on goods you sell to a retailer for resale, if the retailer holds a valid seller's permit and provides you with a resale certificate in connection with the transaction.

Likewise, if your business, as a retailer, buys goods for resale, you need not pay sales tax to the wholesalers if you provide them with resale certificates. You may buy blank resale certificate forms at most stationery stores in states where such certificates are required.

The sales and use tax laws typically require that a business that sells or leases tangible personal property keep complete records of the gross receipts from sales or rentals whether or not the receipts are believed to be taxable. You must also keep adequate and complete records to sub-stantiate all deductions claimed on sales and use tax returns and of the total purchase price of all tangible personal property bought for sale, lease, or consumption in the state.

4.9 Real Estate Taxes

Property Taxes

As a rule, you do not need to worry about contacting the county tax assessor's office regarding payment of any real property taxes on real property acquired for your business. They will usually contact you by mailing a property tax bill to the owner of record. See Section 11.4 for a general description of how state or local real property and personal property taxes are assessed and collected.

FIRPTA Withholding Tax on Purchase of Real Property

In addition to local property taxes, American citizens and other U.S. residents who acquire U.S. real estate from foreign persons — includ-ing partnership interests or stock in certain firms owning U.S. real property — must withhold up to 10% of the purchase price and remit it to the IRS under the Foreign Investment in Real Property Tax Act (FIRPTA). If you fail to withhold the tax, you are liable for it. This is a potentially dangerous tax trap for unsuspecting American buyers of real estate, since it is often difficult to determine whether a seller is a for-eign person.

While there is an exception for residences costing $300,000 or less — if you will live in it for at least 50% of the time for two years — it is far safer to obtain a certificate of nonforeign status from the seller if there is any possibility that the seller is a nonresident alien or a foreign company.

To protect yourself when purchasing real estate — or your client, if you are in the real estate business — you should require, as a condition of closing the transaction, that the seller provide you with an affidavit certi-fying whether or not the seller is a nonresident alien or a foreign company.

If the seller refuses to sign the affidavit and provide the required infor-mation, you should withhold 10% of the gross purchase price and trans-mit it to the IRS within 10 days of the sale along with IRS *Form 8288* and *Form 8288-A*. This can be a real problem in a highly leveraged deal where less than 10% of the purchase price is paid in cash at the closing. Note that some states have recently adopted similar withholding provi-sions with regard to purchases of real estate within such states where the seller is a nonresident of the state.

If the seller is a foreign person, you will owe the IRS 10% of the pur-chase price if you fail to withhold the tax, unless you received a certifi-cate of nonforeign status from the seller.

4.10 Fictitious Business Name Statement

Almost every state has laws requiring any person who regularly transacts business in the state for profit under a fictitious business name to file and publish a fictitious business name statement. For a sole proprietorship or partnership, a business name is generally considered fictitious unless it contains the surname of the owner or all of the general partners and does not suggest the existence of additional owners. Use of a name which includes words like "company," "associates," "group," "brothers," or "sons" will suggest additional owners and will make it necessary for a business to file and publish a fictitious business name statement. Putting a name that would be considered a fictitious name on your company letterhead, on your business cards, in advertising, or on your products will be considered a use of the name.

Many newspapers will provide the form for filing, publish the notice, and file the required affidavit. See Section 11.4 regarding specific requirements for filing a fictitious business name statement in this state.

4.11 Insurance — A Practical Necessity for Businesses

Insurance, like death and taxes, is an inevitable necessity for the owner of any small business. For almost any business, even one that has no employees, insurance coverage for general liability, product liability, fire and similar disasters, robbery, theft, and interruption of business should be considered.

If your business will have employees, workers' compensation insurance is usually mandatory under state law; and employee life, health, and disability insurance have become virtual necessities in many businesses and professions, if you wish to be competitive with other firms in hiring and retaining capable employees.

Fidelity bonding should be considered for employees who will have access to the cash receipts or other funds of the business. If you have an employees' pension or profit-sharing plan subject to the Employee Retirement Income Security Act of 1974 (ERISA), employees involved in administering the plan or handling its funds are required to be covered by a fidelity bond.[23] See Section 5.5 for further information.

Insurance Agents

Since it isn't realistic to expect you to become a sophisticated comparison shopper for insurance while you are trying to get a business off the ground, you should put considerable emphasis on seeking out and finding a good insurance agent whom you can trust and rely upon to give you good advice. There is no easy way to find such an agent, just as there is no sure way of finding a good lawyer or accountant. In general, the best approach will be to ask friends, lawyers, accountants, or other business people you know to refer you to a topflight insurance agent.

Agents who have earned the Chartered Life Underwriter (CLU) designation will, as a rule, be more experienced and capable than those without the CLU credential. This can be an additional factor to consider when selecting your insurance agent.

Agents who deal primarily in property and casualty insurance will not usually have CLU on their business cards. Instead, they may have the initials CPCU — Chartered Property/Casualty Underwriter — after their name, which is a similar mark of distinction in the field of property/casualty insurance.

Another good tip in finding an insurance agent is to analyze your own insurance needs. There are several how-to books that can help you analyze your risks and compare insurance prices.

One such book, *Risk Analysis: How to Reduce Insurance Costs,* written by Gary Robinson, provides insider tips on buying insurance, selecting insurance agents, and lowering your premiums and rates. The book also explains how not to buy any more insurance than your company actually needs. The book can be purchased through your book source or through The Oasis Press.

Insurance Consultants

If you cannot find an agent with whom you feel comfortable, call an insurance consultant. Ask if — and satisfy yourself that — the consultant is a member of the Society of Risk Management Consultants. To belong to the group, the individual or firm cannot be an insurance broker. These consultants are insurance experts and can give you an objective analysis on risk management and insurance.

Society of Risk Management Consultants
58 Diablo View Drive
Orinda, CA 94563
(510) 254-9472

The usual hourly fees may seem high, but most new businesses probably will not need more than an hour of their time. Most will bill in quarter-hour increments.

You will probably recoup the consultant's fee several times over in premium savings in just the first year alone. You should, however, be wary of a consultant who wants to increase the number of hours by offering to create specifications and provide additional services.

Once you have met with an independent consultant and know what is needed, shop for the insurance you need from insurance brokers. Don't let them bid up the amount of coverage or add on additional types of insurance. Use the insurance consultant as you would an attorney or physician — follow his or her advice.

4.12 Requirements Specific to the Legal Form of the Business

Sole Proprietorships

There are no significant government regulatory requirements that apply specifically to sole proprietorships; however, as a sole proprietor of a business, you will need to attach a form *Schedule C* to your individual federal tax return, on which you will report the income or loss from the business.

Also, if your sole proprietorship shows a profit, you will usually have to pay a self-employment tax equal to 15.3% of your net self-employment income from the business or at least on the first $57,600 of such income, plus an additional 2.9% on self-employment income of more than $57,600, up to $135,000, in 1993. The self-employment tax is computed on *Schedule SE*, which must also be attached to your federal income tax return. See Section 11.4 for how to report business profits on your state income tax returns.

Partnerships

Like a sole proprietor, as a partner, you will have to pay a self-employment tax on your share of your partnership's net self-employment income. Net self-employment income usually includes all partnership income less all partnership deductions allowed for income tax purposes. Some types of income, such as interest, may or may not be considered self-employment income. The source of your income and your involvement in the activity from which your income is received will determine whether it is self-employment income.

If your earnings from self-employment is $400 or more for the year, you will have to figure self-employment tax on *Schedule SE* of your federal *Form 1040*. The self-employment tax is a Social Security and Medicare tax for those who work for themselves.

Schedule E of your federal *Form 1040* deals with your personal income tax and includes all other taxable income, such as royalties, rentals, and interest. You report your share of partnership ordinary income or loss on *Schedule E*.

In addition, your partnership must file a partnership information return, federal *Form 1065*, reporting the partnership's income and each partner's share of income and other items. The partnership must also file *Form SS-4* with the IRS to obtain a federal employer identification number, even if it has no employees. See Section 11.4 for state partnership return filing requirements, and the end of this chapter for a sample *Form SS-4*.

When a partner buys, sells, or exchanges a partnership interest, the partnership must file a special information return if the partnership's assets include unrealized receivables or substantially appreciated inventory that might cause the seller to have ordinary gain, rather than all capital gain, on the sale or exchange.[24] Statements also have to be sent to the partners involved in the transaction.[25]

A limited partnership, to qualify as such, is usually required to file a *Certificate of Limited Partnership* with the secretary of state or other state agency. In most states, a limited partnership should also file certified copies in each county where it does business or owns real estate.

Corporations are subject to the following requirements not applicable to other legal forms of business organization: **Corporations**

- Filing articles of incorporation;
- Adopting a set of bylaws;
- Observing other corporate formalities on a regular basis, such as the election of directors by shareholders and appointment of officers by action of the board of directors;
- Filing federal income tax returns on *Form 1120* — or *Form 1120-S* for an S corporation — and state income or franchise tax returns in most states where they do business. See Section 11.4 for various filings, taxes, and fees required of corporations that are incorporated or doing business in this state;
- Reporting certain information relating to the transfer of tax-free property under the Internal Revenue Code Section 351 on the corporation's income tax return for that year;[26]
- Filing *Form SS-4* with the IRS to obtain an employer identification number, even if there are no employees; and
- Qualifying with the secretary of state to do business, if the corporation was organized under the laws of another state.

4.13 Checklist of Requirements for Nearly All New Businesses

- ☐ Obtain local business licenses.
- ☐ Check on local zoning ordinances, regulations, and other land use restrictions.
- ☐ Determine if your particular business requires a state license to operate.
- ☐ Determine whether any type of federal permit or license is required.
- ☐ Be prepared to make estimated income tax payments almost immediately after starting business or incorporating.
- ☐ Apply for a sales and use tax seller's permit if you will sell tangible personal property.
- ☐ File sales and use tax returns, if you must collect sales or use tax.
- ☐ File with the county clerk and publish a fictitious business name statement if the business operates under a fictitious name, and then file an affidavit of publication with the county clerk (in most states).
- ☐ Locate a good insurance agent or retain and meet with an insurance consultant regarding fire, accident, liability, theft, and other types of

commercial insurance you need. Then obtain the necessary insurance coverage.

☐ If you purchase real estate, you must withhold up to 10% of the purchase price and remit it to the IRS if the seller is a foreign individual or foreign-owned company, under the Foreign Investment in Real Property Tax Act.[27] Otherwise, you should insist upon receiving an affidavit that the seller is not a nonresident alien, with his or her taxpayer identification number, unless you are certain that he or she is a U.S. citizen or resident.

☐ For a sole proprietorship, report any self-employment income on *Schedule SE* of federal *Form 1040*, and report income or loss on *Schedule C* of *Form 1040*.

☐ A partnership files *Form 1065* reporting partnership income. Each partner reports his or her share of self-employment income on *Schedule SE* of *Form 1040* and income or loss from partnership operations on *Schedule E* of *Form 1040*.

☐ For a limited partnership, file a *Certificate of Limited Partnership* with the secretary of state and copies in counties where the partnership has places of business or real estate (in most states).

☐ For a corporation, file articles of incorporation, adopt bylaws, and observe necessary corporate formalities. File federal income tax return *Form 1120*; *Form 1120-S* for an S corporation. If property is transferred to the corporation tax-free under IRC Section 351, report required information relating to the transfer on the corporation's income tax return for that year.

☐ For a corporation or a partnership, apply for a federal employer identification number on *Form SS-4*, even if the business has no employees. See sample at the end of this chapter.

☐ File annual tax information returns, *Form 1096* and the *Form 1099* series, for payments of $600 or more for items such as rent, interest, and compensation for services, and send 1099s to the payees. File *Form 1098* for mortgage interest of $600 or more your business receives in a year from an individual. Also, report any cash payments or cash equivalents of more than $10,000 that you receive to the IRS within 15 days. Such filing may have to be done on computer-readable magnetic media.

☐ If your business is a corporation, be sure to obtain an adequate supply of federal tax deposit coupons in time to make your estimated tax payments.

See Section 11.4 for a checklist of additional state law requirements that apply to nearly all new businesses.

The above requirements apply to any business, whether it has employees or not. There are many additional requirements for businesses that do have employees, and these are covered in the next chapter.

4.14 Securities Laws

Inherent in the choice of the legal form of the business is the potential application of federal and state securities laws, if the new business is to have more than one owner or should it become necessary to raise capital for an existing business. Because of the potentially dire consequences of violating federal or state securities laws, it is important to consult with your attorney as early as possible when considering issuing or transferring a security. Corporate stock and limited partnership interests generally are considered securities, and even a general partnership interest can be a security in appropriate circumstances, as can certain types of debt instruments.

Registration of Securities

Since the Securities Act of 1933, federal law has required registration as a prior condition to the issuance or transfer of securities. The law exempts various types of securities and certain types of transactions. The most important of these exemptions for small businesses have been the exemption for securities sold to persons residing within a single state and transactions by an issuer not deemed to involve any public offering. The Securities and Exchange Commission (SEC) from time to time has issued regulations exempting small securities issues, attempting to balance the needs of small businesses to raise capital against the public policy of protecting investors. In 1982, the commission adopted Regulation D as its primary method of regulation of securities offerings by small businesses, although not to the exclusion of other exemptions which might apply.

Rule 504 Exemption

Rule 504[28] under Regulation D exempts the issuance of securities by an entity if the aggregate offering price of all exempt securities sold by the entity during a 12-month period does not exceed $1 million — not more than $500,000 of securities can be offered and sold without registration under some states' securities laws. The securities cannot be offered or sold by any form of general solicitation or general advertising, and the securities so acquired cannot be resold without registration or an exemption from registration.

This rule does not require any specific information to be given to the purchasers of the securities; however, since the anti-fraud provisions of the securities laws apply even though the transaction is exempt from registration, it is helpful to memorialize in writing the material information regarding the offering.

Rule 505 Exemption

Rule 505[29] exempts offers and sales of securities if the offering price for all exempt securities sold over a 12-month period does not exceed $5 million. To obtain this exemption, the issuer must reasonably believe that there are not more than 35 purchasers exclusive of accredited investors.

Examples of accredited investors include banks, insurance companies, a natural person whose net worth at the time of purchase exceeds $1 million, or a person who has individual income in excess of $200,000 — or $300,000 jointly with a spouse — in each of the two most recent years and expects the same in the current year. Exceptions are also made for certain large investors, including corporations, partnerships, or business trusts with total assets in excess of $5 million, unless formed for the specific purpose of acquiring the securities.

For purposes of Rule 505, the issuer must furnish extensive information and certified financial statements to the investors, unless securities were sold only to accredited investors. The prohibition against advertising and solicitation applies to this rule, as do the anti-fraud provisions of the securities laws.

Rule 506 Exemption

Rule 506[30] is similar to the exemptions provided by Rule 505, except that the $5 million limitation does not apply. The 35 purchaser limitation does apply, with the exception for accredited investors, but a separate limitation requires that the issuer must reasonably believe immediately prior to making any sale to a nonaccredited investor that such investor either alone, or with a representative, has such knowledge and experience in financial and business matters that he or she is capable of evaluating the merits and risks of the prospective investment. The prohibition against advertising and solicitation applies to this rule, as do the anti-fraud provisions of the securities laws.

Issuers utilizing any of the above exemptions must file *Form D* with the Securities and Exchange Commission generally no later than 15 days after the first sale of securities and at other specified times thereafter. New Rule 507 disqualifies any issuer found to have violated the *Form D* filing requirement from future use of the Regulation D exemptions, if the issuer has been enjoined by a court for violating the notice filing requirement — but apparently will not disqualify prior issuances of securities merely due to failure to file *Form D*.[31]

It should be kept in mind that the exemptions available under the federal securities laws are more liberal than those available under the securities laws of many states. In connection with any issuance or transfer of securities, it is necessary to consider the possible application of securities laws in the state where the business entity is established or operates, and, if different, the states where purchasers of the securities live. See Section 11.2 for further information concerning state securities laws.

Footnotes

1. *Armstrong Paint and Varnish Works v. New and U-Enamel Corp.* 305 U.S. 315 (1938); *Carter-Wallace, Inc. v. Proctor and Gamble Co.* 434 F.2d 794 (9th Cir. 1970). The author wishes to acknowledge Henry C. Bunsow, esq. of the San Francisco patent and trademark law firm of Townsend and Townsend for alerting him to this important point.

2. I.R.C. §6654.

3. I.R.C. §6041(a).

4. I.R.C. §6724(d)(3).

5. I.R.C. §3406(a).

6. I.R.C. §6041A(b).

7. I.R.C. §§6721–6722.

8. I.R.C. §3509(a).

9. I.R.C. §3509(b).

10. Treas. Regs. §1.6041-3(c).

11. Treas. Regs. §1.6041-3(a).

12. Treas. Regs. §1.6041-3(d).

13. Treas. Regs. §1.6041-3(e).

14. Treas. Regs. §1.6041-3(i).

15. I.R.C. §6041(a) requires filing of information returns for payments made to another "person." As defined in IRC §7701(a)(1), "person" does not include governmental bodies.

16. I.R.C. §6042(a).

17. I.R.C. §6049(a).

18. I.R.C. §6050I.

19. I.R.C. §6722.

20. I.R.C. §6721.

21. I.R.C. §6050H.

22. Rev. Proc. 89-42, 1989-29 I.R.B. 14.

23. 29 U.S.C. §1112 (§412 of ERISA).

24. I.R.C. §6050K(a).

25. I.R.C. §6050K(b).

26. Treas. Regs. §1.351-3.

27. I.R.C. §1445(a).

28. 17 C.F.R. §230.504.

29. 17 C.F.R. §230.505.

30. 17 C.F.R. §230.506.

31. Rule 507, as interpreted in Securities Act Release No. 6825, March 14, 1989 (17 C.F.R. §230.507).

Form SS-4

Form SS-4
(Rev. April 1991)
Department of the Treasury
Internal Revenue Service

Application for Employer Identification Number

(For use by employers and others. Please read the attached instructions before completing this form.)

EIN **SAMPLE**

OMB No. 1545-0003
Expires 4-30-94

Please type or print clearly.

1 Name of applicant (True legal name) (See instructions.)

2 Trade name of business, if different from name in line 1

3 Executor, trustee, "care of" name

4a Mailing address (street address) (room, apt., or suite no.)

5a Address of business (See instructions.)

4b City, state, and ZIP code

5b City, state, and ZIP code

6 County and state where principal business is located

7 Name of principal officer, grantor, or general partner (See instructions.) ▶

8a Type of entity (Check only one box.) (See instructions.)
- ☐ Individual SSN _____
- ☐ REMIC
- ☐ State/local government
- ☐ Other nonprofit organization (specify) _____
- ☐ Other (specify) ▶ _____
- ☐ Personal service corp.
- ☐ National guard
- ☐ Estate
- ☐ Plan administrator SSN _____
- ☐ Other corporation (specify) _____
- ☐ Federal government/military
- ☐ Church or church controlled organization
- If nonprofit organization enter GEN (if applicable) _____
- ☐ Trust
- ☐ Partnership
- ☐ Farmers' cooperative

8b If a corporation, give name of foreign country (if applicable) or state in the U.S. where incorporated ▶

Foreign country

State

9 Reason for applying (Check only one box.)
- ☐ Started new business
- ☐ Hired employees
- ☐ Created a pension plan (specify type) ▶ _____
- ☐ Banking purpose (specify) ▶
- ☐ Changed type of organization (specify) ▶ _____
- ☐ Purchased going business
- ☐ Created a trust (specify) ▶ _____
- ☐ Other (specify) ▶

10 Date business started or acquired (Mo., day, year) (See instructions.)

11 Enter closing month of accounting year. (See instructions.)

12 First date wages or annuities were paid or will be paid (Mo., day, year). **Note:** *If applicant is a withholding agent, enter date income will first be paid to nonresident alien. (Mo., day, year)* . . . . ▶

13 Enter highest number of employees expected in the next 12 months. **Note:** *If the applicant does not expect to have any employees during the period, enter "0."* . . . . ▶

Nonagricultural	Agricultural	Household

14 Principal activity (See instructions.) ▶

15 Is the principal business activity manufacturing? . . . . ☐ Yes ☐ No
If "Yes," principal product and raw material used ▶

16 To whom are most of the products or services sold? Please check the appropriate box. ☐ Business (wholesale)
- ☐ Public (retail)
- ☐ Other (specify) ▶
- ☐ N/A

17a Has the applicant ever applied for an identification number for this or any other business? . . . . ☐ Yes ☐ No
Note: *If "Yes," please complete lines 17b and 17c.*

17b If you checked the "Yes" box in line 17a, give applicant's true name and trade name, if different than name shown on prior application.

True name ▶

Trade name ▶

17c Enter approximate date, city, and state where the application was filed and the previous employer identification number if known.

Approximate date when filed (Mo., day, year)	City and state where filed	Previous EIN

Under penalties of perjury, I declare that I have examined this application, and to the best of my knowledge and belief, it is true, correct, and complete

Telephone number (include area code)

Name and title (Please type or print clearly.) ▶

Signature ▶

Date ▶

Note: *Do not write below this line.   For official use only.*

Please leave blank ▶	Geo.	Ind.	Class	Size	Reason for applying

For Paperwork Reduction Act Notice, see attached instructions.

Cat. No. 16055N

Form **SS-4** (Rev. 4-91)

General Instructions

(Section references are to the Internal Revenue Code unless otherwise noted.)

Paperwork Reduction Act Notice.—We ask for the information on this form to carry out the Internal Revenue laws of the United States. You are required to give us this information. We need it to ensure that you are complying with these laws and to allow us to figure and collect the right amount of tax.

The time needed to complete and file this form will vary depending on individual circumstances. The estimated average time is:

Recordkeeping	7 min.
Learning about the law or the form	21 min.
Preparing the form	42 min.
Copying, assembling, and sending the form to IRS	20 min.

If you have comments concerning the accuracy of these time estimates or suggestions for making this form more simple, we would be happy to hear from you. You can write to both the **Internal Revenue Service,** Washington, DC 20224, Attention: IRS Reports Clearance Officer, T:FP; and the **Office of Management and Budget,** Paperwork Reduction Project (1545-0003), Washington, DC 20503. **DO NOT** send the tax form to either of these offices. Instead, see **Where To Apply.**

Purpose.—Use Form SS-4 to apply for an employer identification number (EIN). The information you provide on this form will establish your filing requirements.

Who Must File.—You must file this form if you have not obtained an EIN before and

• You pay wages to one or more employees.

• You are required to have an EIN to use on any return, statement, or other document, even if you are not an employer.

• You are required to withhold taxes on income, other than wages, paid to a nonresident alien (individual, corporation, partnership, etc.). For example, individuals who file **Form 1042,** Annual Withholding Tax Return for U.S. Source Income of Foreign Persons, to report alimony paid to nonresident aliens must have EINs.

Individuals who file **Schedule C,** Profit or Loss From Business, or **Schedule F,** Profit or Loss From Farming, of **Form 1040,** U.S. Individual Income Tax Return, must use EINs if they have a Keogh plan or are required to file excise, employment, or alcohol, tobacco, or firearms returns.

The following must use EINs even if they do not have any employees:

• Trusts, except an IRA trust, unless the IRA trust is required to file **Form 990-T,** Exempt Organization Business Income Tax Return, to report unrelated business taxable income or is filing Form 990-T to obtain a refund of the credit from a regulated investment company.

• Estates

• Partnerships

• REMICS (real estate mortgage investment conduits)

• Corporations

• Nonprofit organizations (churches, clubs, etc.)

• Farmers' cooperatives

• Plan administrators

New Business.—If you become the new owner of an existing business, **DO NOT** use the EIN of the former owner. If you already have an EIN, use that number. If you do not have an EIN, apply for one on this form. If

you become the "owner" of a corporation by acquiring its stock, use the corporation's EIN.

If you already have an EIN, you may need to get a new one if either the organization or ownership of your business changes. If you incorporate a sole proprietorship or form a partnership, you must get a new EIN. However, **DO NOT** apply for a new EIN if you change only the name of your business.

File Only One Form SS-4.—File only one Form SS-4, regardless of the number of businesses operated or trade names under which a business operates. However, each corporation in an affiliated group must file a separate application.

If you do not have an EIN by the time a return is due, write "Applied for" and the date you applied in the space shown for the number. **DO NOT** show your social security number as an EIN on returns.

If you do not have an EIN by the time a tax deposit is due, send your payment to the Internal Revenue service center for your filing area. (See **Where To Apply** below.) Make your check or money order payable to Internal Revenue Service and show your name (as shown on Form SS-4), address, kind of tax, period covered, and date you applied for an EIN.

For more information about EINs, see **Pub. 583,** Taxpayers Starting a Business.

How To Apply.—You can apply for an EIN either by mail or by telephone. You can get an EIN immediately by calling the Tele-TIN phone number for the service center for your state, or you can send the completed Form SS-4 directly to the service center to receive your EIN in the mail.

Application by Tele-TIN.—The Tele-TIN program is designed to assign EINs by telephone. Under this program, you can receive your EIN over the telephone and use it immediately to file a return or make a payment.

To receive an EIN by phone, complete Form SS-4, then call the Tele-TIN phone number listed for your state under **Where To Apply.** The person making the call must be authorized to sign the form (see **Signature block** on page 3).

An IRS representative will use the information from the Form SS-4 to establish your account and assign you an EIN. Write the number you are given on the upper right-hand corner of the form, sign and date it, and promptly mail it to the Tele-TIN Unit at the service center address for your state.

Application by mail.—Complete Form SS-4 at least 4 to 5 weeks before you will need an EIN. Sign and date the application and mail it to the service center address for your state. You will receive your FIN in the mail in approximately 4 weeks.

Note: *The Tele-TIN phone numbers listed below will involve a long-distance charge to callers outside of the local calling area, and should only be used to apply for an EIN. Use 1-800-829-1040 to ask about an application by mail.*

Where To Apply.—

If your principal business, office or agency, or legal residence in the case of an individual, is located in: ▼	Call the Tele-TIN phone number shown or file with the Internal Revenue service center at: ▼
Florida, Georgia, South Carolina	Atlanta, GA 39901 (404) 455-2360
New Jersey, New York City and counties of Nassau, Rockland, Suffolk, and Westchester	Holtsville, NY 00501 (516) 447-4955

New York (all other counties), Connecticut, Maine, Massachusetts, New Hampshire, Rhode Island, Vermont	Andover, MA 05501 (508) 474-9717
Illinois, Iowa, Minnesota, Missouri, Wisconsin	Kansas City, MO 64999 (816) 926-5999
Delaware, District of Columbia, Maryland, Pennsylvania, Virginia	Philadelphia, PA 19255 (215) 961-3980
Indiana, Kentucky, Michigan, Ohio, West Virginia	Cincinnati, OH 45999 (606) 292-5467
Kansas, New Mexico, Oklahoma, Texas	Austin, TX 73301 (512) 462-7845
Alaska, Arizona, California (counties of Alpine, Amador, Butte, Calaveras, Colusa, Contra Costa, Del Norte, El Dorado, Glenn, Humboldt, Lake, Lassen, Marin, Mendocino, Modoc, Napa, Nevada, Placer, Plumas, Sacramento, San Joaquin, Shasta, Sierra, Siskiyou, Solano, Sonoma, Sutter, Tehama, Trinity, Yolo, and Yuba), Colorado, Idaho, Montana, Nebraska, Nevada, North Dakota, Oregon, South Dakota, Utah, Washington, Wyoming	Ogden, UT 84201 (801) 625-7645
California (all other counties), Hawaii	Fresno, CA 93888 (209) 456-5900
Alabama, Arkansas, Louisiana, Mississippi, North Carolina, Tennessee	Memphis, TN 37501 (901) 365-5970

If you have no legal residence, principal place of business, or principal office or agency in any Internal Revenue District, file your form with the Internal Revenue Service Center, Philadelphia, PA 19255 or call (215) 961-3980.

Specific Instructions

The instructions that follow are for those items that are not self-explanatory. Enter N/A (nonapplicable) on the lines that do not apply.

Line 1.—Enter the legal name of the entity applying for the EIN.

Individuals.—Enter the first name, middle initial, and last name.

Trusts.—Enter the name of the trust.

Estate of a decedent.—Enter the name of the estate.

Partnerships.—Enter the legal name of the partnership as it appears in the partnership agreement.

Corporations.—Enter the corporate name as set forth in the corporation charter or other legal document creating it.

Plan administrators.—Enter the name of the plan administrator. A plan administrator who already has an EIN should use that number.

Line 2.—Enter the trade name of the business if different from the legal name.

Note: *Use the full legal name entered on line 1 on all tax returns to be filed for the entity. However, if a trade name is entered on line 2, use only the name on line 1 **or** the name on line 2 consistently when filing tax returns.*

Line 3.—Trusts enter the name of the trustee. Estates enter the name of the executor, administrator, or other fiduciary. If the entity applying has a designated person to receive tax information, enter that person's name as the "care of" person. Print or type the first name, middle initial, and last name.

Lines 5a and 5b.—If the physical location of the business is different from the mailing address (lines 4a and 4b), enter the address of the physical location on lines 5a and 5b.

Line 7.—Enter the first name, middle initial, and last name of a principal officer if the business is a corporation; of a general partner if a partnership; and of a grantor if a trust.

Line 8a.—Check the box that best describes the type of entity that is applying for the EIN. If not specifically mentioned, check the "other" box and enter the type of entity. Do not enter N/A.

Individual.—Check this box if the individual files Schedule C or F (Form 1040) and has a Keogh plan or is required to file excise, employment, or alcohol, tobacco, or firearms returns. If this box is checked, enter the individual's SSN (social security number) in the space provided.

Plan administrator.—The term plan administrator means the person or group of persons specified as the administrator by the instrument under which the plan is operated. If the plan administrator is an individual, enter the plan administrator's SSN in the space provided.

New withholding agent.—If you are a new withholding agent required to file Form 1042, check the "other" box and enter in the space provided "new withholding agent."

REMICs.—Check this box if the entity is a real estate mortgage investment conduit (REMIC). A REMIC is any entity

1. To which an election to be treated as a REMIC applies for the tax year and all prior tax years,

2. In which all of the interests are regular interests or residual interests,

3. Which has one class of residual interests (and all distributions, if any, with respect to such interests are pro rata),

4. In which as of the close of the 3rd month beginning after the startup date and at all times thereafter, substantially all of its assets consist of qualified mortgages and permitted investments,

5. Which has a tax year that is a calendar year, and

6. With respect to which there are reasonable arrangements designed to ensure that: (a) residual interests are not held by disqualified organizations (as defined in section 860E(e)(5)), and (b) information necessary for the application of section 860E(e) will be made available.

For more information about REMICs see the Instructions for **Form 1066,** U. S. Real Estate Mortgage Investment Conduit Income Tax Return.

Personal service corporations.—Check this box if the entity is a personal service corporation. An entity is a personal service corporation for a tax year only if

1. The entity is a C corporation for the tax year.

2. The principal activity of the entity during the testing period (as defined in Temporary Regulations section 1.441-4T(f)) for the tax year is the performance of personal service.

3. During the testing period for the tax year, such services are substantially performed by employee-owners.

4. The employee-owners own 10 percent of the fair market value of the outstanding stock in the entity on the last day of the testing period for the tax year.

For more information about personal service corporations, see the instructions to **Form 1120,** U.S. Corporation Income Tax Return, and Temporary Regulations section 1.441-4T.

Other corporations.—This box is for any corporation other than a personal service corporation. If you check this box, enter the type of corporation (such as insurance company) in the space provided.

Other nonprofit organizations.—Check this box if the nonprofit organization is other than a church or church-controlled organization and specify the type of nonprofit organization (for example, an educational organization.)

Group exemption number (GEN).—If the applicant is a nonprofit organization that is a subordinate organization to be included in a group exemption letter under Revenue Procedure 80-27, 1980-1 C.B. 677, enter the GEN in the space provided. If you do not know the GEN, contact the parent organization for it. GEN is a four-digit number. Do not confuse it with the nine-digit EIN.

Line 9.—Check only one box. Do not enter N/A.

Started new business.—Check this box if you are starting a new business that requires an EIN. If you check this box, enter the type of business being started. **DO NOT** apply if you already have an EIN and are only adding another place of business.

Changed type of organization.—Check this box if the business is changing its type of organization, for example, if the business was a sole proprietorship and has been incorporated or has become a partnership. If you check this box, specify in the space provided the type of change made, for example, "from sole proprietorship to partnership."

Purchased going business.—Check this box if you acquired a business through purchase. Do not use the former owner's EIN. If you already have an EIN, use that number.

Hired employees.—Check this box if the existing business is requesting an EIN because it has hired or is hiring employees and is therefore required to file employment tax return for which an EIN is required. **DO NOT** apply if you already have an EIN and are only hiring employees.

Created a trust.—Check this box if you created a trust, and enter the type of trust created.

Created a pension plan.—Check this box if you have created a pension plan and need this number for reporting purposes. Also, enter the type of plan created.

Banking purpose.—Check this box if you are requesting an EIN for banking purpose only and enter the banking purpose (for example, checking, loan, etc.).

Other (specify).—Check this box if you are requesting an EIN for any reason other than those for which there are checkboxes and enter the reason.

Line 10.—If you are starting a new business, enter the starting date of the business. If the business you acquired is already operating, enter the date you acquired the business. Trusts should enter the date the trust was legally created. Estates should enter the date of death of the decedent whose name appears on line 1.

Line 11.—Enter the last month of your accounting year or tax year. An accounting year or tax year is usually 12 consecutive months. It may be a calendar year or a fiscal year (including a period of 52 or 53 weeks). A calendar year is 12 consecutive months ending on December 31. A fiscal year is either 12 consecutive months ending on the last day of any month other than December or a 52-53 week year. For more information

on accounting periods, see **Pub. 538,** Accounting Periods and Methods.

Individuals.—Your tax year generally will be a calendar year.

Partnerships.—Partnerships generally should conform to the tax year of either (1) its majority partners; (2) its principal partners; (3) the tax year that results in the least aggregate deferral of income (see Temporary Regulations section 1.706-1T); or (4) some other tax year, if (a) a business purpose is established for the fiscal year, or (b) the fiscal year is a "grandfather" year, or (c) an election is made under section 444 to have a fiscal year. (See the Instructions for **Form 1065,** U.S. Partnership Return of Income, for more information.)

REMICs.—Remics must have a calendar year as their tax year.

Personal service corporations.—A personal service corporation generally must adopt a calendar year unless:

1. It can establish to the satisfaction of the Commissioner that there is a business purpose for having a different tax year, or

2. It elects under section 444 to have a tax year other than a calendar year.

Line 12.—If the business has or will have employees, enter on this line the date on which the business began or will begin to pay wages to the employees. If the business does not have any plans to have employees, enter N/A on this line.

New withholding agent.—Enter the date you began or will begin to pay income to a nonresident alien. This also applies to individuals who are required to file Form 1042 to report alimony paid to a nonresident alien.

Line 14.—Generally, enter the exact type of business being operated (for example, advertising agency, farm, labor union, real estate agency, steam laundry, rental of coin-operated vending machine, investment club, etc.).

Governmental.—Enter the type of organization (state, county, school district, or municipality, etc.)

Nonprofit organization (other than governmental).—Enter whether organized for religious, educational, or humane purposes, and the principal activity (for example, religious organization—hospital, charitable).

Mining and quarrying.—Specify the process and the principal product (for example, mining bituminous coal, contract drilling for oil, quarrying dimension stone, etc.).

Contract construction.—Specify whether general contracting or special trade contracting. Also, show the type of work normally performed (for example, general contractor for residential buildings, electrical subcontractor, etc.).

Trade.—Specify the type of sales and the principal line of goods sold (for example, wholesale dairy products, manufacturer's representative for mining machinery, retail hardware, etc.).

Manufacturing.—Specify the type of establishment operated (for example, sawmill, vegetable cannery, etc.).

Signature block.—The application must be signed by: (1) the individual, if the person is an individual, (2) the president, vice president, or other principal officer, if the person is a corporation, (3) a responsible and duly authorized member or officer having knowledge of its affairs, if the person is a partnership or other unincorporated organization, or (4) the fiduciary, if the person is a trust or estate.

Chapter 5

The Thicket Thickens: Additional Requirements for Businesses with Employees

If anything can go wrong it will. Nature always sides with the hidden flaw.

— Murphy's Law

Murphy was an optimist.

— O'Toole's Law

5.1 General Considerations

As the previous chapter indicated, there is a considerable amount of governmental red tape involved in starting almost any new business. If your business will have any employees — even if it is incorporated and you are the only employee — the level of government regulation and red tape will multiply several times over in the typical case. This chapter outlines the bases you must cover, in addition to those described in Chapter 4, if you start a business that will have employees.

5.2 Social Security and Income Tax Withholding

Once you go into business and begin paying salary or wages to employees, you will find that you have been appointed, as an agent of the government, to collect taxes from your employees. The most significant taxes you will be required to collect are income taxes and Social Security (FICA) tax withheld from employees' wages, which are discussed in this section. You will also find in this and subsequent sections that there are payroll taxes imposed directly on you, as payor of wages.

Employer Identification Number

The first thing you must do is to apply for a federal employer identification number. This number will be used to identify your business on payroll and income tax returns and for most other federal tax purposes. To apply for a number, you need to file a completed *Form SS-4* at the earliest possible time, especially if you have employees. This will ensure that you will get tax deposit coupons in time for depositing federal payroll taxes or corporate income tax. Corporations and partnerships must file *Form SS-4* even if they have no employees. A sample of this form is located at the end of Chapter 4.

As a new employer, you should obtain a business tax kit from your local IRS office. At the same time, you can obtain *Circular E, Employer's Tax Guide,* an IRS publication that explains federal income tax withholding and Social Security tax requirements for employers. *Circular E* also contains up-to-date withholding tables that you must use to determine how much federal income tax and Social Security tax is to be withheld from each employee's paycheck.

Employer Social Security Tax

In addition to withholding Social Security tax from an employee's paycheck — at the rate of 7.65% on gross wages up to $57,600, 1.45% on wages more than $57,600, with a $135,000 limit in 1993 — the employer must also pay an equal amount of employer's Social Security tax. The withheld federal income tax, withheld employee Social Security tax, and employer's Social Security tax are lumped together and paid to the IRS at the same time. In some cases, these taxes can simply be mailed in with your payroll tax return (*Form 941* series) at the end of the calendar quarter or year; however, if you have significant amounts of these taxes to pay, you will generally be required to deposit the taxes with a federal tax deposit form, a precoded coupon, at an authorized commercial bank or a federal reserve bank. As a rule, the greater the amount of taxes due, the sooner they must be paid. How and when federal income and Social Security taxes are to be mailed in or deposited are summarized briefly as follows:[1]

Undeposited Federal Income and FICA Taxes	Deposit with Bank Is Due by:
Less than $500 at the end of a calendar quarter.	Last day of the following month — or mail payment with *Form 941* return.
$500 or more, but less than $3,000 undeposited at end of any eighth-monthly period (a period ending on the 3rd, 7th, 11th, 15th, 19th, 22nd, 25th, or last day of any month).	15th day of the following month.[2]
$3,000 or more undeposited at the end of an eighth-monthly period.	3rd banking day after the end of the eighth-monthly period in which undeposited taxes reach $3,000.[3]
$100,000 or more undeposited at the end of any day.	1st banking day following.[4]

Very large employers may have to make payroll tax deposits frequently. For an employer making eighth-monthly deposits, no penalty for under-deposits will be made if at least 95% of the tax due is deposited when required each month. For a more detailed explanation of federal tax deposits, see IRS *Notice 109*.

Deposits of payroll and withholding taxes may be mailed to a depository bank, if postmarked at least two days prior to the tax deposit due date. But tax deposits of $20,000 or more by employers making more than one deposit a month must reach the bank by the due date, regardless of the postmark date.[5]

New Employees

When a new employee is hired, you must furnish the employee with a federal *Form W-4*, which he or she must complete and return to you. *Form W-4*, when completed, provides the employee's Social Security number and the number of withholding exemptions the employee is claiming, which is used to determine how much income tax you must withhold from his or her wages. You keep *Form W-4*. Neither it nor the information on it is filed with the IRS, except in the case of an employee who claims more than 10 withholding exemptions, or who claims exemption from income tax withholding.

By January 31 of each year, you must furnish each employee with copies of *Form W-2, Annual Wage and Tax Statement*, showing the taxable wages paid to the employee during the preceding calendar year and the taxes withheld, including state income tax. By February 28, the original of each W-2 and a summary form, *Form W-3*, should be filed with the IRS.

Independent Contractors

Not all individuals who perform services for your business will necessarily be employees. In many cases, it is possible to structure your legal relationships with persons who provide services to you so that they are considered to be independent contractors for tax and other legal purposes. From your standpoint as an employer, it is much preferable to be able to treat someone as an independent contractor rather than an employee of your business.

If a person is considered to be an independent contractor, you do not have to pay Social Security tax or federal or state unemployment taxes with respect to his or her compensation. The independent contractor is considered to be self-employed for tax purposes and pays self-employment tax. In addition, you are relieved from the obligation to withhold income and payroll taxes from payments made to independent contractors or to file payroll tax returns with respect to their compensation. You must, however, file a *Form 1099-MISC* for each independent contractor to whom you make payments of $600 or more during a calendar year (with certain exceptions), or, in the case of a direct seller of consumer goods, for each such direct seller to whom you sell $5,000 of goods during a year.

Because of the obvious advantages to employers of treating their employees as independent contractors, the IRS has been very aggressive in attempting to reclassify so-called independent contractors as employees where they perform functions in a manner that is more typical of an employer/employee relationship. Requiring businesses to file *Form 1099-MISC* is an attempt by the IRS to identify those businesses that may be improperly treating employees as independent contractors.

Before you decide to treat anyone who works for you as an independent contractor, you should consult your tax adviser, since there can be serious consequences if those individuals are reclassified as employees by the IRS. See Section 9.11 for a discussion of the risks involved.

State Withholding Taxes

Each state has its own withholding taxes, which vary from state to state. For information on the withholding tax requirements for this state, see Section 11.5.

5.3 Unemployment Taxes

With relatively few exceptions, all businesses with employees must pay both federal and state unemployment taxes. These taxes are imposed entirely on you, the employer. The federal unemployment tax on paper is 6.2% of the first $7,000 of annual wages per employee;[6] however, the federal rate is usually only 0.8% because a credit for up to 5.4% is given for state unemployment taxes paid and for a favorable experience rating for state unemployment tax purposes.[7]

The state unemployment tax rate for an employer can be either more or less than the basic rate, depending upon the amount of unemployment claims by former employees. The more unemployment benefits claimed by your former employees, the higher your unemployment tax rate will be, within certain limits.

Federal Unemployment Tax

Your business will be required to pay federal unemployment tax (FUTA) for any calendar year in which it pays wages of $1,500 or more[8] or if it has one or more employees for at least a portion of the day during any 20 different calendar weeks during the year.[9] Needless to say, this will cover almost any business that has even one employee, even part-time.

If the FUTA liability during any of the first three calendar quarters is more than $100, you must deposit the tax with a federal tax deposit coupon, *Form 8109*, at an authorized bank during the month following the end of the quarter. If the tax is $100 or less, you are not required to make a deposit, but you must add it to the taxes for the next quarter. For the fourth quarter, if the undeposited FUTA tax for the year is more than

$100, deposit the tax with a tax deposit coupon at an authorized bank by January 31. If the balance due is $100 or less, either deposit it with the coupon or mail it in with your federal unemployment tax return, *Form 940*, by January 31. *Form 940* is not due until February 10 if all of the FUTA tax for the prior year has already been deposited when due.

The IRS introduced *Form 940-EZ*, a greatly simplified FUTA return for small employers, in the 1989 tax year. In general, the small employers who can use the new *Form 940-EZ* are those:

Simplified Filing for Small Employers

- Who pay unemployment tax to only one state;
- Who pay state unemployment taxes by the *Form 940-EZ* due date; and
- Whose wages subject to FUTA are also taxable for state unemployment tax purposes.

The state also imposes an unemployment tax which meshes closely with the federal unemployment tax. Refer to Section 11.5 for details on the state unemployment tax, rates, returns, registration as an employer, etc.

State Unemployment Tax

5.4 Workers' Compensation Insurance

A business is generally required by state law to obtain workers' compensation insurance for its employees. This means that you, as an employer, may have to immediately seek out and obtain a workers' compensation insurance policy covering all your employees, or you will be subject to possible legal sanctions. Workers' compensation insurance coverage provides various benefits to an employee who suffers a job-related injury or illness.

There are many insurance companies that offer workers' compensation coverage. Many such companies, however, may be reluctant to write a policy that covers only one or a few employees, unless it is tied to other types of insurance policies. See Section 11.5 for a description of other formal requirements applicable to employers under the workers' compensation laws.

5.5 Compliance with ERISA — Employee Benefit Plans

If you have employees and provide them with fringe benefits, such as group insurance — other than workers' compensation — other types of employee welfare plan benefits, or if you adopt a pension or profit-sharing retirement plan, you will almost certainly have to comply with at least some aspects of the Employee Retirement Income Security Act of 1974 (ERISA). There are criminal penalties for willful failure to comply with two types of ERISA requirements: reporting to government agencies and disclosure to employees.[10] In addition, there are a number of different types of civil penalties which are incredibly numerous and complex, for unintentional failures to comply with ERISA requirements.[11] In short, compliance with ERISA is a nightmare.

This section is an attempt to lay down some relatively simple and straightforward guidelines you, as a layperson, can follow in trying to recognize when you might have an ERISA compliance obligation, so that you will know when to call your attorney, accountant, or benefit consultant for help. ERISA deals with two kinds of employee benefit plans — pension plans and welfare plans.

Pension Plans

Pension plans[12] under ERISA are pretty much what you might expect — tax qualified retirement plans including both pension and profit-sharing plans (including Keogh plans), plus other types of benefit programs that defer payments until after employment has terminated. The ERISA reporting and disclosure requirements for pension plans are quite extensive, and if your business adopts any such plans, you will most definitely need professional assistance in meeting the ERISA requirements that may apply. These are summarized later in this section.

Welfare Plans

Welfare plans[13] under ERISA include most other types of employee benefit plans that are not considered pension plans. These include typical fringe benefit plans adopted by small firms, such as health insurance, long-term disability, group-term life insurance, and accidental death insurance plans. ERISA compliance for welfare plans is usually less of a burden than for pension plans, but is required for almost every business that provides any kind of benefits for employees of the type mentioned above.

Note that a number of so-called fringe benefits that are in the nature of payroll practices, such as paid holidays, vacation pay, bonuses, overtime premium pay, and most kinds of severance pay arrangements, are usually not considered to be either pension or welfare plans under ERISA.[14] Thus, these kinds of payroll practices are not subject to ERISA at all.

Compliance requirements for reporting and disclosure under ERISA are briefly discussed below.

Summary Plan Description

The one ERISA compliance requirement that applies to almost all small businesses is the requirement for you to prepare a summary plan description (SPD) for distribution to all employees covered by any type of welfare plan you sponsor, such as typical health, accident, life, or disability insurance plans.[15] An SPD must contain more than 20 specific items of information listed in the U.S. Department of Labor Regulations,[16] including an ERISA rights statement which must be copied more or less verbatim from the regulations.

An SPD must be prepared for each plan and distributed to covered employees within 120 days after the plan is first adopted.[17] Each new employee must be given a copy of the SPD within 90 days after becoming a participant in the plan.[18] Since an SPD must be prepared for each employee plan subject to ERISA, even a very small business may find that it has to produce three or four of these documents, each of which must meet detailed technical requirements.

One important consideration in taking out insurance coverage for employees should be a firm commitment from the insurance company or brokers that they will prepare the necessary SPDs for the insurance plans they are selling you. Otherwise, you may need to have your attorney or benefit consultant prepare the SPDs, which can result in substantial professional fees.

Other than the need for you to prepare SPDs and distribute them to employees, there are no significant ERISA requirements that apply to most kinds of insured-type welfare plans that cover fewer than 100 employees.[19] You must, however, make available the insurance policies and other plan documents for inspection by your employees and you must furnish copies to them upon request.[20]

Additional ERISA Requirements

If your business should grow to have 100 or more employees who are covered by a plan, or if you adopt any type of uninsured funded welfare plan, you will suddenly become subject to a whole array of additional ERISA requirements, including:

- Filing a copy of the SPD with the U.S. Department of Labor;[21]
- Filing an annual return/report or registration (*Form 5500* series) with the IRS each year;[22]
- Preparing and distributing a summary annual report to covered employees each year;[23]
- Preparing a summary of material modifications of the plan, if necessary, and filing it with the U.S. Department of Labor and distributing it to covered employees;[24] and
- Filing a terminal report if the plan is terminated.[25]

The ERISA compliance requirements for a pension or profit-sharing plan of even a very small business are very onerous, complex, and expensive, despite numerous attempts by the IRS and U.S. Department of Labor to simplify the reporting requirements, in response to a barrage of criticism from small businesses.

Because these compliance requirements are so very complex and are constantly in a state of flux, no attempt to spell them out in detail is made here. Instead, the basic ERISA compliance requirements for most pension and profit-sharing plans are summarized on the next page.

Summary of Basic ERISA Compliance Requirements

Item	Provided to
Summary plan description.	U.S. Department of Labor; participants; beneficiaries
Annual return/report (*Form 5500, 5500-EZ, 5500-C* or *5500-R*).	IRS (now required even for a simple one-person Keogh plan)
Schedule A, Form 5500 series (insurance information).	IRS
Schedule B, Form 5500 series (actuarial information prepared and signed by an enrolled actuary for "defined benefit" plans only).	IRS
Schedule SSA, Form 5500 series (registration statement).	IRS
Form W-2P (report of periodic plan benefit payments made during the year).	IRS; recipient of distribution
Form 1099-R (report of total distribution of benefits during the year).	IRS; recipient of distribution
Form W-3 or *W-3G* (transmittal of *Form W-2P* and *Form 1099-R*).	IRS
Form PBGC-1 (premium payment of required plan termination insurance — for "defined benefit" plans only).	Pension Benefit Guaranty Corporation (a government agency that insures pension plans of corporate employers)
Summary annual report.	Participants; beneficiaries
Individual deferred vested benefit statement to separated employee.	Former participant in plan
Summary of material modifications to a plan.	U.S. Department of Labor; participants; beneficiaries
Terminal report (when plan is terminated).	U.S. Department of Labor; participants; beneficiaries
Written explanation of joint and survivor annuity and financial effect of not electing to receive it (if plan provides benefits in the form of an annuity).	Participants
Written explanation of reasons for denying benefit claim and description of appeal procedures.	Person claiming entitlement to plan benefit
Various documents and information to be provided on request.	U.S. Department of Labor; participants
Various formal notices upon occurrence of certain events.	IRS; U.S. Department of Labor; Pension Benefit Guaranty Corporation; participants

If your business maintains a pension or profit-sharing plan, it should be obvious from this summary of basic ERISA compliance requirements that you need some expert help from an attorney, accountant, or pension consulting firm — or all of them — if you are going to be able to properly comply with the requirements of ERISA and avoid potential fines and other civil and criminal penalties.

The cost of maintaining these plans has unfortunately multiplied several times over since the passage of ERISA in 1974, followed by a labyrinth of ERISA regulations issued by several different federal agencies. In short, unless you make substantial contributions to and obtain significant tax savings from an employee retirement plan, it may not be worth having because of the heavy costs of compliance with ERISA.

Bonding and Withholding Requirements

Besides the ERISA reporting and disclosure requirements discussed above, there are two other points you should be aware of regarding ERISA — the bonding requirement and withholding requirements on pension or profit-sharing plan distributions. All employees who are deemed to handle assets of a pension or welfare plan that is subject to ERISA must be covered by fidelity bond.[26] Consult your attorney or benefit consultant to see if any required bonding needs to be paid regarding any benefit plans you maintain for your employees. This is particularly important if you have a pension or profit-sharing plan.

Secondly, withholding is now mandatory on distributions of pension and profit-sharing benefits,[27] unless the recipient elects in advance not to have any tax withheld.

In addition to reporting and disclosure requirements under ERISA, there are other federal reporting and recordkeeping requirements for certain types of fringe benefit plans.[28] For example, employers maintaining educational assistance programs, group legal services plans, and so-called cafeteria plans are currently required to file annual reports with the IRS on *Form 5500*, *Form 5500-C*, or *Form 5500-R* and, if needed, to maintain records to show that those plans qualified for tax purposes for each year after 1984.[29]

5.6 Employee Safety and Health Regulations

As has been discussed in Section 5.4, employers are required by state law in many states to carry workers' compensation insurance for the protection of employees who develop job-related illnesses or who are injured on the job. In addition, there are comprehensive and far-reaching federal laws that set safety standards designed to prevent injuries arising from unsafe or unhealthy working conditions. The primary federal law regulating job safety, the Occupational Safety and Health Act of 1970 (OSHA), imposes several reporting and recordkeeping obligations for employers.

Federal OSHA

Over the years, the Occupational Safety and Health Administration has issued reams of regulations and standards for workplace safety. If you have employees, you will need to consult an attorney, preferably one with OSHA expertise, to determine what, if any, steps you must take to comply with federal and state safety standards at your place of business. Otherwise, you may be subject to fines and other legal sanctions if any employee is injured on the job or OSHA inspectors find that you are not in compliance with applicable safety standards at your place of business.

You may also want to contact the nearest regional U.S. Department of Labor–OSHA office and request information on any free consultative services or publications the office may have available. Many state occupational safety and health agencies provide confidential, on-site consultations for no charge. These consultations point out state compliance issues at your place of business. These state agencies would also know if any federal OSHA consultants are available.

Notices to Employees

OSHA requires that you post a permanent notice to employees regarding job safety.[30] In addition, OSHA rules require the posting of a second official poster regarding the rights of employees who are punished for objecting to unsafe working conditions.

Recordkeeping Requirements

Under OSHA, it is necessary to keep a log of industrial injuries and illnesses.[31] The federal *Form 200* can be used to satisfy this requirement.[32] The information in the log must also be summarized and posted prominently in your workplace from February 1 to March 1.[33] This requirement was eliminated January 1, 1983 for most retail, financial, insurance, and service firms,[34] but not for:

- Building material and garden supply stores
- General merchandise stores
- Foodstores
- Hotels and other lodging places
- Repair, amusement, and recreation services
- Health services[35]

Under OSHA, a supplementary record must be prepared after a recordable injury or illness occurs, using federal *Form 101* or any of the substitutes state law permits to be used for this purpose.[36]

Neither of the above recordkeeping forms are ordinarily filed with the government. Instead, these records must be retained and kept available for inspection for five years.[37] In addition, special recordkeeping requirements will generally apply if your employees are exposed to toxic substances, asbestos, radiation, or carcinogens on the job. You can obtain more detailed information on OSHA recordkeeping requirements by calling the nearest OSHA office (usually listed in the phone book under U. S. Government – Department of Labor) and asking for the booklet entitled *Recordkeeping Requirements for Occupational Injuries and Illnesses.*

OSHA exempts any employer with 10 or fewer employees from most of its reporting and recordkeeping requirements;[38] however, these small employers are not exempt from keeping a log of all injuries and accidents or reporting job-related fatalities and multiple injuries.

Exemption from Recordkeeping

Federal OSHA reporting requirements include:

Reporting Requirements

- The Bureau of Labor Statistics may require certain selected employers, including small employers, to report certain summary information on job-related injuries and illnesses annually on an occupational injuries and illness survey form.[39]
- In the event of a fatality or an accident resulting in the hospitalization of five or more employees, you must notify the area OSHA director within 48 hours, describing the circumstances of the accident, the extent of any injuries, and the number of fatalities.[40] There are penalties in the event you fail to give notice as required.[41]

See Section 11.5 for a discussion of laws this state may have that govern employee health and safety.

State Employee Safety and Health Regulations

5.7 Employee Wage-Hour and Child Labor Laws

Not all businesses nor all employees of a given business are covered by federal and state wage-hour and child labor laws. The coverage of these laws is a crazy quilt patchwork of exceptions. Thus, there is no simple way to tell you whether your business will be subject to one or more of the federal and state laws relating to minimum wage, overtime pay, and child labor, or, if it is, which employees are covered and which are not. To find out which laws apply to your business, contact your attorney or the local wage-hour office.

The Federal Fair Labor Standards Act (FLSA) includes a number of requirements regarding compensation of employees covered under the act. There are two major requirements you need to know about.

Federal Wage-Hour Laws

The minimum wage provisions of the FLSA set an hourly minimum wage that you can pay to an employee. The current federal minimum wage is $4.25 per hour.[42] Certain states provide for a minimum wage in excess of the federal requirement or that applies to some employees who are not covered under the federal minimum wage law. Refer to Section 11.5 for the requirements in this state.

Minimum Wage Requirement

The overtime pay requirement rule states you must pay a covered employee at one and one-half times the employee's regular hourly rate

Overtime Pay Requirement

for any hours worked in excess of 40 in a week.[43] The regular hourly rate cannot be less than the minimum wage. For the overtime pay requirement, the FLSA takes a single workweek as its measuring period and does not permit averaging of hours over two or more weeks. For example, if an employee works 30 hours one week and 50 hours during the next, he or she must receive overtime compensation (time and one-half) for the 10 overtime hours worked in the second week, even though the average number of hours worked in the two weeks is 40. Note that the FLSA only requires overtime pay based on the number of hours worked during a week and not for working long hours on a particular day.

The above rules generally apply to salaried workers as well as to those paid on an hourly basis. To determine the regular hourly rate for a salaried employee, it is necessary to divide the employee's weekly salary by the number of hours in his or her regular workweek (40 or less).

Employee Exemptions

Executives, administrators, professionals, and outside salespeople are not covered and thus are not entitled by law to any pay for overtime hours worked.[44] The theory behind this exemption is apparently the view that these types of employees are independent and sophisticated enough to take care of themselves and do not need to be protected by the government from exploitation by their employers.

Under the Code of Federal Regulations (Section 541.5), an employee qualifying for the exemption as an outside salesperson must meet the two requirements listed below.

- The employee customarily and regularly works away from the employer's place of business while making sales or obtaining orders or contracts for services or for the use of facilities for which a consideration will be paid by the client or customer.
- The employee cannot do any other kind of work for the company (besides that of selling) for more than 20% of the usual workweek put in by the company's nonexempt employees; for example, the outside salesperson or exempted employee could do receptionist work for only 8 hours of each 40-hour workweek.

Various indicators of an employee's bona fide status as an outside salesperson include:

- A contractual designation or job title that reflects involvement in sales;
- Significant compensation on a commission basis;
- Special sales training; and
- Little or no direct or constant supervision in carrying out daily tasks.

Small Enterprise Exemption

Employees of certain small companies, other than those enterprises engaged in commerce, are exempt from coverage under the wage-hour laws. What this really means, translated from the legalese, is that certain smaller businesses that do not significantly affect the flow of goods and services in interstate commerce are exempted. An "enterprise engaged in commerce" is one that "has employees engaged in commerce or in the production of goods for commerce, or that has employees handling, selling, or otherwise working on goods or materials that have been moved in commerce or produced for commerce by any person," and "is an enterprise whose annual gross volume of sales made or business done is not less than $500,000."[45]

All of which means that, if your firm does less than a half million dollars in sales a year, it will generally be exempt from FLSA overtime and minimum wage requirements.[46]

Even if you are exempt from the FLSA wage-hour rules, state wage-hour laws may apply and may be more stringent than federal laws in many states.

Numerous other exemptions from the wage-hour laws are based on the type of business, the nature of the work performed by the employee, where the work is done, and other factors.[47] Before you assume that your employees are covered by the FLSA, you should consult your attorney, or at least call the local wage and hour office on an anonymous basis and ask for an informal and nonbinding opinion over the phone.

Detailed Records Required

Probably the most important thing you should be aware of, if you have employees subject to FLSA standards, is the need to keep detailed records of hours worked, the type of work, and wages or salary paid. Under the law, if an employee files a claim against you for alleged failure to pay required wages in the past, you will need to be able to produce proof that you met the statutory requirements. Keeping detailed pay and work records for each employee is the only way to protect yourself against such claims for back pay. In addition, the FLSA requires employers to preserve such records for up to three years.

Poster Requirement

If you have employees whose wages, hours, and working conditions are subject to FLSA regulations, you will need to post the official wage-hour poster provided by the U.S. Department of Labor.

State Wage-Hour Laws

Refer to Section 11.5 for a discussion of the basic wage-hour and other significant labor law requirements under state law.

Child Labor Laws

Both the FLSA and various state laws regulate or prohibit the employment of children in businesses, with very few exceptions. If you intend to hire children to work in your business — other than hiring your own children, which is usually permitted, except in hazardous situations — you need to be aware of the following basic child labor law provisions.

Federal Child Labor Laws

As a general rule, the FLSA prohibits the employment of children under 16 years of age;[48] although, there are a number of exceptions to this rule.[49] All children under age 18, however, are excluded from certain occupations that are designated as hazardous by the secretary of labor.[50]

Children under 16 years of age cannot be hired under any of the following circumstances:

- To work in any workplace where mining, manufacturing, or processing operations take place;
- To operate power machinery, other than office equipment;
- To operate or serve as a helper on motor vehicles;
- To work in public messenger services; and
- To work in the following occupations: transportation; warehousing or storage; communications or public utilities; or construction (except in sales or office work).[51]

Children 14 or 15 years of age can be hired in other occupations not considered to be hazardous, but there are numerous limitations on the hours and times when they may work, particularly when schools are in session. A few occupations, such as delivering newspapers and doing theatrical work, are exempt from the federal child labor laws, even for children under 14 years of age.[52]

State Child Labor Laws

Most states also strictly regulate the employment of children. See Section 11.5 regarding state child labor laws in this state. Thus, if you intend to employ children under 18 years of age in a business, you will probably need legal guidance as to the conditions under which they may work, if at all, under federal and state child labor laws.

5.8 Fair Employment Practices

As an employer, you will also need to be alert to your obligations under a number of federal and state laws that prohibit discrimination in employment on the basis of sex, age, race, color, national origin, religion, or on account of mental or physical handicaps. These anti-discrimination laws are not just limited to hiring practices, but relate to almost every aspect of the relationship between employer and employee, including compensation, promotions, type of work assigned, and working conditions.

In addition to outlawing discrimination in employment, companies contracting for business with the federal government are generally required to adopt affirmative action programs in employment of minorities, women, the handicapped, and Vietnam veterans. Affirmative action programs are employment programs that go beyond elimination of discrimination. Under such programs, employers consciously make an effort to hire more women and minority group members and to upgrade the pay and responsibility levels of women and other groups that have historically been subject to patterns of discrimination.

Affirmative action programs are generally required for businesses that are government contractors. Most businesses are only required to refrain from discriminating in employment.

There are several anti-discrimination requirements that, as a small business owner, you should be aware of; however, if your small business employs less than 15 employees and is not working on government contracts or subcontracts, the federal anti-discrimination laws listed below generally do not apply to you. The one exception to this would be the Equal Pay Act of 1963 which provides equal pay for equal work for women. This act is applicable to employers with two or more employees.

Federal Anti-Discrimination Laws

Employers Subject to Federal Anti-Discrimination Laws

Name of Law	Employers Who Are Covered	What the Law Requires
Title VII of the Civil Rights Act of 1964 and Americans with Disabilities Act (ADA)	Employers with 15 or more employees during 20 weeks of a calendar year (25 employees under ADA until 1994)	No discrimination in employment practices based on race, religion, disability or national origin
Pregnancy Discrimination Act	Same as for Title VII above	Equal treatment for pregnant women and new mothers for all employment-related purposes, including fringe benefits
Executive Order 11246 as amended	Employers with federal contracts or subcontracts of $10,000 or more	No discrimination in employment practices based on race, sex, color, religion, or national origin
Equal Pay Act of 1963	Nearly all employers with two or more employees	Equal pay for women
Age Discrimination in Employment Act of 1967	Employers with 20 or more employees, 20 or more weeks in a calendar year	No discrimination in hiring or firing on account of age, for persons age 40 to 70
Rehabilitation Act of 1973	Employers with federal contracts or subcontracts of $2,500 or more	No discrimination in employment practices on account of mental health or physical handicaps
Vietnam-Era Veteran Readjustment Assistance Act of 1974	Employers with federal contracts or subcontracts of $10,000 or more	Affirmative action programs for certain disabled veterans

Employers who violate any of the above laws may be sued by either the complaining individuals or by the various government enforcement agencies, or both.

Formal Compliance Requirements

Small businesses are not required to do a lot of paperwork or filling out of forms when it comes to federal anti-discrimination laws. An employer with more than 100 employees, however, must file *Form EEO-1* with the Equal Employment Opportunity Commission (EEOC) each year.[53]

As an employer you are required to keep detailed records — and should, for your own protection — as to reasons for hiring or not hiring, promoting or not promoting, any employee or job applicant. In the event it is ever necessary to demonstrate that your firm has not discriminated against any group or individual member of a group in violation of federal laws, these records will provide the needed documentation.

Besides these requirements, there are a number of official posters you may be required to post in your place of business. These may include:

Display Posters

Type of Poster	Who Must Post	Source of Poster
Civil rights poster regarding sexual, racial, religious, and ethnic discrimination or because of physical or mental disability (*WH Publication 1088*)	Employers with 15 or more employees during 20 weeks of the year or with federal contracts or subcontracts of $10,000 or more[54]	EEOC offices, the nearest Office of Compliance
Age discrimination poster	Employers with 20 or more employees who work 20 or more weeks a year[55]	EEOC offices
Notice to employees working on government contracts (*WH Publication 1313*)	Any employer performing government contract work subject to the Service Contract Act or the Public Contracts Act	U.S. Department of Labor, Employment Standards Division
Poster required under the Vietnam Era Veterans Readjustment Assistance Act	Employers with federal contracts or subcontracts of $10,000 or more	From the federal contracting officer administering the contract

To obtain these posters, you can contact each of the appropriate federal agencies and request a copy of their required poster.

The civil rights poster and the age discrimination poster — plus two other required posters mentioned earlier, the Fair Labor Standards Act (FLSA) and the Occupational Safety and Health Act (OSHA) posters — are available through a company called Remarkable Products. This company has conveniently laminated these four posters onto one, easy-to-mount poster.

These laminated posters are available for a nominal fee. For more information on these posters, contact:

Remarkable Products
(201) 784-0900

Sexual Harassment

You need to be keenly aware of your potential liability for sexual harassment in the workplace, another increasingly significant area of the anti-discrimination laws, under Title VII of the Civil Rights Act. While the federal Civil Rights Act does not specifically refer to sexual harassment as a form of discrimination, the courts and the Equal Employment Opportunity Commission (EEOC) have long accepted it as such. There are two types of sexual harassment under Title VII, as it has been interpreted over the years.

One type of sexual harassment is where tangible job benefits are granted or withheld based on an employee's receptiveness to unwelcome requests or conduct. For example, a male supervisor tells a female employee to meet him in the hot tub of his mountain chalet on a Saturday afternoon to discuss a business contract. She refuses to meet him at his place and later receives a bad rating from him for "poor attitude and unwillingness to work overtime," which costs her a raise or promotion. The female employee in such a case has been denied a tangible job benefit due to sexual harassment.

The second type of sexual harassment involves a hostile work environment; that is, a situation in which the work environment is oppressive and hostile to members of one sex. This occurs when such conditions either unreasonably interfere with the individual's work performance or create an intimidating, hostile, or offensive environment. This type of harassment may not have any economic effects on the individual, and management or supervisory personnel may not be involved. Nevertheless, an employer who allows such a condition to persist may still be liable if management was aware of the harassment by co-workers (or even by customers) and fails to take appropriate actions to remedy the situation.

Merely having a company policy that prohibits sexual harassment at your company won't automatically stop such activity or protect the firm from liability if harassment occurs, but the absence of such a policy makes such conduct somewhat more likely to occur and will also tend to strengthen an employee's claim against you if your firm is sued for allowing such acts to occur. Adopt a sexual harassment policy that not only prohibits such conduct, but which sets up a grievance mechanism for employees who are victims of any such harassment, and communicate this company policy strongly and clearly to your employees.

Note that, in addition to federal civil rights case law, the statutes of many states, or the regulations of many state civil rights commissions, now specifically prohibit sexual harassment in the workplace, and some of these laws go well beyond the protections afforded under federal law.

State Anti-Discrimination Laws

Many states have additional statutes or regulations, which may go beyond federal laws. For a more detailed discussion of anti-discrimination laws in this state, refer to Section 11.5.

5.9 Immigration Law Restrictions on Hiring

The Immigration Reform and Control Act of 1986 represents a major governmental requirement regarding the relationship between the employer and employee. Under this law, you are prohibited from hiring illegal aliens and, depending on the number of any prior violations, are subject to fines of $250 to $20,000 for each illegal alien hired after November 6, 1986. At the same time, the act also prohibits employment discrimination on the basis of citizenship status and national origin; you may not fire or fail to hire anyone on the basis of foreign appearance, language, or name.

For all employees hired after November 6, 1986, you are required to verify their eligibility for employment within three business days of each new hire. As an employer, you will need to fill out and retain *Form I-9*. The employee fills out the top portion of the form, indicating whether he or she is a citizen or national of the United States; an alien lawfully admitted for permanent residence; or an alien authorized by the U.S. Immigration and Naturalization Service (INS) to work in the United States.

On the bottom portion of *Form I-9*, there are three separate lists of various forms of identification and employment eligibility documents the employee must provide for you. You must check off the documents you have examined, such as passport, certificate of naturalization, etc. These papers must include either one document in List A or one each in lists B and C. Both you and the employee must sign the form under penalty of perjury, and you must retain the completed form and make it available if the INS or U.S. Department of Labor requests it during an inspection.

You may obtain copies of *Form I-9* and a related *Employer's Handbook* from the nearest office of the U.S. Immigration and Naturalization Service. A sample *Form I-9* is also included at the end of this chapter. For more information on employer responsibilities, call and request Category 3.

U.S. Immigration and Naturalization Service
(800) 755-0777

5.10 Restrictions on Layoffs of Employees

The WARN Act

If your business grows to the size where you have 100 or more full-time employees — or the equivalent, based on 40-hour workweeks — at a single location, you may be subject to the potentially onerous provisions of the plant closing bill that was enacted by Congress in 1988 and went into effect on February 4, 1989. This law, called the Worker Adjustment and Retraining Notification Act, or WARN Act,[56] would affect you if you laid off 50 or more employees, or one-third of the work force, in a 30-day period. It applies to virtually any plant closing or major layoff for any reason, with a few obvious exceptions, such as due to an earthquake or flood, or due to a labor dispute, e.g., a strike or lockout for which no notice need be given.

A "layoff" under this act includes any of the following:

- A permanent termination of employment;
- A layoff of an employee for more than six months; or
- A loss of half the employees' working hours for six consecutive months.

In case of any major layoff or shutdown, the law requires you to give at least 60 days advance notice. If you give less than that, you are required to pay the laid-off workers for 60 days minus the actual number of days' notice you gave. The law requires you to notify the labor union that represents the employees, or, if none, the individual employees by mailing the notice to their last known address or including it in their pay envelope. You must also notify the local city or county government and state labor agency of the planned shutdown or cutback.

The WARN Act doesn't generally prohibit a company from making layoffs or shutting down a money-losing plant, but it makes it more costly for the employer to do so, and also gives local unions and politicians time to find some way to attempt to coerce a company into maintaining an antiquated facility that may no longer be economically viable.

The WARN law does impose stiff restrictions on a firm's ability to sell off, reorganize, merge, or consolidate operations, if such a decision would adversely affect the jobs of 50 or more employees. In other words, if your Japanese competition renders your plant obsolete, you will not be allowed to sell it off to a competitor, if doing so would cost 50 or more employees their jobs. The act has made it much more costly to take a risk on building a plant in the United States — if it fails, you may have to close shop rather than restructure or sell.

As a result, there is expected to be a great deal of litigation over what does and does not constitute a mass layoff or shutdown under WARN.

5.11 The Americans with Disabilities Act

In July of 1990, Congress enacted a revolutionary and wide-reaching piece of legislation, the Americans with Disabilities Act (ADA), which is designed to make both the workplace and most public facilities much more accessible to disabled persons.

This new law[57] and related regulations,[58] which are being phased in over several years, will have a significant impact on a great many businesses, both in terms of employment practices and in terms or removing architectural barriers and other physical features that have limiting effects on the lives of disabled persons.

Anti-Discrimination Rules Regarding the Disabled

Title I of the ADA, which became effective for larger firms on July 26, 1992, prohibits discrimination against any "qualified individual with a disability" in all aspects of employment, including hiring and discharge of workers, compensation and benefits. In addition, you must reasonably accommodate employees' or applicants' disabilities, which may mean modifying facilities, restructuring work schedules, or transferring disabled workers to vacant positions for which they are qualified, in appropriate circumstances. You are not required to accommodate a disabled worker, however, if doing so would impose an "undue hardship" on yourself.

Medical Screening Tests

One area that will be significantly affected in the hiring process is the limitation on medical screening of applicants. Under the ADA, companies can no longer screen out prospective employees with disabilities because the applicant has an elevated risk of an on-the-job injury or a medical condition that might be aggravated because of job demands. The law specifically bans questions about a job applicant's physical or mental condition either on an employment application form or during a job interview. This would include general questions such as, "Do you have any mental or physical conditions that would prevent you from performing your job functions?"

Medical exams are still allowed, but they are greatly restricted. Pre-offer exams are prohibited, but an offer may be conditioned upon the satisfactory results of a medical examination. Results, however, cannot be used to withdraw an offer, unless they show that the individual in question is not able to perform the tasks required by the position.

You should be aware that the definition of "disabled" under the ADA includes people with AIDS, those who test positive for the HIV virus, and rehabilitated drug abusers and alcoholics; however, you should also note that the ADA does not:

- Prohibit voluntary tests, such as employer-sponsored cholesterol or blood pressure tests; nor
- Require employers to hire persons who are drug users or who have contagious diseases.

The ADA is neutral on the issue of drug testing of employees, in effect leaving that up to regulation by the states.

Effective Dates

The ADA's employment-related rules slated to become effective between mid-1992 and mid-1994 are:

- July 26, 1992 — Equal employment rules with regard to the disabled, effective for employers with 25 or more employees during 20 weeks of the year;

- January 26, 1993 — Newly built facilities must be accessible to both disabled employees and customers; and
- July 26, 1994 — Equal employment rules with regard to the disabled, effective for employers with 15 or more employees during 20 weeks of the year.

Title III of the ADA requires practically all businesses to make their facilities accessible to disabled employees and customers. Examples of various accessibility requirements with regard to public accommodations include:

Public Accommodations for the Disabled

- One designated parking space for the disabled must be provided for every 25 or fewer spaces. A lesser ratio applies if there are more than 100 total spaces.
- Hotels and motels must have 5% of their rooms accessible to wheelchairs and another 5% must be equipped with devices such as visual alarms for the hearing-impaired.
- Access ramps must be in place where the floor level changes more than one-half of an inch.
- Elevators must be provided in three-story or taller buildings and in those with more than 3,000 square feet per story.
- In retail or grocery stores, checkout aisles must be at least 36 inches wide. This is wide enough for wheelchairs.
- Theaters and similar places of assembly for 50 or more persons must have at least three wheelchair spaces dispersed throughout the seating area.

The new public access requirements became effective:

Effective Dates

- January 26, 1992 — For all larger employers with more than 25 employers or more than $1 million of gross annual receipts;
- July 26, 1992 — For companies with 25 or fewer employees and gross annual receipts of $1 million or less; and
- January 26, 1993 — For companies with 10 or fewer employees and gross annual receipts of $500,000 or less.

Companies spending money to remove architectural and transportation barriers to the disabled can deduct up to $15,000 a year of such expenses.[59] In addition, small firms — those with gross receipts under $1 million or fewer than 30 full-time employees — who spend between $250 and $10,250 a year on access for the disabled, can claim a tax credit for up to 50% of the cost of such expenditures, a maximum annual credit of $5,000.[60] For more information on the ADA, contact:

Tax Incentives

Equal Employment Opportunity Commission   or   **U.S. Department of Justice**
2401 E Street   (202) 514-0301
Washington, DC 20506
(202) 663-4264

Footnotes

1. Treasury Decision 7701, 1980-28 I.R.B. 20.
2. Treas. Regs. § 31.6302(c)-1(a)(1)(i)(a).
3. Treas. Regs. § 31.6302(c)-1(a)(1)(i)(b).
4. I.R.C. § 6302(g).
5. I.R.C. § 7502(e)(3).
6. I.R.C. §§ 3301(1) and 3306(b)(1).
7. I.R.C. §§ 3301(1) and 3302(b).
8. I.R.C. § 3306(a)(1)(A).
9. I.R.C. § 3306(a)(1)(B).
10. 29 U.S.C. § 1131.
11. 29 U.S.C. § 1132; I.R.C. §§ 4971, 4975, 6057–6059, and 6652.
12. 29 U.S.C. § 1002(2); 29 C.F.R. § 2510.3-2.
13. 29 U.S.C. § 1002(1); 29 C.F.R. § 2510.3-1.
14. 29 C.F.R. § 2510.3-1(b); 29 C.F.R. § 2510.3-2(b).
15. 29 C.F.R. § 2520.104b-2.
16. 29 C.F.R. § 2520.102-3.
17. 29 C.F.R. § 2520.104b-2(a)(2).
18. 29 C.F.R. § 2520.104b-2(a)(1).
19. 29 C.F.R. § 2520.104-20.
20. 29 U.S.C. § 1024(b)(4); 29 C.F.R. § 2520.104b-1.
21. 29 C.F.R. § 2520.104a-3.
22. 29 C.F.R. § 2520.104a-5.
23. 29 C.F.R. § 2520.104b-10.
24. 29 C.F.R. §§ 2520.104a-4 and 2520.104b-3.
25. 29 U.S.C. § 1021(c).
26. 29 U.S.C. § 1112.
27. I.R.C. § 3405(a).
28. I.R.C. § 6039 D.
29. Announcement 86-20, I.R.B. 1986–87, 34.
30. 29 C.F.R. § 1903.2.
31. 29 C.F.R. § 1904.2.
32. 29 C.F.R. § 1904.10.
33. 29 C.F.R. § 1904.5.
34. 29 C.F.R. § 1904.16.
35. 29 C.F.R. § 1904.12.
36. 29 C.F.R. § 1904.4.
37. 29 C.F.R. § 1904.6.
38. 29 C.F.R. § 1904.15.
39. 29 C.F.R. §§ 1904.15 and 1904.21.
40. 29 C.F.R. § 1904.8.
41. 29 C.F.R. § 1904.9.
42. 29 U.S.C. § 206(a)(1).
43. 29 U.S.C. § 207(a)(1).
44. 29 U.S.C. § 213(a)(1).
45. 29 U.S.C. § 203(s).
46. 29 U.S.C. § 207(a)(1).
47. 29 U.S.C. § 213.
48. 29 U.S.C. §§ 203(1) and 212.
49. 29 U.S.C. § 213.
50. 29 C.F.R. § 570.50–570.71.
51. 29 C.F.R. § 570.33.
52. 29 U.S.C. § 213(c) and (d).
53. 29 C.F.R. § 1602.7.
54. 29 C.F.R. § 1601.30.
55. 29 U.S.C. § 627 and 29 C.F.R. § 1627.10.
56. 29 U.S.C. §§ 2101–2109.
57. 42 U.S.C. § 12101 *et seq.*
58. 29 C.F.R. § 1630.
59. I.R.C. § 190.

EMPLOYMENT ELIGIBILITY VERIFICATION (Form I-9)

1 **EMPLOYEE INFORMATION AND VERIFICATION:** (To be completed and signed by employee.)

Name: (Print or Type) Last	First	Middle	Birth Name
Address: Street Name and Number	City	State	ZIP Code

Date of Birth (Month/Day/Year)	Social Security Number

I attest, under penalty of perjury, that I am (check a box):

☐ 1. A citizen or national of the United States.

☐ 2. An alien lawfully admitted for permanent residence (Alien Number A _____).

☐ 3. An alien authorized by the Immigration and Naturalization Service to work in the United States (Alien Number A _____ ,
or Admission Number _____ , expiration of employment authorization, if any _____).

I attest, under penalty of perjury, the documents that I have presented as evidence of identity and employment eligibility are genuine and relate to me. I am aware that federal law provides for imprisonment and/or fine for any false statements or use of false documents in connection with this certificate.

Signature	Date (Month/Day/Year)

PREPARER/TRANSLATOR CERTIFICATION (To be completed if prepared by person other than the employee). I attest, under penalty of perjury, that the above was prepared by me at the request of the named individual and is based on all information of which I have any knowledge.

Signature	Name (Print or Type)		
Address (Street Name and Number)	City	State	Zip Code

2 **EMPLOYER REVIEW AND VERIFICATION:** (To be completed and signed by employer.)

Instructions:

Examine one document from List A and check the appropriate box, _OR_ examine one document from List B _and_ one from List C and check the appropriate boxes. Provide the *Document Identification Number* and *Expiration Date* for the document checked.

List A Documents that Establish Identity and Employment Eligibility	List B Documents that Establish Identity	**and**	List C Documents that Establish Employment Eligibility
☐ 1. United States Passport ☐ 2. Certificate of United States Citizenship ☐ 3. Certificate of Naturalization ☐ 4. Unexpired foreign passport with attached Employment Authorization ☐ 5. Alien Registration Card with photograph	☐ 1. A State-issued driver's license or a State-issued I.D. card with a photograph, or information, including name, sex, date of birth, height, weight, and color of eyes. (Specify State)_____) ☐ 2. U.S. Military Card ☐ 3. Other (Specify document and issuing authority) _____		☐ 1. Original Social Security Number Card (other than a card stating it is not valid for employment) ☐ 2. A birth certificate issued by State, county, or municipal authority bearing a seal or other certification ☐ 3. Unexpired INS Employment Authorization Specify form # _____
Document Identification # _____	*Document Identification* # _____		*Document Identification* # _____
Expiration Date (if any) _____	*Expiration Date (if any)* _____		*Expiration Date (if any)* _____

CERTIFICATION: I attest, under penalty of perjury, that I have examined the documents presented by the above individual, that they appear to be genuine and to relate to the individual named, and that the individual, to the best of my knowledge, is eligible to work in the United States.

Signature	Name (Print or Type)	Title
Employer Name	Address	Date

Employment Eligibility Verification

> **NOTICE:** Authority for collecting the information on this form is in Title 8, United States Code, Section 1324A, which requires employers to verify employment eligibility of individuals on a form approved by the Attorney General. This form will be used to verify the individual's eligibility for employment in the United States. Failure to present this form for inspection to officers of the Immigration and Naturalization Service or Department of Labor within the time period specified by regulation, or improper completion or retention of this form, may be a violation of the above law and may result in a civil money penalty.

Section 1. Instructions to Employee/Preparer for completing this form

Instructions for the employee.

All employees, upon being hired, must complete Section 1 of this form. Any person hired after November 6, 1986 must complete this form. (For the purpose of completion of this form the term "hired" applies to those employed, recruited or referred for a fee.)

All employees must print or type their complete name, address, date of birth, and Social Security Number. The block which correctly indicates the employee's immigration status must be checked. If the second block is checked, the employee's Alien Registration Number must be provided. If the third block is checked, the employee's Alien Registration Number *or* Admission Number must be provided, as well as the date of expiration of that status, if it expires.

All employees whose present names differ from birth names, because of marriage or other reasons, must print or type their birth names in the appropriate space of Section 1. Also, employees whose names change after employment verification should report these changes to their employer.

All employees must sign and date the form.

Instructions for the preparer of the form, if not the employee.

If a person assists the employee with completing this form, the preparer must certify the form by signing it and printing or typing his or her complete name and address.

Section 2. Instructions to Employer for completing this form

(For the purpose of completion of this form, the term "employer" applies to employers and those who recruit or refer for a fee.)

Employers must complete this section by examining evidence of identity and employment eligibility, and:
- checking the appropriate box in List A *or* boxes in both Lists B and C;
- recording the document identification number and expiration date (if any);
- recording the type of form if not specifically identified in the list;
- signing the certification section.

NOTE: Employers are responsible for reverifying employment eligibility of employees whose employment eligibility documents carry an expiration date.

Copies of documentation presented by an individual for the purpose of establishing identity and employment eligibility may be copied and retained for the purpose of complying with the requirements of this form and no other purpose. Any copies of documentation made for this purpose should be maintained with this form.

Name changes of employees which occur after preparation of this form should be recorded on the form by lining through the old name, printing the new name and the reason (such as marriage), and dating and initialing the changes. Employers should not attempt to delete or erase the old name in any fashion.

RETENTION OF RECORDS.

The completed form must be retained by the employer for:
- three years after the date of hiring; or
- one year after the date the employment is terminated, whichever is later.

> Employers may photocopy or reprint this form as necessary.

U.S. Department of Justice
Immigration and Naturalization Service

OMB #1115-0136
Form I-9 (05/07 87)
☆ USGPO 1987- 183-918/69085

For sale by the Superintendent of Documents, U.S. Government Printing Office
Washington, D.C. 20402

Chapter 6

Businesses that Require Licenses to Operate

The bureaucrat who smiles when something serious has gone wrong
has already found someone to blame it on.

— Anonymous

6.1 General Licensing

Almost any kind of business activity you engage in will require a city or
county business license, which is usually fairly simple to obtain. In addition, some types of businesses will have to obtain licenses from the federal government to operate; while other businesses, occupations, and professions are also licensed and regulated by the state.

Even though there are tremendous variations regarding the requirements
for obtaining necessary federal and state licenses, these requirements
generally relate to educational attainments, experience in the particular
field, passage of examinations, submission of detailed applications,
meeting financial or bonding requirements, or some combination of the
foregoing, plus payment of a licensing fee or tax.

In addition to the federal and state licensing requirements, you need to be
aware of certain local city or county permits that you may have to obtain.
For example, if you will be in the food business, you may have to get a
license from the county health department; or, if your business would
like to do any construction or remodeling, you might have to get approval from your local planning commission.

Before you begin to operate any kind of business, find out whether you
will be required to obtain any special government licenses or permits,
since in most cases you must obtain the particular license before com-
mencing operation.

This chapter and Section 11.6, respectively, provide a partial listing of the federal and state licensing requirements you are most likely to encounter as a small business owner. Because the number of activities that may require federal or state licenses is so large, no attempt has been made to try to list all of them in this book.

Thus, the lists of licensing agencies and businesses that require licenses found in this chapter and in Chapter 11 should be helpful in alerting you, as a small business owner, to possible licensing needs, but you should remember that these lists are not complete and are not a substitute for individualized legal advice.

6.2 Federal Licenses

If you are starting a small business, it is relatively unlikely that you will need any type of license or permit from the federal government; however, the following is a list of the federal licensing requirements you might possibly encounter:

Federal Licensing Requirements

Activity	Federal Agency
Rendering investment advice	Securities and Exchange Commission
Providing ground transportation as a common carrier	Interstate Commerce Commission
Preparation of meat products	Food and Drug Administration
Production of drugs or biological products	Food and Drug Administration
Making tobacco products or alcohol	Treasury Department, Bureau of Alcohol, Tobacco, and Firearms
Making or dealing in firearms	Treasury Department, Bureau of Alcohol, Tobacco, and Firearms
Radio or television broadcasting	Federal Communications Commission

6.3 State Licenses

For a partial listing of businesses and professions required to be licensed in this state, see Section 11.6.

Operating the Business

Chapter 7

Excise Taxes

Taxation without representation is tyranny.

— Patrick Henry

Taxation with representation is worse.

— Will Rogers

7.1 General Considerations

Both federal and state tax laws impose excise or similar taxes on a number of different types of businesses, products, services, and occupations. These taxes are usually imposed without any assessment or notice to the taxpayer. Thus, it is up to you to find out if you are subject to any of these taxes and, if so, to obtain the proper tax return forms and pay the tax on time.

It is not uncommon for a small business to operate for several years without the owner ever being aware of the need to pay excise taxes. Then comes the day of reckoning, when a formal notice is received from the government demanding immediate payment of several years' worth of back taxes on some particular item subject to excise tax, plus interest and penalties for not filing the returns and not paying the tax. This can be a disastrous surprise, especially since the business owner has not factored the cost of paying the excise into the price of his or her goods or services.

Therefore, this chapter is designed to alert you in advance to the types of federal and state excise — and similar — taxes that you may need to know about. Some excise taxes, such as those on telephone service and insurance companies, are not discussed below since they are passed along or absorbed by the telephone company, insurance company, or other large institution with which your business may deal, and you have no obligation to file any returns or make any direct payment to the government of such taxes.

7.2 State Excise Taxes

See Section 11.7 for a summary of various state excise taxes that may affect your business.

7.3 Federal Excise Taxes

Federal excise taxes on many products and transactions have been repealed over the last 20 years, so these taxes are much less pervasive now than in the past. The excise tax that the largest number of small businesses are likely to be subject to is the motor vehicle highway use tax on vehicles of more than 55,000 pounds gross weight.[1] *Form 2290* must be filed by owners of trucks and buses subject to the highway use tax. If you want information about the highway use tax, you should request a copy of IRS *Publication 349* from any IRS office. The federal government imposes a number of excise taxes on various types of business activities. Some excise taxes are on the production or sale of certain goods. Some are on services or the use of certain products or facilities. Still others are imposed on businesses of a certain type. Most federal excise taxes are reported on *Form 720, Quarterly Federal Excise Tax Return*, the most common excise tax form.

Environmental taxes on petroleum and 42 designated chemical substances are reported on *Form 6627* and attached to *Form 720*. The windfall profits tax on crude oil was repealed by Congress in 1988.

Federal excise taxes can be broken down into several major categories:

- The motor vehicle highway use tax — This tax is imposed on vehicles of more than 55,000 pounds gross weight.[2]
- Retailer taxes on certain fuels[3] — The federal gasoline tax is now $0.14 (14 cents) per gallon on gasoline, and the tax on diesel is $0.20 (20 cents) per gallon. In addition, both of the taxes are increased by $0.01 ($1/10$ of a cent) per gallon to create a Leaking Underground Storage Tank Trust Fund. A reduced tax rate applies to qualified methane and ethanol fuel.
- Other retail excise taxes are now imposed on sales of:

- Heavy trucks and trailers;[4]
- Tires and tubes;[5]
- Recreation equipment such as bows, arrows, fishing rods, reels, lures, and creels;[6] and
- Firearms and ammunition.[7]

- Transportation taxes on air transportation[8] — If you are in the business of transporting people by air, you may have to collect an excise tax.
- Communications taxes on telephone and teletype services.[9]
- Wagering taxes.[10]
- Tax on coal mined in the United States.[11]
- Environmental taxes on petroleum products, various chemicals, and hazardous wastes.[12]
- Taxes on alcohol, firearms, ammunition, and tobacco products.[13]
- Manufacturer's excise tax on vaccines — Certain vaccines manufactured or imported into the United States are subject to an excise tax in order to create a Vaccine Injury Compensation Trust Fund, a no-fault program for compensating persons who are injured by, or die from, certain vaccines.[14]

The Revenue Reconciliation Act of 1989:

- Created an excise tax on ozone-depleting chemicals; and
- Increased the oil spill liability excise tax to $0.05 (5 cents) a barrel.[15]

Luxury Taxes

So-called luxury taxes, which were all repealed in 1965, have come back to life in the Revenue Reconciliation Act of 1990. In general, the newly enacted luxury taxes apply to retail purchases of certain items after December 31, 1990 and apply at a rate of 10% of the amount by which the retail price exceeds certain exempt amounts.[16] The new luxury taxes are as follows:

- Automobiles — The 10% tax applies to the portion of the retail purchase price in excess of $30,000. It does not apply to vehicles of more than 6,000 pounds unloaded gross weight, or to any vehicle, such as a taxicab, that is used exclusively in the active conduct of a trade or business of transporting people or property for compensation or hire.
- Boats — The 10% tax applies to the portion of the retail purchase price that exceeds $100,000, but not to boats used commercially for fishing or transporting persons or property for compensation or hire.
- Aircraft — The 10% tax applies to the portion of the retail purchase price that exceeds $250,000. The tax can be avoided if the aircraft is to be used at least 80% for business.
- Furs and Jewelry — The 10% tax applies to the portion of the retail purchase price that exceeds $10,000 per item.

The new luxury taxes, which are collected by the retailer who sells the item, apply only to the first retail sale of an item. Thus, for example, if you buy a used $50,000 automobile, there is no luxury tax on the purchase.

For further information on excise taxes and other federal taxes, you may wish to obtain IRS *Publication 334, Tax Guide for Small Business,* or, for more detailed information on excise taxes, IRS *Publication 510, Excise Taxes.*

Footnotes

1. I.R.C. § 4481(a).
2. Id.
3. I.R.C. §§ 4041, 4081, and 4091.
4. I.R.C. § 4051.
5. I.R.C. § 4071(a).
6. I.R.C. § 4161(a) and (b).
7. I.R.C. § 4181.
8. I.R.C. §§ 4261(a) and 4271(a).
9. I.R.C. § 4251.
10. I.R.C. §§ 4401 and 4411.
11. I.R.C. § 4121(a).
12. I.R.C. §§ 4611 and 4661.
13. I.R.C. §§ 5001, 5041(b), 5701, and 5801–5822.
14. I.R.C. §§ 4131–4132.
15. I.R.C. §§ 4611(c)(2) and 4681.
16. I.R.C. §§ 4001–4012.

Chapter 8

Planning for Tax Savings in a Business

*The words of such an act as the income tax merely dance
before my eyes in a meaningless procession: cross-reference
to cross-reference, exception upon exception — couched in
abstract terms that offer no handle to seize hold of — leave in
my mind only a confused sense of some vitally important, but
successfully concealed, purport, which it is my duty to extract,
but which is within my power, if at all, only after the most
inordinate expenditure of time. I know that these monsters are
the result of fabulous industry and ingenuity, plugging up this
hole and casting out that net against all possible evasion; yet
at times I cannot help recalling a saying of William James'
about certain passages of Hegel: that they were no doubt
written with a passion of rationality; but that one cannot help
wondering whether to the reader they have any significance
save that the words are strung together with syntactical
correctness.*

— Judge Learned Hand

referring to the 1939 Internal Revenue Code, a statute which was
almost childlike in its simplicity compared to our current tax law.

8.1 General Considerations

One of the most shocking and unpleasant realizations of many successful
small business owners comes when they finally grasp the fact that they
have acquired an unwanted silent partner — a partner who contributes
nothing to the business but who often lays claim to half or more of the

owner's hard-earned profits. That silent partner, of course, is the government income tax collector, and this chapter is a summary of many of the best and most effective legal ways to reduce that silent partner's share of the profits from your business.

This chapter is not intended to be a substitute for professional tax advice regarding your individual situation. Because the tax laws are so enormously complex, a technique that may work brilliantly in most cases might be useless or even disastrous in your particular tax situation. This chapter will provide you with a working understanding of some of the key ways to plan for tax savings and to avoid tax pitfalls in your business.

After you have read this chapter, you may want to talk to your tax adviser about one or more of the ideas discussed, if you feel they might be useful for applying to your business. Your tax adviser should be able to tell you whether a particular idea will work in your situation. If it will, he or she can help you implement it.

Tax attorneys and accountants, particularly the most competent ones, often have a very heavy workload and a large number of clients to serve. An unfortunate result of this situation is that your tax adviser may tend to spend most of the time responding to inquiries by clients and meeting tax deadlines rather than taking the initiative in seeking out ways to minimize your taxes. Thus, by having some understanding of what you would like to do in the way of reducing taxes on your business income, you can propose ideas to your tax advisers and maximize the effectiveness of their expert knowledge and advice. In tax planning, as in so many areas of life, it pays to be assertive. "The wheel that squeaks is the one that gets the grease."

8.2 Using a Corporation as a Tax Shelter

One of the most effective ways to reduce your taxes, in many cases, is to incorporate your business. Incorporation is most likely to be advantageous if the business is generating about $75,000 or less in annual profits and salary for the owner — or per owner, if there is more than one. There are three basic ways, other than the adoption of employee fringe benefit plans, that incorporation can reduce your taxes on business income:

- Leaving profits in the corporation;
- Income-splitting; and
- Investing in stock.

Leaving Profits in the Corporation

By leaving your first $75,000 of profits in your corporation, they are taxed at corporate rates — 15% for the first $50,000 and 25% for the next $25,000 — that are lower than the current individual income tax rate of 31%. Note that after the first $75,000 of profits, the corporate tax rate jumps to 34%, 3% more than the individual rate. An additional 5% is added on profits over $100,000, making the tax rate 39%. Keep this in mind when deciding how much of your profits to leave in your corporation. In Section 2.4, there is more information on federal corporate income taxes and a tax table. Sections 8.5 and 8.9 discuss the potential benefits and risks of having your profits accumulate in your corporation.

Income-Splitting

Splitting income between you and the corporation is done by paying yourself a salary and leaving the remaining profit after salary in the corporation, so it can be taxed at lower corporate rates, if less than $75,000. Thus, both you and the corporation may be taxed at relatively low tax brackets on the business income. More details are located in Section 2.4.

Investing in Stocks

By investing accumulated corporate funds in dividend-paying stocks, you can take advantage of the 70% deduction corporations are entitled to on dividends they receive.[1] Because this special deduction makes most dividends received by a corporation — other than an S corporation — practically tax-free to the recipient corporation, your incorporated business can be an excellent place to hold stocks you wish to invest in, if you do not need the dividend income to live on.

Before you get too excited about putting your whole stock portfolio into your incorporated business, you should be aware of several potential drawbacks:

- If you decide to later withdraw your corporate dividends or the stocks themselves, the withdrawal will usually be taxable to you as ordinary income[2] or perhaps, if you liquidate the corporation, as capital gains.[3] After 1990, capital gains are taxed at a maximum rate of 28% for individuals;[4] although, proposed legislation may change this rate in 1992 or 1993.

- If you should accumulate more than $250,000 — $150,000 for professional and certain personal service firms — in after-tax earnings in your corporation, including the 70% of dividends that the corporation doesn't pay income tax on, and invest part of those earnings in liquid, nonbusiness investment assets like stocks, you may be inviting an IRS audit and a potential penalty tax[5] for unreasonably accumulating earnings and profits in the corporation. See the discussion of the accumulated earnings tax in Section 8.9.

- If too much of your corporation's income is in the form of dividends and other passive types of investment income, the corporation may be classified as a personal holding company[6] for tax purposes, and this can have drastic tax consequences, as outlined in Section 8.9. As long as more than 40%[7] of your corporation's gross income is from sales of goods and services, however, as a general rule, you should not have to be concerned about personal holding company taxes.

- Putting your personal assets that are not needed in the business into your corporation will subject those assets to the risk of the business. That is, anything you put into the corporation will be subject to the claims of the corporation's creditors if it goes bankrupt. If you put all of your assets into the corporation, you will in effect have given up the benefits of limited liability.

- If your corporation borrows money to invest in or carry stock investments, the 70% dividend exclusion will be reduced in part by the interest paid on the borrowed funds.[8]

Your accountant will probably be the best person to consult for determining how and whether you can use a corporation to reduce taxes on your business profits.

8.3 Retirement Plans and Other Fringe Benefits

One advantage of being your own boss, either as a sole proprietor, a partner, or a shareholder of a closely held corporation, is the opportunity to be able to set up a Keogh plan or corporate retirement plan. In a corporation, other than an S corporation, you can obtain insurance and other important fringe benefits as an officer and employee of the corporation on a tax-favored basis. At this point, you may wish to refer to Section 2.4, where retirement plans for businesses and corporate fringe benefits are discussed in greater detail.

In the past, corporate retirement plans offered very substantial tax and practical advantages to corporation owners compared to the Keogh plans available to unincorporated owners; however, since 1984, it has become a whole new ball game. You should be aware that corporate and Keogh retirement plans are now almost identical under the tax law in all major respects, except for the ability to borrow one's retirement funds from the plan, which still will be subject to an excise or penalty tax in the case of a Keogh. It no longer pays to incorporate your business just for pension and profit-sharing plan purposes.

If you decide to establish a retirement plan, there are several practical points you should consider before reaching a decision.

Model SEP Plans from Financial Institutions

If you are setting up a Simplified Employee Pension (SEP) plan for yourself, or a Keogh plan, you should consider obtaining a "canned" plan from a bank, savings and loan, insurance company, or mutual fund. Usually, these preapproved plans will be suitable for you unless you have a significant number of employees to cover under your Keogh, in which case you probably should be incorporated anyway. The great advantages of getting a canned SEP or Keogh plan from a financial institution are cost and simplicity. Most such institutions will charge you only $10–$25 to adopt their plan. Their profit comes from investing your funds for a management fee, in the case of a mutual fund; or maintaining your deposits in interest-bearing accounts, in the case of a bank or savings and loan.

By contrast, hiring a lawyer or benefit consultant to draw up a customized SEP or Keogh plan for you could cost anywhere from a few hundred to a few thousand dollars in fees. In addition, since the pension laws seem to be rewritten every time Congress meets, you may find yourself paying hundreds or even thousands of dollars each year to your attorney or benefit consultant to revise or amend a custom-designed plan, just to keep it in compliance with the never-ending changes in the tax and other laws affecting pension plans.

Model SEP and Keogh Plans from Stockbrokerages

If you are not content to invest your SEP or Keogh funds in or with a financial institution, you can still participate in a canned plan offered by some stockbrokerage firms. These plans usually permit you to direct your own stock and bond investments.

Model Corporate Plans

If you are setting up a corporate retirement plan, it is also possible to obtain canned prototype plans from banks, if you allow them to act as trustee — or from insurance companies, if you buy their insurance or managed fund accounts through the plan. These plans usually have variable terms that can be tailored somewhat to suit your needs, unless you want to do something out of the ordinary, such as allow each participant to direct the investment of his or her portion of the plan's funds. Other institutions, such as stockbrokerages and mutual funds, also offer corporate plans.

Customized Plans

Even if you do need something unusual that requires a customized retirement plan for your corporation, you will probably find it more cost-effective to have a benefit consulting firm draw up the plan for you. This way, your attorney would only be involved in reviewing the plan and obtaining approval of the plan from the IRS. Typically, benefit consultants or pension consultants will charge only a fraction of what a law firm would charge to draw up the plan, and the larger benefit consulting firms are generally quite competent. Most of their fees come from helping you administer the plan under ERISA after it is set up — a service you will need anyway.

Saving with SEPs

Simplified Employee Pension (SEP) plans have gotten very little use since they were created by Congress several years ago; however, they now offer most of the attractive features of typical Keogh and corporate plans with virtually no administrative costs, unlike a Keogh or corporate plan that may cost up to $2,000 or $3,000 a year to maintain for only 5 or 10 employees.

A SEP is basically a glorified individual retirement account (IRA), but it is one where you contribute to each employee's IRA account an amount of up to 15% of an employee's compensation with a maximum of $30,000.

The amount contributed is not taxed to the employee and can be invested in any type of IRA account the employee chooses. SEPs can be set up by corporations, partnerships, or sole proprietorships. Participants can still contribute up to $2,000 a year to their SEP/IRA or to another IRA plan.

SEP participants with taxable income in excess of $25,000 (single) or $40,000 (married filing jointly), however, will have their IRA deductions reduced or eliminated.

The main existing drawback of an SEP is that any distributions from the plan at retirement are taxed as ordinary income. The special five-year averaging — which can result in a lower tax rate — for lump sum distributions from a Keogh or corporate qualified plan is not available for IRAs or SEPs. Even so, they strongly merit consideration as an alternative to Keogh or corporate retirement plans, due to their relative simplicity.

Section 401(k) Plans

An increasingly popular form of qualified retirement plan is the Section 401(k) plan. This type of plan generally permits employees to elect to have a percentage of their salary — with various limitations — deducted from their paychecks, free of income tax, and deposited on their behalf in a profit-sharing-type plan. In many cases, as an additional incentive to employees to make such tax-favored savings, you, as an employer, may provide some degree of matching contribution to the plan on behalf of the employee.

For example, a typical situation would be where you contribute $0.50 (50 cents) for every dollar the employee elects to have withheld from his or her pay. Your contribution is placed in the 401(k) plan and is tax-free to the employee.

Various Nonretirement Fringe Benefit Plans

The federal tax laws are replete with a whole host of tax-favored employee fringe benefits, which are characterized as being deductible to you and nontaxable to the employee. In addition to the fairly standard health care, disability, and group-term life insurance plans discussed in Chapter 2, some of the other most common and important nontaxable fringes are discussed below.

Section 132 Excludable Fringe Benefits

The following fringe benefits are excludable both from income and employment taxes (FUTA and FICA) for you and the employee:

- No-additional-cost services provided to an employee — These services consist of benefits such as free airline, rail or bus transportation, provided by companies in those industries; rooms for hotel employees; or free phone service for telephone company employees.

- Employee discounts — Service companies can provide their services to employees at up to a 20% discount. For companies selling goods, the discount may not exceed the employer's gross profit percentage multiplied by the usual selling price of the item to customers.

- Working condition fringes — These fringe benefits are tax-free, up to the amounts that would have been deductible if paid by the employee. Benefits include such items as a company car or plane used for business purposes; subscriptions to trade or professional publications; on-the-job training; business travel; parking; and others.

- Minor fringes — These benefits are items that are considered to be minimal to justify the administrative costs for them, such as using the company's copier machine or having a secretary type a personal letter.

- On-premises athletic facilities — Providing and operating facilities such as gyms, pools, tennis or golf courses on the business premises, for employees, their spouses, and dependents is a nontaxable fringe benefit.[9]

Meals on Premises

If meals are provided on-premises to employees, for your convenience as the employer, the value of such meals is usually not taxable to the employee for income tax purposes;[10] however, you can only deduct 80% of the cost of furnishing such meals.

Educational Assistance Plans

You may pay educational expenses on behalf of an employee — free of employment taxes or income tax to the employee — if the purpose of such education meets one of the two following tests:

- The education maintains or improves skills required by the job.
- The education meets requirements set by you or applicable laws, where such requirements are imposed as a condition of the retention of employment or rate of compensation.

You may also set up tax-qualified educational assistance plans to provide other — not necessarily job-related — educational benefits for employees, in amounts up to $5,250 a year per employee.[11] To qualify, such a plan must be in writing, disclosed to employees, and no more than 5% of benefits paid under the plan can go to 5% owners of the firm or their spouses or dependents.

This tax benefit expired on June 30, 1992, but will probably be retroactively extended again by Congress, which has routinely occurred several times during recent years.

Legal Services Plans

As an employer, you may also set up a qualified group legal services plan, whereby prepaid legal services are provided to employees. If the value of such coverage is no more than $70 a year to the employee, no part of any legal services actually provided to the employee under the plan — which may be worth thousands of dollars in some instances — is taxable to the employee.[12] If the value of such coverage exceeds $70, then a proportional part of benefits are taxable. Under a group legal services plan, benefits may not be provided to highly compensated employees on a discriminatory basis, and not more than 25% of amounts contributed under the plan may be on behalf of 5% owners of the company or their spouses or dependents.

Similar to the educational assistance plans, this tax benefit expired on June 30, 1992, but will probably be retroactively extended again by Congress.

Dependent Care Plans

Dependent care plans are one of the most popular and rapidly growing types of employee fringe benefit plans in recent years, providing up to $5,000 a year of dependent care benefits for children or elderly dependents per employee. Not more than 25% of benefits provided, however, can be on behalf of 5% owners of the employer company, and other technical nondiscrimination rules also apply.[13]

Stock Option Plans

Companies have devised, or Congress has provided, a number of different stock option plans with various tax advantages, all of which are designed to encourage employees to acquire a proprietary stake in the companies they work for. Major types of such plans include:

- Nonqualified stock options — In this plan, you usually grant favored employees options to acquire stock of the company at a bargain price during a period of several years. Such an option is usually not a taxable event, although the excess of the value over the option price of the stock received, when the option is eventually exercised, is then taxed as ordinary compensation income in most cases — unless the stock is restricted or forfeitable.

- Incentive stock options (ISOs) — ISOs are options granted under a plan that meets IRS requirements, where the term of the option is limited and the option price is not less than the value of the stock at the day the option is granted. That is, with an ISO, there is no bargain element built into the option. If the stock is worth, say, $20 a share the day the option is granted to the employee, the option must be at an exercise price of no less than $20. Thus, the employee will not stand to profit from exercising the option unless the value of the stock subsequently rises to above $20 a share — which is good incentive for the employee to help make the company as profitable as possible, so its stock goes up. If certain requirements are met, the employee does not recognize taxable income when he or she exercises an ISO and may qualify for subsequent capital gains treatment if the stock received from exercise of the option is sold at a gain.[14]

- Employee stock purchase plans — Under a tax-qualified employee stock purchase plan, a company may allow employees to purchase its stock, directly from the company, for up to a 15% discount from the fair market value of the stock. The employee is not taxed when exercising the right to purchase stock under such a plan and may receive capital gain treatment when the stock is eventually sold at a gain.[15]

In the last few years, the flexible spending plan, or flex plan, has become another increasingly popular type of tax-favored employee benefit plan. Each of the three flex plans below are designed to permit employees to choose how much to spend on a tax-free basis for various employee benefits, such as health care or dependent care. Please note that flex plans are for employees only and cannot cover sole proprietors, partners in a partnership, or 2% shareholders in an S corporation.

Flexible Spending Plans

- Premium-conversion accounts — This is the simplest kind of flex account. It primarily is set up to allow employees to pay for their share of health, disability, or group-term life insurance premiums with untaxed dollars by deducting specified amounts out of their regular paychecks to pay for such coverage. The amounts the employees agree to have withheld from their salaries or wages to pay such insurance premiums are excluded from their taxable income, but deductible by the corporation or unincorporated employer. Such plans, in effect, convert part of wages directly into insurance payments, without having the government first remove a slice for taxes. Premium-conversion accounts are practical for even the smallest companies with only one or two employees.

- Flexible reimbursement accounts — Flexible reimbursement accounts are accounts where an employee may agree to contribute a specified amount to each year and draw on the account to pay for health care expenses not covered by the company. Health care expenses could include medical insurance deductibles, vision care, dental coverage, etc., or for up to $5,000 a year for dependent care expenses.

  Here's how these accounts work: Before the start of each year, the employees must estimate their medical and dependent care costs for the coming year that they want paid out of their accounts. The amount designated by an employee is withheld from his or her paycheck during the year (tax-free). As expenses are incurred during the year for health and dependent care, the employee submits requests for reimbursement out of the account to the plan administrator, up to the specified maximum. Employers may choose to supplement or match amounts employees choose to have withheld from their pay, as an additional tax-free benefit to the employee.

  Flexible reimbursement accounts may stand alone, or may be combined with premium-conversion accounts. They are feasible for fairly small employers, as well, although administrative costs may tend to be greater than for premium-conversion accounts.

- Cafeteria plans — Cafeteria plans are more complex and are rarely adopted by companies with fewer than 50 employees. Under a cafeteria plan, a company gives employees a menu of benefit choices, provides a fixed number of tax-free dollars per employee each year, and allows the employees to each select or buy the particular benefits desired, such as:

  - 401(k) contributions
  - Health insurance

- Life insurance
- Disability insurance
- Vision or dental care, or both
- Vacation time

If the costs of the benefits selected exceeds the dollar amount provided by you, the employee may fund the balance with salary reduction amounts through premium-conversion or reimbursement accounts, or both, also on an untaxed basis.

Under flex plans, the golden rule is "use it or lose it." Any amount in an employee's account that is not utilized by the employee during the year is forfeited, and reverts back to you at the end of the year. Note that flex plans are required to meet nondiscrimination tests to ensure that highly compensated employees do not receive a disproportionate share of the benefits provided.[16] For more information on flex plans, contact:

Employers Council on Flexible Compensation
927 15th Street NW, Suite 1000
Washington, DC 20005
(202) 659-4300

8.4 Sheltering Profits on Export Sales

Many small and large American businesses have an unfortunate tendency to look at the United States as their only market and to ignore the vast potential markets for their products or services that lie outside the borders of this country. One way in which Congress has taken constructive steps to encourage more exports and to make American goods and services more competitive in foreign markets is to provide a form of indirect tax subsidy to American firms that export.

While this export subsidy has not succeeded in stemming the unfavorable trend in the balance of trade the United States has experienced in recent years, it does provide a very attractive tax benefit for U.S. companies that export.

If your business is one of the many small firms that does sell its goods or services overseas, you may be able to qualify for this tax incentive by setting up either a Domestic International Sales Corporation (DISC) or another type of entity permitted by the Tax Reform Act of 1984, called a Foreign Sales Corporation (FSC).

In general, a DISC will allow you to accumulate profits earned from export sales in a specially treated corporation, free of U.S. taxes until you eventually choose to distribute the deferred income. An FSC will allow you to accumulate such income, whether or not distributed, free (in part) of U.S. corporate taxes. For an FSC, the exempt foreign trade income will not even be taxed when paid out as a dividend, if the shareholder is a corporation.[17] For small companies, DISCs may often be much simpler to operate and preferable to the FSCs, at least for the first few years of operation.

A DISC is usually just a dummy corporation that has no employees and does not carry on any sort of business, except on paper.

DISCs — In a Nutshell

The tax law allows a U.S. firm that has qualified export receipts to set aside part of its profits on the export transactions by paying a so-called sales commission to a DISC.[18] As a corporation without any employees, the DISC does not actually do anything to earn the commissions; your firm pays the DISC the largest commission permitted by the tax law on each qualifying export sale. It is usually advisable to have a written commission agreement between your firm and the DISC for legal purposes, although not required for tax purposes.

The commission that can be paid to the DISC on an export sale is the larger of 4% of the gross sales price or 50% of the profit on the sale[19] — so long as the commission does not create a loss on the sale for your firm.[20] In addition, the DISC's commission income can be increased by 10% of certain export promotion expenses, if any, incurred by the DISC.[21] As you might suspect, some fairly elaborate tax accounting rules[22] determine how much profit you have on an export sale, for purposes of computing the DISC's maximum commission.

The tax benefits for your business arise from the fact that you or your business owns the DISC stock, and the commissions your business pays to the DISC are deducted from the business taxable income, while the DISC pays no tax on income it receives.

However, about 6% (or $1/17$) of the DISC's income each year is taxed to its corporate (but not individual) shareholders,[23] so the DISC will usually pay about 6% of its income back as a dividend to the business that owns the stock of the DISC — which is usually, but not necessarily — your corporation that paid the DISC the commissions. Thus, 94% (or $16/17$) of the income that is shifted to the DISC as export sales commissions escapes federal income tax indefinitely, until the DISC either pays out the accumulated income as dividends or is disqualified and loses its status as a DISC.[24]

For deferred DISC income that accumulates after 1984, however, each DISC shareholder must compute the amount of additional tax it would pay each year if all the deferred DISC income were taxed and pay the IRS interest on the deferred tax.[25] This interest will apparently be tax-deductible if paid by a corporation. The interest rate is based on the going rate for one-year T-bills.

Conceptually, having a DISC can be thought of as taking $100 of pre-tax income out of your left-hand pocket and putting it in your right-hand pocket, then putting $6 back into the left-hand pocket. You do not have to pay tax on the $94 that remains in the right-hand pocket as long as you leave it there. In fact, there are even legal ways in which you can borrow the $94 and put it back in the left-hand pocket (your business) without paying tax on it — another example of having your cake and eating it, too.[26] But as long as you keep the $94 in the right-hand pocket, you pay interest on the tax saved.

Another advantage of having a DISC is that the DISC can continue to accumulate its undistributed profits year after year without fear of incurring an accumulated earnings tax, since a DISC is exempt from the accumulated earnings tax as well as the regular federal income tax.[27]

FSCs — In a Nutshell

A Foreign Sales Corporation (FSC) is somewhat similar to a DISC, but will probably be too great of an administrative burden for it to be worthwhile for your small business to consider.

Unlike a DISC, an FSC cannot be a dummy or paper corporation set up in the United States. Instead, it must meet all of the following requirements:

- It must be a foreign corporation, incorporated in a U.S. possession or in a foreign country that, in general, has arrangements to swap tax information with the IRS.
- There can be no more than 25 shareholders in an FSC.
- An FSC cannot issue preferred stock.
- An FSC must maintain a foreign office, at which there is a permanent set of tax records, including invoices.
- The FSC's board of directors must include at least one person who is not a resident of the United States — although the nonresident member can apparently be a U.S. citizen.
- An FSC cannot be part of a controlled group of corporations that also includes a DISC. That is, you can set up either an FSC or a DISC, but not both.[28]

Summary

Here is a brief summary of this section on DISC and FSC tax benefits.

- If your business will be engaged or is engaged in selling goods or services abroad, you should consult your tax adviser as to the advisability of establishing a DISC or FSC to shelter a large portion of your export profits.
- Both DISCs and FSCs are extremely complex entities to establish and administer, although a DISC will probably be much less of a headache for a small business to operate than an FSC. In either case, you will need to hire some very sophisticated accounting talent, so unless you earn some fairly substantial export profits, the administrative costs of having a DISC or FSC may well exceed any tax savings you will generate.
- State tax treatment of DISCs and FSCs is discussed in Section 11.8.

8.5 Planning for Withdrawal of Corporate Funds with Minimum Tax Cost

Because of the many tax and other advantages of operating a corporation, there is a good chance you will choose, either initially or later on, to incorporate your business. If you do, and your business becomes profitable to the extent that it has significant profits even after paying you the largest salary that can be justified as "reasonable compensation" under the circumstances, you will eventually be faced with the problem of how to remove the accumulated profits from the corporation without excessive tax costs. That is, unless you decide to liquidate the corporation at some point and operate as an unincorporated business or decide to sell your stock to someone else. The proceeds you receive from liquidation or selling your stock would probably result in capital gains tax in most cases, in addition to a tax at the corporate level upon liquidation. For a definition of unreasonable compensation, see Section 8.9.

If the corporation simply pays dividends to you, that will normally be a tax disaster, since the dividends you receive will probably be taxable to you as ordinary income at federal income tax rates up to 31% or somewhat more. Since the corporation will have already paid tax on the money it distributes to you as dividends, double taxation will result. If both you and the corporation are in the maximum tax brackets, the result can be an effective tax rate of approximately 58% (federal corporate and individual taxes) on the income that is paid out as dividends and an even higher rate if there are also state income taxes. There are better ways to get the money out of the corporation.

Personal Loans from the Corporation

Your corporation can often serve as a bank for your short-term financial needs; however, if you continually borrow from your corporation, the IRS can in some cases treat the loans as dividends to you, which is just what you want to avoid. Or, if your corporation has an accumulated earnings problem, as described in Section 8.9, the existence of loans to shareholders can make it very difficult to argue that the corporation is accumulating earnings for the reasonable needs of the business. So, while a loan from your corporation can be a very good way to tap its funds on a temporary basis, it is not a long-term solution.

If you do borrow, you should normally pay interest if the loan is greater than $10,000. The interest rate should not be less than the applicable federal rate established by the IRS.[29] This rate is announced by the IRS each month of the year for transactions that occur during the following month.

Preliminary Structuring

A number of different ways of structuring your corporation at its inception can give you a great deal of potential flexibility in getting money out of the corporation for yourself or family members later at no tax cost or, at worst, as only partially taxable. Some of these approaches can also make it possible to keep a great deal of the value of the corporation's stock out of your taxable estate for estate tax and inheritance tax purposes. Discuss the structuring of your corporation with your tax adviser before you form the corporation. Here are some of the strategies you might explore.

Putting Stock in Names of Spouse and Children

When the corporation is formed, consider putting a substantial part of the stock in the name of your spouse or children, or both. Later, when or if the business has prospered and the stock has become valuable, it may be possible to bail out a large chunk of the corporation's accumulated profits at a child's lower tax rates by having the corporation redeem (purchase) all of the stock of your spouse or child.

The redemption will usually be treated as a sale for a capital gain if your spouse or child agrees to notify the IRS if he or she reacquires any interest in the corporation within 10 years after the redemption.[30] Working as an employee of the corporation would be an "interest" that would prevent the spouse or child from receiving favorable capital gains treatment. So if you want your son or daughter to work for you in the business, do not count on being able to redeem his or her stock as a capital gain.

Note that while capital gains are taxed at only slightly lower rates than ordinary income after 1990, it is still very desirable to have a stock redemption qualify for capital gains treatment, since part of the money received will be a nontaxable recovery of the shareholder's tax basis in the stock that is being redeemed. This is usually not the case if the redemption payment is treated as an ordinary income dividend.

Such redemption of stock as a capital gain could even be made on an installment basis.[31] For example, if your daughter had all her stock redeemed by the corporation for $150,000, the corporation could pay the $150,000 price, plus interest, in 15 annual installments of $10,000 each, so that your daughter would not have a "bunching" of all the capital gain on the sale in one tax year. Instead, the capital gains tax would be spread over a 15-year period, and the corporation should be able to deduct interest paid on the note held by the daughter.

Constraints in Community Property States

Unfortunately, this tactic does not work as well in community property states if you attempt to redeem your spouse's stock. Under the community property laws, half of your stock will generally be treated as owned by your spouse. This makes it difficult to completely terminate his or her interest, unless all of the stock that is community property is first split in half between you by agreement, so that you each own your shares as separate property.

Even in that case, your spouse may be considered to have reacquired a community property interest in your separately owned stock if you continue to work for the corporation and the value of the stock increases on account of your efforts. Thus, if you live in a community property state, you probably should not count on trying to redeem your spouse's interest in the corporation as a capital gain. The states that have community property laws are Arizona, California, Idaho, Louisiana, Nevada, New Mexico, Texas, Washington, and Wisconsin.

Even if the corporation never redeems your children's stock, it is useful to put some of the stock in their names when you form the corporation — especially at a time when a gift to them of the stock will be subject to little or no gift tax because of its low value. When you die many years later, the stock owned by your children may then be very valuable and will not be included in your estate in most instances, which could save your children a great deal in estate and inheritance taxes. The federal gift tax laws now permit you to make gifts worth up to $10,000 per child per year free of federal gift tax. If you are married, you and your spouse can jointly make gifts of up to $20,000 per year per child; however, you may be subject to state gift taxes in some states.

Gifts of Stock to Children

Until the Revenue Reconciliation Act of 1989 was passed, it was considered astute tax planning — when setting up a new corporation — to capitalize the company with both equity capital (stock) and debt capital (an interest-bearing note from the corporation to you); however, such a tactic can now be a tax trap.

Debt Capitalization Drawback

This type of structuring can still be done without adverse tax consequences, but only if the assets you are transferring to the corporation are cash or other assets on which you would not have a taxable gain if sold at current fair market value. Otherwise, under the 1989 law, any notes or other debt capital you take back from the corporation will cause you to pay tax on appreciated assets (land, equipment, etc.) that you transfer to the corporation in return for the stock and debt instruments.

If, however, the only asset you are putting in the corporation to start it up is, for example, cash, you will not be affected by the 1989 tax law change mentioned in the preceding paragraph. As an illustration, if you plan to put $10,000 in the corporation to get the business started, you might take back stock for $5,000 and a $5,000 note when the corporation is set up, rather than having the corporation issue you stock for the whole $10,000. While the note is outstanding, you will be able to siphon off some funds from the corporation as interest on the note, which the corporation can deduct. By contrast, if the corporation distributed profits to you as dividends on its stock, it would result in double taxation of those profits, since, unlike interest, the corporation cannot deduct dividends it pays.

Debt Capitalization Still Can Be Advantageous

More importantly, when the note becomes due, the corporation will repay you the $5,000 principal of the note; if things have been handled properly, you should pay no tax on that $5,000. In contrast, if the corporation attempted to return part of your investment in the stock, whatever you received would probably be fully taxable to you as a dividend, even if you surrendered some of your stock in a redemption. Lending the corporation part of its start-up capital allows you to withdraw part of your investment without paying tax.

Thus, there are considerable advantages in partially capitalizing your corporation with debt in the form of a note or notes that you will hold from the corporation. You will need competent tax advice before you do so, however, since there are hundreds of court cases that have tried to define when debt instruments will be considered debt and when they will be considered stock.

For example, if you capitalize your corporation with more than $3 of debt for each $1 of stock — say a $6,000 note and $2,000 of stock — the note (debt) may be treated as though it were stock for tax purposes. Thus, if the corporation paid you interest or principal on the note, whatever payments you received would be treated as dividends to you, and the corporation's deduction for the interest payments would be disallowed. So you must tread very lightly in lending money to your corporation. See the discussion of the distinction between debt and equity for tax purposes in Section 8.9.

Post-Incorporation Planning

Whether or not you take advantage of the above planning suggestions at the time you incorporate, there are a number of other ways you can get cash out of your corporation at a low tax cost later on.

Leasing to the Corporation

One way is to lease real property or equipment to the corporation. Instead of putting enough of your own money into the corporation for it to buy property it needs for its business, keep the money outside the corporation, and buy the property yourself and lease it all at a reasonable rental to the corporation. This way, you will be able to directly obtain the tax depreciation and other benefits of owning the property. At the same time, by keeping the property out of the corporation, you will be putting less of your assets at risk in the business, especially if the corporation goes broke. Also, if the leased property is real estate, it will probably appreciate in value.

You can personally and directly benefit from that appreciation, including the increased rent you will be able to charge the corporation as inflation continues. Furthermore, if you have used straight-line depreciation and sell the property at a gain, all of the gain will be capital gain. By contrast, if the corporation sells real property at a gain, 20% of the straight-line depreciation is recaptured as ordinary income.[32] Although a corporation's capital gains are currently taxed at the same rate as ordinary income, Congress restored preferential tax rates for capital gains in 1990 tax legislation. It may do the same for corporations in the near future, if regular corporate tax rates are increased.

Trusts for Your Children

You could make a gift of business property — or the funds to buy it — to a trust and have a bank or other independent trustee negotiate a reasonable lease of the property to the business, with the rental income going to the trust for distribution to your children. Upon the trust's termination, the property can be distributed to the children, revert to the trust grantor, or be distributed in accordance with the trust terms.

This can be a useful way of taking cash out of the corporation for the benefit of your children, who have lower tax brackets; however, since the IRS regularly attempts to attack these types of arrangements, you should go into this only with the help of an astute tax adviser. Be aware that the Tax Reform Act of 1986 eliminated nearly all the tax advantages of trusts for children under 14 years of age.

Consider setting up a DISC corporation if your corporation has foreign sales. You can then hold the DISC stock yourself or give it to your children. This will not only enable you to indefinitely defer federal income taxes on part of the profits from export sales, it will also, in effect, allow you or your children to siphon off part of the profits on export sales — dividends paid by the DISC — in a manner that allows your corporation to deduct those dividends, thereby avoiding double taxation.

DISC Deferrals

Consider adopting corporate pension or profit-sharing plans and various corporate fringe benefit plans. These types of benefit plans, in appropriate circumstances, can provide deferred retirement benefits or current insurance benefits to you tax-free — or on a tax-deferred basis, in the case of retirement plans — while reducing the corporation's current taxable income. See the discussion of these kinds of employee benefit plans in Section 8.3.

Benefit Plans

8.6 Deducting Expenses Related to Your Business

One major advantage of operating your own business is the opportunity it may give you to enjoy certain luxuries as deductible business expenses. Some of the tax benefits that were available in the past, however, such as costs of attending foreign conventions[33] and treating part of your home as a business office,[34] have been severely curtailed, and there are strict recordkeeping requirements[35] for others.

Deductions for attending foreign conventions are now completely disallowed, unless you can show that:

- It is just as reasonable for the convention to be held abroad as it would be to hold it in North America; and
- The meeting is directly related to your trade or business.

If these two requirements are met, you must then meet the general requirements for traveling outside the United States. Deductions for conventions or seminars on cruise ships are limited to $2,000, and other travel by "luxury water transportation" is deductible only up to certain per diem amounts.[36]

Some other items you may be entitled to write off as business expenses for tax purposes are discussed on the following page.

Travel, Entertainment, and Meal Expenses

It is still possible to deduct business travel expenses, entertainment of your clients or customers, and business-related meals, but only 80% of qualifying business meals and entertainment are deductible. This 80% rule considerably complicates recordkeeping for expenses. For instance, if you stay in a hotel on a business trip and charge your meals to your room, you are required to separately break out your meal expenses from the rest of your hotel bill for tax purposes, since your meal expenses are only 80% deductible.

Note that if you are an employee of your business, the 20% disallowance of meal and entertainment expenses does not apply to you individually, if your company reimburses you for the expenses; it applies only at the company level.

Detailed Records Required

To claim any of these kinds of deductions, you must keep daily, detailed records of such expenditures, including bills, receipts, and the following information for each expense:

- The relationship of the expenditure to the business;
- The time when the expense was incurred;
- Where the money was spent, and to whom it was paid;
- The amount of the expenditure; and
- The identities of the persons involved, including persons entertained.[37]

It is strongly recommended that you pick up a daily expense record book or diary and enter all expenses for travel, meals, and entertainment you think should be deductible. Include the above information for each item.

The Tax Reform Act of 1984 would have required contemporaneous written records to substantiate all such travel and entertainment expenses, beginning in 1985. The issuance of IRS regulations on October 15, 1984, however, provoked a massive outcry among taxpayers that was heard all the way to the District of Columbia. Senator William Roth (R–Del.) said, "I've never had an outrage at home as I've had with this legislation."

Accordingly, by mid-1985, Congress retroactively repealed the contemporaneous part of the recordkeeping requirement for travel and entertainment deductions, replacing it with the requirement that taxpayers keep "adequate records or . . . sufficient evidence corroborating the taxpayer's own statement."[38]

This is a return to the old substantiation requirements as they existed before the 1984 act, except that these substantiation requirements now also apply to local travel expenses, which was not the case in the past.

Not All Expenses Deductible

Not all expenses for entertaining clients or customers will be deductible, even if you keep meticulous records. As a general rule, your records must show that you were engaged in a substantial and bona fide business discussion during or immediately before or after the entertainment.[39] Expenses of entertaining people just to create a good impression on them, in the hope they might send some business your way someday, are classified as goodwill entertainment and are not deductible.

The rule allowing quiet business meals with clients or potential customers to be deductible, even if no business is discussed, has been repealed.[40] For more information on business-related expenses you can deduct, contact your local IRS office and request *Publication 463, Travel, Entertainment, and Gift Expenses.*

Automobile Expenses

If you use an automobile more than 50% of the time for business purposes, you will generally be able to deduct a percentage of the costs of owning and operating the car, if you can substantiate the business mileage. The expenses of using the car for commuting to and from work and for personal travel are not deductible.[41] For example, if your business purchases a new car for your use as a business car, and 80% of the mileage on the car can be shown to be for business trips, and only 20% for commuting to work and other personal use, you should be able to deduct 80% of the gas, oil, insurance, and maintenance costs relating to the car. You can also depreciate the cost of the car, less 20% for personal use.

Rules are even more drastic for any automobile, airplane, boat or computer not kept in your place of business if you can't establish a business-use percentage in excess of 50%. Automobile depreciation is stretched out over at least six years, straight-line: 10% the first year; 20% a year thereafter, for four years; and 10% the final year. For boats, planes, or computers, it can be stretched out for longer periods.[42]

For luxury automobiles, the maximum annual depreciation deduction allowed is limited to the amounts below.

Luxury Automobile Depreciation

1991 Acquisitions	1992 Acquisitions
$2,660 for the first year	$2,760 for the first year
$4,300 for the second year	$4,400 for the second year
$2,550 for the third year	$2,650 for the third year
$1,575 for each succeeding year[43]	$1,575 for each succeeding year

Exemptions

These restrictions don't apply to business vehicles such as ambulances, hearses, taxis, delivery vans, or heavy trucks.[44]

Mileage Deduction

If you drive an inexpensive economy car on business, it may be simpler and better to elect to deduct a flat $0.28 (28 cents) per mile for 1993[45] for your business mileage rather than keep records of your various kinds of automobile expenses. You will, however, still be required to keep records to substantiate that the car was used for business purposes for the mileage you claim. If you use this method, you can still deduct tolls and parking incurred on business trips. If you drive an expensive car, you will probably get much larger tax deductions by reporting your actual operating expenses, plus depreciation, than by electing the mileage allowance.

Form 4562 of your annual tax return requires you to answer certain questions if you claim an automobile deduction.

Questions to Be Answered if You Claim an Automobile Deduction:

Total miles driven during the year: _____

Total business miles driven during the year: _____

Total commuting miles driven during the year: _____

Total other personal (noncommuting) miles driven: _____

Was the vehicle available for personal use during off-duty hours? Yes ☐ No ☐

Was the vehicle used primarily by a more than 5% owner or related person? Yes ☐ No ☐

Is another vehicle available for personal use? Yes ☐ No ☐

Do you have evidence to support the business-use percentage claimed? Yes ☐ No ☐

If yes, is the evidence written? Yes ☐ No ☐

8.7 Choosing the Best Taxable Year for a Corporation

If your business is an S corporation or is considered a personal service corporation, you will generally have no choice but to operate on a calendar-year basis, and you can skip over the following discussion of how to select a taxable year. If, however, your business is incorporated and is neither an S corporation or a personal service corporation in which the services performed are "substantially performed" by owner/employees,[46] you will have an opportunity to choose any tax fiscal-year period you desire during your initial year of operation as a corporation. There are significant tax deferral and savings opportunities in selecting the right year end.

Unfortunately, in some cases, it will be necessary to be able to project with some accuracy how much your corporation will earn or lose each month for several months to a year ahead. If you expect to have start-up losses and show an overall net profit for your first year as an incorporated business, one good rule is to cut off your first taxable year at the end of the month in which you first get back to break even for the year-to-date.

For example, assume your first tax year starts on January 1, 1993, and you show a cumulative tax loss of $20,000 at the end of June. You then have taxable income of $10,000 a month in July, August, and September, and expect profits to continue. If you chose June 30 as your tax year end, you would have a $20,000 loss for your first tax period ending June 30,

1993. For federal income tax purposes, it's no problem, since you can carry over the loss and use it to offset $20,000 of taxable income during the next tax year. Some states, however, do not allow a carryover of losses.

Another approach would be to choose an August 31 year end, so that you would show no taxable income for your first year, assuming the corporation continued to net $10,000 a month.

If you do not mind paying some tax earlier, it might pay, in the above example, to wait until the end of October, November, or even December to cut off the first tax year. This would enable the corporation to isolate $20,000 to $40,000 or so of profit in a tax period subject to low federal corporate income tax rates, which are only 15% on the first $50,000 of corporate income.

If you do so, however, you are making an assumption that the corporation will be in a higher tax bracket in the following year, which cannot be known with any certainty. Also, the existence of tax credits would somewhat complicate the simple picture portrayed above. Obviously, your accountant can help you decide which tax year will produce the best result.

Start-up Losses Must Be Capitalized, Not Deducted

Remember, when projecting your start-up losses, you can't immediately deduct preopening expenses; instead, you must capitalize those costs and write them off (straight-line) over 60 months.[47] For example, if you are starting a restaurant and are paying salaries, etc. to a manager and to employees being trained prior to the day the restaurant opens for business, you might well think those expenses are immediately deductible. Not so! All such preopening expenses must be capitalized, and you can't begin to amortize them until opening day.

Benefits of Adopting January 31 Year End

Another planning approach in adopting a year end, which may sometimes conflict with the above strategy, is to adopt a January 31 year end. If you structure your employment contract with your corporation so that you receive a substantial part of your compensation in January each year, you can, in effect, defer the bonus to your following tax year, while the corporation can deduct it — if paid in January — for its fiscal year ending just after the bonus is paid. Naturally, the corporation will be required to withhold income tax from your bonus, but at reduced rates, compared to regular monthly salary payments. Federal income tax withholding on bonuses is at a flat rate of only 20%.

Seasonal Businesses

If you have a seasonal business, you may want to defer taxes by selecting a tax year that ends just before your most profitable season begins. For example, if you are in the business of selling Christmas tree ornaments and do most of your business from October through December each year, you might choose a September 30 tax year end.

Remember, though, that tax considerations are not the only factors to take into account in choosing a fiscal year. If taking an annual inventory is a major task, consider adopting a year end that occurs when inventory is at a low ebb and when business is slow, if possible. You may also find that you will get somewhat quicker and better service from your CPA firm for annual tax returns, audits, etc. if you pick a fiscal year that ends several months before or after December. Most CPAs are at their busiest during their annual tax season from about February to May, preparing 1040s and doing audits for their many clients who have December year ends.

8.8 Selecting Tax Accounting Methods

Rely on your tax accountant's advice when choosing which tax accounting methods you should adopt in your business. This section is provided for your information in case you are not sure whether your accountant has recommended the method that will produce the best results for you.

The two overall tax accounting methods most commonly used are the cash method and the accrual method. There are, however, other special overall methods, plus a number of special kinds of accounting elections a business can make with regard to particular items, such as installment sales, inventory valuations, and deduction of accrued vacation pay.

Cash Method

The cash receipts and disbursements method of accounting, called the cash method, is the simplest accounting method in use. Under this method, you include income only as it is actually or constructively received.

Likewise, you only become entitled to deductions when you actually pay expenses — except for certain special items like depreciation or amortization of certain kinds of expenditures — rather than when you receive bills for the expenses. Thus, you usually do not have to report your year-end accounts receivable in income for the year and cannot deduct your year-end accounts payable. This will normally allow you to defer some taxable income each year if your year-end receivables are larger than accounts payable and other accrued but unpaid expenses. Obviously, this gives you some flexibility, too, if you want to pay off a number of payables at year end to reduce your taxable income for the current year.

The cash method is the method used by most individual taxpayers and by businesses in the real estate, financial, and service fields, where inventories of goods are not material factors in producing income.

Businesses with significant inventories, such as manufacturers and wholesale or retail firms, are usually required to use an accrual method of tax accounting.[48] In some cases, however, it is possible even for those businesses to use a hybrid accounting method — accounting for income and the cost of goods sold on an accrual method — while using the cash method to report selling expenses and administrative expenses.

The Tax Reform Act of 1986 disallowed use of the cash method for C corporations — regular corporations — and for partnerships that have C corporations as partners. One exception is for small firms with an average gross receipts of $5 million or less during the three preceding years.[49] Another exception is made for larger firms in the farming business and for certain employee-owned qualified personal service corporations in fields such as law, medicine, accounting, architecture, or consulting.

Sole proprietorships, S corporations, and partnerships with no C corporation partners are not affected by these restrictions, unless they are considered tax shelters, and may remain on the cash method if that is a permissible accounting method for their particular type of business. Firms that are forbidden from using the cash method must adopt the more complex accrual method of accounting.

As noted above, most large corporations and businesses with significant inventories are required to report income on the accrual method of accounting for tax purposes. This method requires you to report income when income is earned rather than when you receive it. Similarly, expenses can be deducted when all events have occurred that fix the amount and the fact of your business' liability for a particular expense, even if it is paid in a subsequent tax year. However, if economic performance required of the other party does not occur until a subsequent tax year, you may not be able to deduct an accrued expense until economic performance occurs.

Accrual Method

For example, if you sign a contract with your accountant in 1993 to prepare your tax return in 1994, "economic performance" does not occur until 1994, and you may be unable to accrue the deduction in 1993, unless you meet several requirements — recurring expenses, performance occurs within a reasonable time after the end of the tax year, etc.[50]

A once-in-a-lifetime tax election was required to be made on your first tax year after 1989 — the 1990 tax return for existing businesses. Under the economic performance rules, if you wish to deduct, in advance, items that you prepay under the recurring items exception, you must elect to deduct such items on the first return on which the item recurs, or you will be unable to use that exception for the item in question, forever.

The new tax regulations covering this exception to the economic performance rules went into effect for tax years that began after 1989. This means that if you had some recurring item that you were in the habit of prepaying before year end each year, you had to deduct it on your 1990 tax return. If you didn't, you will never again be able to deduct it in advance in any subsequent year. The IRS announced in 1991 that the one-time election that was required to be adopted on 1990 tax returns was delayed for one more year, for certain types of expenses.[51]

Even though the accrual method may not be required for your business, you may find it preferable to use, if most or all of your income is from cash sales and you pay a large part of your expenses on a delayed credit basis. In this case, you would have few, if any, receivables at year end but might have substantial accrued payables you could deduct in the current year without having to actually make payment before year end.

Accrual of bonuses to employees, in an incorporated business, is a good example of a deduction that can be accelerated by a business using the accrual method. But expenses owed to you or a related owner of the business can't be deducted until actually paid.[52]

Special Accounting Methods
Long-term Contracts

If your business is engaged in heavy construction work on a long-term contract basis, it may be difficult to tell in advance whether a particular contract will result in a profit or loss, since many unforeseen difficulties may arise. The tax regulations recognize this problem and allow such contractors to utilize special methods of accounting which may delay the time at which profit or loss is recognized on a long-term contract. They are:

- The percentage of completion method; and
- The completed contract method.[53]

The Tax Reform Act of 1986, however, and subsequent legislation has eliminated the use of the completed contract method of accounting for most large companies, except for certain ship contracts and for some home construction and other residential building contractors. Fortunately, small businesses, whose average annual gross receipts for the three preceding years do not exceed $10 million, are still allowed to use completed contract accounting for tax purposes, at least for contracts that are estimated to take no more than two years to complete.[54]

Even those completed contract method deferrals that survive the new restrictions are now mostly considered tax preference items under the alternative minimum tax rules.[55] In other words, heads you lose, tails the tax collector wins.

Installment Sales

If your business makes casual or occasional sales of personal property — other than merchandise held for sale — or makes sales of real estate it owns, the profit on any such sale can, in general, be reported on the installment basis as and when payments are received, rather than in the year of sale.[56] The installment method of reporting, however, is not available for "dealers," such as retailers, in personal or real property, except for certain dealers in real property. This is an election that sellers of residential lots or time-shares may make to use the installment method. The catch is that the dealer making such an election must agree to pay interest on any tax that is deferred by using installment reporting.[57]

In the case of nondealer sales of property for more than $150,000, if the total face amount of all installment notes exceeds $5 million for the year, at the end of the year, the seller must pay interest on the deferred tax liability.[58]

Sales of personal-use property or of farm property, for any amount, are exempt from the interest-on-deferred-tax provisions.[59]

Inventory Valuation Methods

If you maintain substantial inventories, discuss with your accountant the pros and cons of using the last-in-first-out (LIFO) method of valuing year-end inventories[60] versus the more common and simpler first-in-first-out (FIFO) method.

FIFO Method

Under the FIFO method, the cost of ending inventory is calculated under the assumption that the first items of inventory bought were the first ones to be sold, so that only the most recently purchased items are assumed to be left in inventory at the end of each year. This usually means the highest-cost items, in times of inflation. That is, if a company turns all its inventory over every three months each year, FIFO assumes, in effect, that the inventory remaining on hand at December 31 was all bought in the last three months of the year, rather than at some earlier date when prices may have been lower.

Most companies use the FIFO method because:

- FIFO is much simpler to use in terms of maintaining accounting records;
- When prices of goods are generally rising, FIFO has the effect of making a company's net income appear to be greater than if the more conservative LIFO method were used — but it also tends to inflate the amount of a company's taxable income; and
- Their accountants never mention to them that there is an alternative method (LIFO) of inventory accounting that can be used.

LIFO Method

In contrast to FIFO, the LIFO method assumes that the items in your ending inventory are the first or oldest ones that were acquired. Thus, under LIFO, ending inventory values for many of the items of inventory will be based on what that item cost in the very first year in which the business began using the LIFO method. The difference in inventory valuation can be dramatic if, for example, a business using LIFO for 10 years was paying $10 each 10 years earlier for the widgets it keeps in inventory versus a current price of $75 per widget. Under LIFO, the widgets would still be carried on the accounting records at a cost of $10 apiece versus $75 under FIFO.

Accordingly, the difference in inventory cost, or $65 per widget in the above example — called the LIFO reserve — would be the amount of taxable income per widget that the company has deferred over the 10 years. Thus, for a company with large amounts of capital invested in inventories, it is easy to see how LIFO can result in a huge tax saving.

At present, using the LIFO method is extremely complex, and the tax savings may in some cases be offset by increased accounting fees incurred and additional management time spent in attempting to comply with the LIFO tax regulations. The tax requirements for using LIFO, however, are somewhat relaxed for those small businesses with less than $5 million a year in sales.[61]

Any firm with inventories may elect to use either FIFO or LIFO. If a firm is already using FIFO, it may be able to change over to LIFO, if a number of technical requirements set by the IRS are met. Or, a company using LIFO may also change over to FIFO. Note, however, that if a firm uses LIFO and changes to FIFO for some reason, it will usually have to pay a large amount of tax, when it recaptures the LIFO reserve described above, at the time of the changeover. Any such changes in inventory accounting methods should not be attempted without the assistance of a competent tax advisor. If your C corporation already uses LIFO inventory accounting and elects S corporation status, your corporation will be required to pay tax, in four annual installments, on the LIFO reserve at the time of the changeover to an S corporation.[62]

Regardless of whether a company uses LIFO or FIFO for inventory accounting, it generally must allocate a wide range of its indirect costs to inventory, rather than simply deducting them as expenses, under the IRS's uniform capitalization rules. The practical effect of this is that any such costs that have been absorbed into the cost of inventory on hand at the end of the tax year do not get deducted currently for tax purposes. Manufacturing and processing operations of any size are subject to these complex capitalization rules. Fortunately, the uniform capitalization rules do not apply to a wholesale or retail business in any year when the company's annual gross receipts for the preceding three years have averaged $10 million or less.[63]

Vacation Pay Accrual Method

If you accrue employees' vacation pay for internal business purposes, you normally can only deduct your liability for such accruals when an employee actually uses his or her vacation pay. Before 1988, under certain circumstances, you were able to deduct the vacation pay liability that was accrued as of the end of each year;[64] however, this method of accounting was repealed in 1987. Vacation pay is now generally deductible only in the year it is paid out. The exception is for accrual-basis taxpayers, where vacation pay is vested at the end of a tax year and paid within two-and-a-half months afterwards.

Bad Debt Deductions

Before 1987, if your business extended credit to customers you could accelerate your business' bad debt deductions by electing to create a bad debt reserve for tax purposes. By doing so, you could deduct the amount that you expected to have to write off in the future, without waiting until the debts became uncollectible.

Since 1987, the reserve method of accounting has been abolished except for certain small financial institutions.[65] For all other taxpayers, bad debts are now only deductible when they actually become uncollectible.

8.9 Tax Problems Unique to Corporations

While this book has outlined some of the many tax and other advantages inherent in operating a corporation, you need to be aware that there are a number of traps in the tax law if you go overboard in trying to take advantage of the tax benefits bestowed on corporations.

For many years, the most basic goal in corporate tax planning for many high-income individuals was to leave as much profit in the corporation as possible so it could be taxed at the relatively low corporate tax rates and later withdrawn tax-free or at capital gains rates, such as by selling or having the corporation redeem the stock or by liquidating the corporation.

The government's role is to prevent the taxpayer from reaching these goals except where the corporation has good business reasons — as opposed to the individual's tax and investment reasons — for virtually everything it does. In attempting to plug up all the possible loopholes taxpayers might use to take advantage of low corporate rates, the tax law contains a whole array of penalties for corporations:

- That unreasonably accumulate earnings;[66]
- That are used as "incorporated pocket books" for holding personal investments;[67] or
- That are capitalized too heavily with debt.[68]

These and other operating problems of corporations under the tax law are briefly outlined below to give you a sense of what the limits are and how far you can go in utilizing corporate tax advantages.

Tax Problems Specific to C Corporations

None of the pitfalls and problems discussed below are of concern if your business is not incorporated or taxed as a corporation, and most of them are not applicable or are of only minor concern to corporations operating under S corporation elections.

Penalty Tax on Accumulated Earnings

The accumulated earnings tax[69] might well be called the scourge of the overly successful small corporation. This tax potentially applies to almost every corporation that accumulates more than $250,000[70] in after-tax profits (with certain adjustments),[71] unless the corporation can demonstrate that it needs to retain the profits for use in its business operations.[72]

Your corporation can accumulate up to $250,000 — $150,000 for professional and certain personal service firms — in earnings without having to be concerned about this penalty tax.[73] If additional accumulations cannot be justified as being made for the "reasonable needs of the business," however, the corporation will be faced with the choice of paying out the excess earnings as dividends or paying the accumulated earnings tax. The tax is imposed at the rate of 28% on the improperly accumulated earnings.[74] Since this is a tax that is imposed in addition to the corporate income tax, it is one you probably do not ever want to be forced to pay.

As long as you are able to keep plowing profits back into your business, buying more facilities, equipment, and inventory, and maintaining needed working capital, you will not have much cause for worry about the accumulated earnings tax. If, however, you reach a point where the corporation has more liquid funds than it needs, and you are beginning to look for places to invest the surplus cash, like real estate or the stock market, that should serve as a signal to you that there may be a potential accumulated earnings problem. In that case, you will need some good tax advice as to what you can do to protect the corporation from imposition of the penalty tax.

Justifiable Accumulations

Fortunately, there are a number of acceptable reasons that can justify accumulating funds that are not currently being used in the corporation's business. Some of the more important ones include:

- Setting up a reserve to redeem enough of the stock of a shareholder (yourself, for example) who dies, in order to enable the individual's estate to pay certain expenses related to his or her death — estate and inheritance taxes, funeral expenses, and expenses of administering the estate.[75] This reserve can only be created by the corporation after the death of a shareholder, prior to the repurchase of the shareholder's stock;

- Creating a fund to allow for a bona fide plan to replace facilities or expand the business, including the acquisition of another business;[76]

- Creating a reasonable reserve fund to pay potential uninsured product liability claims;[77]

- Accumulating funds to retire indebtedness created in connection with the business of the corporation;[78] and

- Setting up a defined benefit pension plan with an initial "past service liability" to be funded over a number of years.

A number of ways also exist to reduce the accumulated earnings without paying them out as dividends. Some typical examples would be to redeem part of the stock of the corporation, such as the stock of one of your children. This will not only reduce accumulated earnings but will reduce the amount of excess cash not needed in the business.

Another useful approach is to have the corporation purchase real estate that it might currently be leasing. This can sometimes be particularly advantageous where you are the landlord who is leasing the property to the corporation, as suggested in Section 8.5. This tactic technically will not reduce the corporation's accumulated earnings, but will use up excess cash that would otherwise raise questions by IRS auditors.

S Corporations

S corporations are not subject to the accumulated earnings tax because all their earnings are deemed to be distributed to shareholders. Thus, in some cases, an S corporation election may be a solution to the accumulated earnings problem. In the past, one frequent objection to electing

S corporation status was that it limited pension plan contributions for shareholder/employees to the lesser limits allowed for Keogh plans. Since 1984, this has ceased to be a problem since pension and profit-sharing plans of S corporations are treated almost exactly like those of regular corporations.

Penalty Tax on Personal Holding Company Income

If a closely held corporation gets a large proportion of its gross income, usually 60% or more, in the form of personal holding company income,[79] such as dividends, interest, rents, and royalties, it will generally be considered a personal holding company for tax purposes.[80]

Other kinds of income considered personal holding company income include income received by a service business from anyone (other than the corporation) who has the right under a contract to designate a particular individual to perform the contracted services. The person designated, however, must own at least 25% of the corporate stock.[81] Also, payments a corporation receives from a 25% shareholder for use of its property is personal holding company income.[82] This puts a damper on schemes such as having your corporation buy a yacht and charter it to you.

As a rule, if a corporation comes within the definition of a personal holding company, the tax law imposes a 28% penalty tax on any personal holding company income not distributed as a dividend.[83] This tax rate is expected to be raised to 31% by Congress in the very near future.

Most actively conducted small businesses will not need to be very concerned about being treated as personal holding companies since they will seldom get 60% or more of their gross income from passive sources like dividends and interest.

The kind of small business most likely to have a personal holding company problem is the incorporated personal service business — when the corporation enters into contracts and agrees to provide the services of an employee who is a major shareholder.

The best way to avoid this problem is to specify in the contract that the corporation reserves the right to designate the person who will provide the services. You will need to consult your tax adviser, however, before entering into any such personal service contract since the tax rules in this area are quite subtle and the tax penalty is very heavy if the income under the personal service contract is considered to be personal holding company income.

Another type of operating company that frequently encounters personal holding company tax problems is the developer of computer software that generates much of its income from software licensing agreements.

While the Tax Reform Act of 1986 included a special exemption from the personal holding company provisions for corporations actively engaged in the computer software business, the terms of this exception[84] are quite technical and many software firms will not be able to qualify for this relief without very careful planning.

Possible Treatment of Corporate Debt as Stock

As discussed in Section 8.5, there are two significant advantages to putting part of your investment in an incorporated business into the corporation in the form of debt, rather than all of it in exchange for stock. These advantages are:

- The interest paid to you is normally deductible by the corporation, unlike dividends paid on its stock.
- Repayment of the money you loaned to the corporation allows you to take part of your investment out of the corporation free of tax.

Because the use of debt in structuring a closely held corporation is so advantageous, Congress[85] has taken steps to limit the extent to which you can use debt to capitalize a corporation and still enjoy these advantages.

Over the last few years, the IRS has proposed several sets of new and complex regulations as to when loans to a corporation by its shareholders will be treated as equivalent to an investment in its stock — in which case interest payments will not be deductible by the corporation and principal payments would be taxable to the recipient.

Debt-Equity Distinction

These regulations raised such a storm of protest each time they were proposed that the IRS has finally withdrawn them. So, to determine what constitutes debt and stock, guidelines are used from hundreds of different court decisions. Nevertheless, there are a few generally accepted ground rules that you should follow to avoid having corporate debt reclassified by the IRS as equity or stock:

- The loan should not have any equity-type features, such as interest or payments, pegged to the corporation's income.
- The loan should be made at a reasonable interest rate, such as the rate at which the IRS imputes interest between related parties.
- The corporation's total debts — other than trade accounts payable — should not be more than about three times its net worth.
- The loan should be documented by a written note and should have a specified maturity date. All interest and principal payments on the note should be made on time.

If you follow each of the above rules, you will generally avoid the problem of having debt reclassified as stock. If you fail to comply with one or more of those rules when lending money to your corporation, the loan may be treated as a stock investment. This can be a serious tax trap if, when the loan is to be repaid, you are unaware that the repayment to you may constitute taxable income.

Double Taxation of Corporate Income

The most basic tax problem resulting from incorporating a business is the possibility of double taxation of the business income if it is paid out as dividends. That is, if the corporation has any profit after payment of salaries and other expenses, it must pay tax on those profits, unless it is an S corporation. Then, if those profits left after taxes are distributed to stockholders as dividends, the stockholders must also pay tax on the dividends they receive.

Fortunately, the problem of double taxation is generally quite manageable and most small incorporated businesses never pay dividends. The owners normally are also the officers of the corporation and can take enough income out in the form of salary and fringe benefits to live on, usually leaving some profit in the corporation to be plowed back into the business.

Also, as outlined briefly in Section 8.5, there are a number of better ways to get the accumulated profits out of the corporation than by paying dividends.

Unreasonable Compensation

If you own an incorporated business or own a portion of its stock and are actively involved in operating the business, you will be an employee of the corporation and will draw a salary. Drawing a large salary from the corporation may enable you to withdraw much of the profits of the business without any problem of double taxation, since the corporation can deduct reasonable compensation it pays to you as your salary.[86]

Thus, taking salary out of the corporation is preferable to taking money out in the form of dividends, since the corporation cannot deduct dividends it pays. The salary you receive, if reasonable, is deductible by the corporation; however, the key word here is reasonable. If you try to take too much income out of the corporation as salary, including bonuses and fringe benefits like pension and profit-sharing contributions, the IRS may try to treat part of your salary as unreasonable compensation.

There are no hard and fast rules as to how much compensation is reasonable, but if you are taking no more than the officers in similar businesses of the same size are paid, you should not have any problem establishing that your compensation from the corporation is reasonable under the circumstances.

If, however, the IRS does succeed in treating part of your compensation as excessive, there will be two serious tax consequences:

- The deduction by the corporation for the unreasonable portion of your salary will be disallowed.
- Part of your salary will be reclassified as dividend income, and thus pension and profit-sharing plan contributions based on that salary may not be fully deductible, which could even result in disqualification of your pension or profit-sharing plan.

8.10 Estate Planning in Connection with Your Business

As the owner of part or all of even a moderately successful business, you may find that after a few years the value of your business accounts for a very large portion of your personal net worth. As such, your business will probably be the most important single asset you have to be concerned with for estate planning purposes, both during your lifetime and at the time of your death. No attempt will be made here to go into the intricacies of the estate-planning possibilities that may be available; instead, the fundamental approaches you need to be aware of are outlined below. Discuss how to relate these concepts to your own situation with your tax adviser and attorney.

Income-Splitting

A useful method of reducing lifetime income taxes is to split the taxable income from your business between two or more persons or entities. Usually a corporation, particularly an S corporation, is a useful vehicle for doing this; you can split income between you and your children by giving them stock in the corporation. A corporation that has not elected S corporation treatment can also be used to split income between you and the corporation. See Section 2.4.

Remember, however, that income-splitting only works if your children are 14 years of age or older. Otherwise, any unearned income of your children in excess of $1,000 a year is taxed at your marginal tax bracket, eliminating any tax savings.[87]

Reducing Estate and Gift Taxes

Often the best time to remove potential wealth from your taxable estate at death is by giving your children part of the stock in your incorporated business when the business is formed — when the value of the stock is likely to be negligible. If you wait until the business has become a valuable and profitable enterprise, gifts of stock at that time may result in substantial taxable gifts for gift tax purposes, even though the tax cost of those gifts may not be felt until you die, in some cases. You can now make gifts of up to $10,000 ($20,000 if married) per year to each of your children completely free of federal gift taxes.

Assuming that you want part of your stock in your incorporated business to pass to your children at your death, it obviously makes sense to give them a portion of the stock — but not enough to affect your control of the corporation — during your lifetime. By doing this, there will be little or no gift tax cost if it is done when the business is started. Thus, they will already own the stock when you die, and that valuable asset will have passed to them free of death taxes in most instances. Also, as noted above, lifetime gifts of stock to your children may also save income taxes.

Buy-Sell Agreements

If you have one or more partners or business associates who also own a part of the business, it is highly important that you enter into a buy-sell agreement with them that spells out what happens if one of you dies, becomes disabled, or wants to sell his or her interest in the business.

Often these agreements are funded by life insurance on the owners, so that if you die, the business or the other owners will collect the life insurance proceeds and use those funds to buy out your interest in the business. Otherwise, your surviving family members might find it very difficult to sell the interest in the business they inherit from you, except at a give-away price.

Many small business owners ignore the need for buy-sell agreements or, like having a will drawn up, they keep putting it off. When one of the partners or shareholders dies, the survivors may have a problem in raising enough cash to pay the death taxes. This is only one of the problems that may arise when there is no buy-sell agreement.

The few hundred dollars you may spend in legal fees to have a buy-sell agreement with your business partners or associates drawn up is probably one of the best investments you and your associates will ever make.

Prior to 1983, there were unlimited statutory exemptions from the estate tax for retirement plan benefits if you left your interest in any such plan or IRA to a designated beneficiary, other than your estate, and if certain other requirements were met;[88] however, Congress repealed this exemption entirely in 1984.

Retirement Plan Exemptions

Accordingly, if you have already done some estate planning based on obtaining this estate tax exemption for retirement benefits you planned to leave to a beneficiary other than your spouse, you had better go back to the drawing board now that this exemption has expired. If, however, you were already receiving retirement benefits before 1984, the benefits may still be eligible for the above exclusions — if you don't change the form in which benefits are being paid.

Since 1982, it has been possible to leave your entire estate to your surviving spouse free of federal estate taxes. In some cases, however, it is not the best strategy to fully use the unlimited estate tax marital deduction, so see a lawyer to get a current will that takes the best approach for your situation.

Unlimited Estate Tax Marital Deduction

This exemption from the estate tax also applies to pension benefits you leave to your spouse when you die, unless the accrued value of your pension benefits exceeds $750,000 (less in some instances). If so, your estate will have to pay a special 15% excise tax on the amount over $750,000.[89]

Since not all state inheritance tax laws permit an unlimited marital deduction, it can create inheritance tax problems in those states if you leave too much property to your spouse. Refer to Section 11.8 for details regarding this state's marital deduction rules under its inheritance tax laws.

Wills or trusts executed before September 13, 1981 may not qualify for the unlimited estate tax marital deduction.[90] If you have such a will or trust, have it updated immediately. See the discussion in Section 2.4 under the sidehead, Exemptions from Estate Tax, for more information.

8.11 Targeted Jobs Tax Credit

Are you aware that if you hire members of certain economically disadvantaged groups, the federal government will pay you a subsidy of up to $2,400 in the form of tax credits per employee? Unfortunately, most employers, particularly small businesses, seem to be unaware of this substantial tax subsidy.

Part of the reason so many employers fail to take advantage of this tax incentive appears to be on account of a Catch-22 in the way the program works. To qualify for the targeted jobs tax credit for hiring a disadvantaged category person, he or she must be certified as such by a designated state employment security agency, and the certification must be received by the employer (or requested in writing) at least one day before the employee begins work.[91]

At the same time, state and federal anti-discrimination laws make it very difficult for you as an employer to ask prospective job applicants if they belong to any of the disadvantaged groups that are eligible for the targeted jobs tax credits, since to do so could be considered a discriminatory hiring practice.

Your best bet is to check first with your local state employment department or division to find out how to take advantage of state and federal job credit programs. The department will either refer you to the proper agency or organization that can assist you, or the department itself will help you find an individual who qualifies under this program and matches your specific job requirements.

Targeted Groups

The targeted group individuals for whom you can claim the jobs tax credit are:

- Vocational rehabilitation referrals — These referrals are for certain handicapped individuals who have completed rehabilitation programs. Tax credits aside, handicapped individuals often are extremely good and conscientious employees.
- Economically disadvantaged youths — These individuals are between 18 and 22 years of age and are certified as members of economically disadvantaged families.
- Economically disadvantaged Vietnam veterans.
- Supplemental Security Income (SSI) recipients — SSI recipients are people who are 65 or older, or blind, or have a disability and who don't

own much or have a lot of income. SSI payments are not just for adults; they can also go to disabled and blind children.

- General assistance recipients — These persons receive state or local welfare payments.
- Economically disadvantaged ex-convicts.
- Youths participating in a cooperative education program — Youths in this category are 16–20 years of age and have not finished high school.
- Eligible work incentive program employees.
- Qualified summer youth employees — These economically disadvantaged youths are 16 or 17 years old and are hired to work between May 1 and September 15, and they were not previously employed by you.

On the first $6,000 you pay an eligible target group employee, you will earn tax credits of 40% of the wages. This is limited to $3,000 of wages for qualified summer youth employees during the first 90 days they work for you.

Here is how the federal targeted jobs tax credits apply for eligible and certified new employees:

Category of Employee	Federal Tax Credit	Minimum Work Period
All qualified employees as listed above	40% of wages on first $6,000 of wages or a maximum credit of $2,400 per employee	90 days or 120 hours
Qualified summer youth employees	40% of first 90 days' wages for up to $3,000 of wages or maximum credit of $1,200	14 days or 20 hours

Drawbacks

One drawback with all of these tax credits is that you must reduce the wages you can deduct dollar-for-dollar for credits you claim.[92] That is, if you pay someone $1,000 and claim a $400 targeted jobs tax credit, you can only deduct $600 for wage expense, not the full $1,000. The credit is not allowed for wages paid to strikebreakers.

The targeted jobs credit expired on June 30, 1992, but will most likely be retroactively extended again by Congress.

8.12 Hiring a Spouse as an Employee

If you run an unincorporated business and your spouse works with or for you, there are three ways your spouse can be treated for tax purposes:

- As an employee;
- As a partner in the firm; and
- As an uncompensated employee — probably the most common approach.

Social Security Tax

Congress, by enacting the Omnibus Budget Reconciliation Act of 1987, ended the exemption from Social Security (FICA) taxes for wages paid to a spouse, parent, or minor child — with the exception of a child under 18 years of age. There are, however, still some advantages to having your spouse be a paid employee of your proprietorship, as described below.

Individual Retirement Account for Spouse

If your spouse works for you without pay and has no other income from an outside job, the most the two of you can put into an individual retirement account (IRA) is $2,250. If you start compensating your spouse, even as little as $2,000 a year, you should each qualify for a $2,000 IRA deduction or a total of $4,000 a year, rather than only $2,250. Note that IRA deductions may be limited if either of you is an active participant in another retirement plan.

Medical Insurance

You can deduct any medical insurance premiums that you pay for employees, but you can only deduct 25% of your own medical insurance premiums. If your spouse works for you, however, you can put your spouse on the payroll and provide a medical expense reimbursement plan or medical insurance for your spouse and his or her family — which includes you — you can then deduct the payments or premiums in full since your spouse is an employee.[93] See Section 11.8 regarding state tax exemptions and other implications of hiring a spouse as an employee.

8.13 How to Save on Unemployment Taxes

The unemployment tax rate you pay as an employer is one of the few taxes where you have some control over the rate you pay. The state maintains a reserve account for each employer, in which it monitors the unemployment taxes you pay in and the unemployment benefits it pays out to your former employees. The more benefits the state pays to your former employees, the higher your individual company's tax rate will be and vice versa. So it pays for you to have as few former employees as possible who are collecting unemployment benefits, since these are charged to your reserve account.

To succeed in keeping down the unemployment claims charged to your account, you need to challenge any former employees' claims that appear to be unjustified. Often you will be surprised to learn that an employee you had fired for stealing or who had quit on you has filed for benefits and has lied about his or her reasons for leaving. In general, an ex-employee can't collect unemployment from you if he or she left your employment for one of these reasons:

- Refusal to work;
- Voluntarily quitting;

- Inability to continue work due to illness, injury, etc; or
- Misconduct, such as theft, not showing up for work, or the like.

An employee who leaves your employ for virtually any other reason, such as being fired for incompetence, can generally collect benefits, which will cost you money by raising your unemployment tax rate. Here are some tips on how you can keep down the number of unemployment claims filed against your account.

Reducing Claims

- When you are hiring, be aware of the cost you may have if you lay off these people in the future. You may hire a number of new employees for an expansion or new project with the view that if things don't work out as planned, you will simply lay them off and cancel the project with no further cost. Count the cost. Remember that if you do have to lay them off, you may pay a much higher unemployment tax rate for several years.
- Document in writing your reasons for firing an employee, if for reasons such as theft, insubordination, absence, or intoxication on the job. This will buttress your argument that the fired employee is not entitled to benefits if he or she should file a claim.
- Be aware that if you change an employee's hours of work and he or she quits as a result, it will be considered involuntary dismissal and the employee will probably be eligible for benefits. So it pays to have a written agreement signed by the employee to work any shift, hours, weekends, etc., that are required, if needed. Then if the employee quits it will not be due to a change in job conditions, in the eyes of the law.
- If you decide to fire someone for misconduct, do it on the spot. If you keep them on at your convenience until you find a replacement, it will not usually be considered a discharge for misconduct, and the fired employee will most likely be eligible for benefits.
- If new employees do not work out, consider firing them before they have worked three months. In most states, a person has to work for you at least three months before they can earn unemployment benefits that are chargeable to your reserve account.

In general, it pays to keep a close eye on your employer reserve account and be aware of who is filing benefit claims that will cost you money. Contest any claims that you do not feel are legitimate.

8.14 Deductions for Office-in-the-Home Expenses

If you use part of your residence for business purposes, you may be able to deduct part of your office-in-the-home expenses; however, the rules are rather stringent, and the general rule is that office-in-the-home expenses are not deductible for tax purposes, unless you meet a number of quite technical requirements. There are several types of situations under which you may be able to claim deductions for part of your rent or expenses related to ownership of your residence, as well as other occupancy expenses, despite the home-office deduction limitations.

Exclusive-Use Tests

If you use part of your residence exclusively for business purposes and on a regular basis, you may be able to claim office-in-the-home deductions, if you also qualify under one of these tests:[94]

- You use a portion of your home as your principal place of business.
- You use your home as a place to meet clients, customers, patients, etc.
- Your home office is a separate structure that is not attached to your house or living quarters.

Note, however, that the definition of "principal place of business" has been strictly limited by a 1993 Supreme Court decision.

Nonexclusive Uses that Qualify

Two special exceptions are made where part of a home is regularly, but not exclusively, used for business purposes.

- Storage of inventory — A wholesaler or retailer who uses part of a home to store inventory that is being held for sale; if the dwelling unit is the taxpayer's sole fixed location of the trade or business; or
- Day care facility — Part of the home is used for day care of children, physically and mentally handicapped persons, or individuals age 65 or older.

If you can show that a portion of your residence qualifies as a home office, you have cleared the first hurdle. But note that, even if you don't meet any of the above requirements, these rules will not disallow your deductions that are otherwise allowed for tax purposes, such as interest on your home mortgage, real estate taxes, or casualty losses from damage to your residence. Also, business expenses that are not home-related, such as business supplies, cost of goods sold, wages paid to business employees, and other such operating expenses, are not affected by the limitation on home office-related deductions.

If the business use of your home qualifies under one of the above tests, then you may be able to deduct part of the home office expenses that are allocable to the portion of your home that is used in your business, in addition to home mortgage interest, property taxes, and casualty losses.

For example, if 15% of your home is used exclusively and regularly as your principal place of business, you could possibly deduct up to 15% of your occupancy costs, such as gas, electricity, insurance, repairs, and similar expenses, as well as 15% of your rent or depreciation expense on 15% of the tax basis of your house. The IRS and the tax court don't agree on the deductibility of certain other types of expenses, e.g., lawn care.

Note, however, that the amount of qualifying home office expense you can actually deduct for the year is limited to the gross income from your home business, reduced by regular operating expenses (wages, supplies, etc.) and an allocable portion (15% in the above example) of your mortgage interest, property taxes, and casualty loss deductions. If you still have net business income after taking those deductions, then you may deduct the allocable portion of your home office expenses, up to the amount of such net income.

Any portion of your home office expenses that aren't deducted due to the income limit in one year can be carried over to future years until usable, if ever. Thus, it pays to keep track of any such disallowed expenses, in case your home-based business becomes more profitable in the future, and you are then able to deduct the carried-over expenses from earlier years.

On 1992 individual returns, *Schedule C* no longer asks you whether expenses for business use of a home are being deducted. Instead, you must determine a tentative profit or loss on *Schedule C*, without taking into account home use expenses. Home office expenses must be computed separately on a new schedule, *Form 8829*, on which you must compute the amount of deductible expenses for business use of the home, which (if any) can then be deducted from the net *Schedule C* income. This will make it impossible, or at least illegal, for taxpayers filing *Schedule C* to simply bury the home office expenses in with other business expenses.

Deductions Limited to Income

The downside of taking home office deductions is a potential tax bite when you sell your home. For example, if 15% of your home has been used for business and you sell your home for a gain, you will have to pay tax on 15% of the gain, even if you reinvest in a new house, or even if you qualify for the once-in-a-lifetime $125,000 exclusion of gain — for persons over age 55 — when you sell the house. Thus, a few hundred dollars of home office deductions now, could later result in many thousands of dollars of tax on the "business" part of your house, if you sell it for a gain a few years down the road.

Potential Tax Trap

Footnotes

1. I.R.C. §243(a).
2. I.R.C. §§301 and 302(d).
3. I.R.C. §331.
4. I.R.C. §1(h).
5. I.R.C. §531.
6. I.R.C. §542.
7. I.R.C. §542(a)(1).
8. I.R.C. §246A.
9. I.R.C. §132.
10. I.R.C. §119.
11. I.R.C. §127.
12. I.R.C. §120.

13. I.R.C. §129.
14. I.R.C. §422.
15. I.R.C. §423.
16. I.R.C. §125.
17. I.R.C. §245(c)(1).
18. I.R.C. §§991–997.
19. I.R.C. §994(a).
20. Treas. Reg. §1.994-1(e).
21. I.R.C. §994(a).
22. Treas. Reg. §1.994.
23. I.R.C. §995(b)(1)(F)(i) (as amended by The Tax Reform Act of '86).
24. I.R.C. §995.
25. I.R.C. §995(f).
26. Rev. Rul. 75-430, 1975-2 C.B. 313; Rev. Rul. 76-284, 1976-2 C.B. 236.
27. Treas. Reg. §1.991-1(a).
28. I.R.C. §922(a)(1).
29. I.R.C. §7872.
30. I.R.C. §302(c)(2) permits the complete termination of the interest of a family member in a corporation by means of a stock redemption to qualify for capital gains treatment, if certain conditions are met.
31. I.R.C. §453(g).
32. I.R.C. §291(a).
33. I.R.C. §274(h).
34. I.R.C. §280A.
35. I.R.C. §274(d).
36. I.R.C. §274(m)(1).
37. I.R.C. §274(d).
38. I.R.C. §274(d), as amended by Pub. L. No. 99-44.
39. I.R.C. §274(a)(1)(A).
40. I.R.C. §274(e)(1). (Repealed as of 1-1-87.)
41. I.R.C. §262.
42. I.R.C. §280F(b)(2).
43. I.R.C. §280F(a)(2)(A) as amended in 1986 by Pub. L. No. 99-514.
44. I.R.C. §280F(d)(5)(B).
45. Rev. Proc. 89-66, 1989-2 C.B. 792.
46. I.R.C. §441(i).
47. I.R.C. §195.
48. Treas. Reg. §1.446-1(c)(2)(i).
49. I.R.C. §448.
50. I.R.C. §461(h).
51. Notice 91-10, 1991-11 I.R.B.
52. I.R.C. §267(a)(2).
53. Treas. Reg. §1.451-3.
54. I.R.C. §460.
55. I.R.C. §56(a)(3).
56. I.R.C. §453(b).
57. I.R.C. §§453(1)(2)(B) and 453(1)(3).
58. I.R.C. §453A(b).
59. I.R.C. §453A(b)(3).
60. I.R.C. §472.
61. I.R.C. §474.
62. I.R.C. §1363(d).
63. I.R.C. §263A(b)(2)(B).
64. I.R.C. §463(a). (Repealed by '87 Act.)
65. The Tax Reform Act of 1986 §805.
66. I.R.C. §531.
67. I.R.C. §541.
68. I.R.C. §385.
69. I.R.C. §531.
70. I.R.C. §535(c)(2).
71. I.R.C. §535(a) and (b).
72. I.R.C. §537(a).
73. I.R.C. §535(c)(2).
74. I.R.C. §531.
75. I.R.C. §537(a)(2).
76. Treas. Reg. §§1.537-1(b)(1) and 1.537-2(b)(2).
77. I.R.C. §537(b)(4).
78. Treas. Reg. §1.537-2(b)(3).
79. As defined in I.R.C. §543.
80. I.R.C. §542.
81. I.R.C. §543(a)(7).
82. I.R.C. §543(a)(6).
83. I.R.C. §541.
84. I.R.C. §543(d).
85. I.R.C. §385.
86. I.R.C. §162(a)(1).
87. I.R.C. §1(g).
88. I.R.C. §2039(c) and (e). (Repealed after 1984.)
89. I.R.C. §4980A(d).
90. Economic Recovery Tax Act of 1981, Pub. L. No. 97-34, §403(e)(3).
91. I.R.C. §51.
92. I.R.C. §280C(a).
93. Rev. Rul. 71-588, 1971-2 C.B. 91.
94. I.R.C. §280A(c)(1).

Chapter 9

Miscellaneous Business Pointers

Money is not the root of all evil. The lack of money is the root of all evil.

—Reverend Ike

9.1 General Considerations

This chapter provides a number of general pointers and suggestions in connection with operating a small business, some of which may be of interest to you.

9.2 Accounting — Some Basics

Maintaining good accounting records is a must for any small business. Without accurate and up-to-date records, you will be operating your business without vitally important information. Meaningful financial statements can only be prepared if the underlying records of transactions are accurate and current.

Accounting Systems

It may help to think of your accounting system as being like an airplane's radar system. If you are not getting current and correct feedback from either system, you will not have enough time to react to prevent a potential crash.

While most schools and colleges teach only the double-entry method of bookkeeping, which provides a series of checks and balances in recording

Single-Entry Method

income and expenditures, some small business owners use a single-entry method of accounting.

If you are not knowledgeable about double-entry bookkeeping and handle most of the funds directly yourself, you may find that a single-entry system is acceptable for your needs and much simpler to use. The single-entry method is only slightly more involved than keeping a checkbook record of cash income and disbursements and usually consists of three basic records:

- A daily cash receipts summary, which may come from a cash register tape or sales slips. This will not only give you a total of your daily cash receipts, but it will break down your sales by product, by salesperson, by store, etc., depending on how much detail you need.
- A monthly cash receipts summary, which is simply a summary of the daily summaries.
- A monthly cash disbursements report of expenses and other payments, such as debt repayments, purchases of capital assets or distributions of profits.

A number of simplified write-it-once systems for all different kinds of businesses are available at office supply stores.

Double-Entry Method

Be aware that while a single-entry system is easy to use, it is not a complete accounting system since it focuses mainly on profit and loss and does not provide a balance sheet. For all but the very smallest of businesses, a single-entry accounting system is likely to be inadequate. Even if your business is very small, but expects to grow, it is usually advisable to start out with a full set of books, using the double-entry method.

You can avoid many future problems if you get a CPA to help you set up the accounting system for your business. He or she will tailor a chart of accounts to your specific needs and build in internal controls to record all transactions and to reduce the possibilities of employee theft or embezzlement that might go undetected with a poorly designed system.

If you use a personal computer in your business, there are any number of general ledger accounting software packages you can buy if your accounting needs are fairly straightforward and if you have a reasonable understanding of how double-entry accounting works. For a very small business, there are adequate software packages available for under $100.

Business Owner's Guide to Accounting & Bookkeeping, published by The Oasis Press, is a valuable resource for the beginning small business owner, manager, or accountant. This book explains the why's and how's of small business accounting, from preparing financial statements to interpreting the numbers. To obtain this book, contact your book source or:

The Oasis Press
(800) 228-2275

If you are going to use an outside accounting firm to prepare financial statements, you need to be aware of the three different levels of service that they will provide: compilations, reviews, and audits.

Accounting Firm Services

Most financial statements prepared for small businesses are compilations for the simple reason that a compilation is far less expensive than an audit or review. In a compilation, the outside accountant has no obligation to do any investigation unless he or she becomes aware of something that looks suspicious or that could be misleading. Generally, all an accountant is required to do in preparing compilation statements is to take the financial data you give him or her and present it in a manner that conforms with generally accepted accounting principles (GAAP).

Compilations

In a compilation, the accountant expresses no opinion on the accuracy of the information presented. The accountant is simply taking what you gave him or her and putting it in a proper financial statement format. It is important for you to remember that regardless of what type of assurance your accountant expresses, they are your financial statements and it is your ultimate responsibility to see that they are accurately prepared.

A review involves some limited analysis or testing of the financial records, but the certified public accountant (CPA) expresses only a very limited opinion as to the accuracy of the information in the financial statements. A review is somewhat less expensive than an audit but more expensive than a compilation. Most small businesses hire a CPA firm to do a review only if their bankers or other lenders or financial backers insist on a review rather than a compilation.

Reviews

An audit is invariably the most involved and most expensive level of service in connection with financial statements. An accounting firm that audits financial statements must not only verify that your financial statements are presented fairly and in accordance with GAAP, but it also checks and verifies some or all of the actual accounts to satisfy itself that they are for real. It does this, for instance, by requesting confirmations of bank accounts or receivable and payable account balances from banks, customers, and vendors to uncover possible errors or fraud in recordkeeping. Because audits are relatively expensive, many small businesses elect to have review or compilation statements done; however, lenders or bonding companies often insist that you have a certified audit.

Audits

The Tax Reform Act of 1986 effectively repealed the highly favorable accelerated cost recovery system (ACRS) tax depreciation system that was in force from 1981 until the end of 1986. In January 1987, taxpayers learned to live with another whole new complex system of depreciation. Unfortunately, it is still necessary to know the former ACRS rules for assets acquired during the 1981–86 period, as well as the old depreciation rules for items acquired before 1981, to compute current depreciation on those assets.

Depreciation

The Modified ACRS System

The modified ACRS (MACRS) law from 1986 does not provide depreciation tables, unlike the previous ACRS system. Instead, all assets (with a few special exceptions) placed in service after 1986 are assigned to 3-, 5-, 7-, 10-, 15-, or 20-year recovery period categories, except for real estate, which must be depreciated over 31.5 years — 27.5 years for residential rental property.[1]

Under the MACRS system, all personal property is depreciated under the 200% declining balance method over its recovery period, except for 15- or 20-year property, for which the 150% declining balance method is used. Real estate may only be depreciated under the straight-line method.

Assets other than real estate are mostly assigned to the various recovery periods based on the former asset depreciation range (ADR) "midpoint" class lives,[2] which were published by the IRS back in the 1970s. These ADR class life guidelines vary from industry to industry and are far too voluminous, technical, and detailed to reproduce in a book of this nature. The MACRS, however, specifically assigns some types of assets to recovery classes. For example, autos and light trucks are five-year property. The MACRS provisions have also reduced the maximum annual depreciation deductions on luxury automobiles as discussed in Section 8.6.

One small ray of sunshine in the MACRS tax depreciation nightmare is a liberalization of the former $5,000 first-year expending election for tangible personal property. You may elect to expense up to $10,000 in cost of furniture, equipment, etc. in the year such assets are placed in service.[3] For example, if the only depreciable items you buy in 1992 are $10,000 of office equipment, you may be able to deduct the full $10,000 in 1992. Note, however, that this special deduction is not allowed to the extent that it would create a loss for your trade(s) or business(es) for the year. Also, the deduction is phased out if you acquire more than $200,000 of eligible property during the tax year.

The Previous ACRS System

The previous accelerated cost recovery system of depreciation applied to all tangible depreciable property acquired after 1980 and before 1987, except certain pre-1981 assets acquired from a related person or entity.

Property Other Than Real Estate

Under the previous ACRS system, depreciation calculations for most kinds of property were extremely simple. Assets other than real property fell into several categories, each with a prescribed percentage for each year of the recovery period:

- Three-year property
- Five-year property
- Ten-year property
- Fifteen-year public utility property

Fifteen-, Eighteen-, or Nineteen-year Real Property

The previous ACRS system allowed buildings to be depreciated over 15, 18, or 19 years, compared to the 27.5 or 31.5 years required after 1986.

Real estate acquired during the period from 1981 through March 15, 1984 is depreciable over 15 years. In general, real estate acquired or constructed after March 15, 1984 and before May 9, 1985 must be written off in 18 years. Real estate acquired or constructed on or after May 8, 1985 and before 1987 generally must be written off over a period of 19 years. A taxpayer could either elect straight-line depreciation or use accelerated depreciation tables for real property — that is, other than for low-income housing units.

Poor internal controls and recordkeeping procedures are a weakness for many small business owners. Lax procedures are frequently to blame when a secretary or bookkeeper departs for Brazil with thousands of dollars of stolen or embezzled funds belonging to his or her employer. Ideally, you would consult a good accountant to set up and review your internal financial controls; however, that will cost you a good deal of money, so before you do so, you may want to do your own review of your internal controls, utilizing this checklist.

Internal Accounting Controls

Internal Controls Checklist

☐ The same person who handles your cash receipts should not be the same person who makes the bank deposits. Cash is too easily misappropriated. Don't tempt an employee by letting him or her handle both of these duties.

☐ The person who writes checks should not also sign them or have the authority to sign checks. A different person should sign checks.

☐ Whoever signs checks should only sign them when the bill that is being paid is presented at the same time. The check number should be written on the bill to avoid double payments or payments to a nonexistent vendor. When you sign the check, be sure you know what the bill is for.

☐ Consider using some type of mechanical check imprinting equipment for all checks that are written, as a further means of preventing unauthorized payments. Such machines keep a record of the amount of any checks written.

☐ Use only prenumbered checks and keep all of the cancelled or voided checks in your records. This will help make it readily apparent if any additional checks are written without your knowledge.

☐ Complete a monthly bank reconciliation yourself or have your outside accountant do it. Never let the person who writes checks do the reconciliation.

☐ Deposit your daily cash receipts in the bank each day. Do not let cash collections for one day get mingled with the next day's collections.

☐ Use prenumbered sets of sales checks, invoices, and receipts to keep control of payments made and received. Duplicates will be kept track of by the individuals making sales, etc., and the master copy will enable you to make sure they account for all of their transactions.

(continued)

Internal Controls Checklist (continued)

☐ Use a petty cash fund and voucher system for stamps, small bills, and other small cash outlays. Do not use cash from the day's receipts to pay bills! Put a voucher or bill in the petty cash box each time money is taken out. When the fund is depleted, write a check to bring it back up to the maximum amount (say $50), and record all the vouchers at the time the check is cashed to replenish the fund.

☐ Maintain a master or control account for all of your accounts receivable, and reconcile it each month to the subsidiary accounts receivable. If someone is stealing money from customer payments, it will be easier to spot if the master and subsidiary accounts are reconciled regularly.

9.3 Cash-Flow Management

Cash flow is the lifeblood of any business organization; yet, often small business operators are so concerned with other matters that they fail to pay proper attention to managing their cash resources properly. Good cash management can make a significant contribution to the competitiveness and profitability of your business. Poor cash management is one of the main causes of business failures, particularly among smaller firms, since a cash shortage due to poor planning can set off a chain reaction of disastrous consequences, even in a profitable business.

Cash-flow management has two aspects: projecting future cash flow and controlling and maximizing the cash available from operations at all times.

Projecting Cash Flow

Perhaps the most important part of cash-flow management is accurately projecting your business' near- and long-term cash needs and making your business decisions reflect those needs. Often, to project what your sales will be in coming months, it will be necessary to rely on what has happened in the past — what percentage will be credit sales and when your receivables are likely to be collected. Similarly, you have to estimate and project what you will have to pay out in the way of payroll, rent, taxes, servicing debts, purchasing inventory, and paying off existing payables, plus extraordinary outlays you can anticipate.

The purpose of making these detailed projections of expected cash inflows and outflows is to point out any future cash shortages or deficits, so you can take steps in advance to prevent such occurrences. For example, if your projections indicated that you were going to experience a severe cash crunch in about three months, you might take any of a number of steps to avert it, such as:

- Seeking to raise new capital;
- Borrowing money;
- Liquidating some of your inventory by cutting prices; or
- Cutting back on planned expenditures.

If you have a computer, be aware that there are microcomputer models available to assist in preparing projections of cash flows. If you don't own a computer, your accountant may have such models available to assist you.

PSI Successful Business Software has developed an inexpensive and simple-to-use program that can help you manage all financial aspects of your business. *Financial Templates for Small Business* lets you monitor cash flow; generate financial statements; track monthly, quarterly, or three-year cash flow and income; and plan for the future by analyzing past and present performance. These multipurpose templates run on either IBM PC (or compatible) or with Macintosh computers, along with spreadsheet programs, such as Lotus 1-2-3 or Excel. For more information, contact:

PSI Successful Business Software
(800) 228-2275

Controlling and Maximizing Cash Flow

If you are able to increase available cash by speeding up collections, delaying payments, or by other means, you can use the extra cash to reduce your borrowings — thus saving interest expenses — or you can invest the surplus cash to earn interest. Either way, improving your cash flow should increase your net earnings and should also help you avert cash shortages.

Here are some basic ways to improve your business' cash flow.

- Bill your customers promptly. The later they receive the bill, the later you will usually collect for a particular sale.
- If you know that certain large customers must receive bills by certain days of the month so you can get paid in that month, try to bill them before those deadlines.
- Deposit your cash receipts daily, if possible.
- Keep close tabs on credit customers. Send them past due notices as soon as payments become overdue.
- If you can do so without hurting business, add late charges to overdue accounts.
- Never pay bills until just before they become due, unless there is a worthwhile discount for quick payment.
- Try to keep inventories as lean as possible. Even if you occasionally lose a small sale because you are temporarily out of an item, you should be far ahead of the game by substantially reducing the amount of cash you have tied up in inventory.

- Look for items in your inventory that are moving slowly or not at all. Consider slashing the price on those articles to convert them to cash and also to reduce the cost of storing them or taking up valuable shelf space.

- Consider leasing equipment items instead of buying.

- Be sure that you are not paying more on your estimated income taxes than you have to. You may qualify — without incurring interest charges or late payment penalties — under one or more exceptions that will allow you to delay paying much of your tax for the year until the tax return is due. If you realize that you have already overpaid your corporate estimated tax for the year, there is a procedure for obtaining a refund prior to the time when you can file a return.[4]

- If your business has a net operating loss for tax purposes that can be carried back to prior years, a procedure exists for filing a claim for a quick refund of the prior years' taxes. And file it as early as you can, since the IRS no longer pays interest on these refunds.

- Instead of keeping all your business cash in a local bank account, consider putting a significant portion of your cash in an out-of-town money market-type fund that pays interest and allows you to write checks against the account. Since you continue to earn interest on funds on deposit until the checks clear, consider using a fund in a distant part of the country, since it will take longer for your checks to clear when you make payments to local firms.

9.4 Protecting Your Assets

Starting a new business is almost always a risky proposition, and you should not overlook the fact that, if the business fails, you may be forced into bankruptcy and could lose everything except what the bankruptcy laws allow you to keep. This is one reason why many small businesses incorporate at the outset, since a corporation will generally limit your liability to business creditors to the amount you invest in the corporation, plus any loans to the corporation you guarantee.

Accordingly, if you incorporate, you should be cautious about unnecessarily committing too much of your personal assets to the business. For example, instead of putting a building or piece of land you own into the corporation, it may be better — and may save income and property taxes — for you to keep the property and lease it to the corporation.

Even if you incorporate, the leases or bank loans you find it necessary to guarantee on behalf of the corporation could still wipe out your personal assets if the business folds. Thus, it often makes sense to have your corporation set up a tax-qualified pension or profit-sharing plan and to have it contribute as much as possible to the plan on your behalf. Not only does this provide substantial tax savings and deferral, but the law in most states will in many cases protect your account under such a plan from your creditors or the corporation's creditors.

So, if you can build up a significant retirement fund in your corporation's pension plan, you have at least some degree of assurance that the failure of the business or a disastrous lawsuit will not touch that nest egg — but in a divorce, your spouse may be able to claim his or her share of the pension plan account.

9.5 Protecting Trade Names and Trademarks

If you intend to use some type of distinctive trade name for your business or trademark for your product or in advertising your services, it will usually be advisable to consider taking steps to protect the use of the name or mark by registration under state or federal law, or both. Also, it may be necessary to perform a search, which can be expensive, to determine whether someone else has already registered the same or a very similar name or symbol.

You do not want to open yourself up to a lawsuit for infringement. Since not every trade name can be registered, you will need to consult a trademark attorney if you are interested in protecting a particular name used by your business. Federal registration of a name confers a number of significant benefits, including:

- Nationwide notice to others of your exclusive right to use the name or mark.
- *Prima facie* evidence of the validity of the registration and your exclusive right to use the mark throughout the country.
- With certain exceptions, registration gives you an unquestionable right to use the name or mark.
- If you prove in court that someone violated your rights under the Trademark Act of 1946,[5] you will be entitled to recover their profits and damages from its use.
- The right to sue in federal court for trademark infringement regardless of the amount at stake and whether or not there is diversity of citizenship, i.e., regardless of whether you and the defendant operate in the same or different states.
- The right to have customs officials halt importation of counterfeit goods using your trademark.

The Oasis Press' *How to Develop & Market Creative Business Ideas* can explain, step-by-step, how to protect your ideas, as well as, trademarks and names. To obtain this book, contact your book source or:

The Oasis Press
(800) 228-2275

9.6 Section 1244 Stock

If you invest directly in a small corporation by transferring money or property (other than securities) to the corporation in exchange for its common stock — or preferred stock, if issued after July 18, 1984 — the stock will usually qualify as Section 1244 stock.[6] If it does, and the stock later becomes worthless or you sell it at a loss, Section 1244 of the Internal Revenue Code permits you to deduct up to $50,000 of your loss — $100,000 for a couple filing a joint return — as an ordinary deduction instead of as a capital loss for that year.

This can be very important, since you can fully deduct an ordinary loss from your taxable income, while capital losses can only be used to offset capital gains, if you have any, or $3,000 of ordinary income per year until your capital losses are used up.[7]

Any stock issued by a small business corporation will generally qualify as Section 1244 stock unless the corporation obtained half or more of its gross receipts from passive kinds of income, such as interest, dividends, and the like, in the five years before your loss is incurred.[8] A corporation qualifies as a small business corporation if the total invested in its stock is $1 million or less.[9]

In the past, for its stock to qualify for this special tax treatment, it was necessary for a corporation to adopt a plan to issue Section 1244 stock. This is no longer required. If the stock issued by your corporation meets the requirements of Section 1244, it will automatically qualify for ordinary loss treatment, up to the first one million dollars of stock issued. You should be aware, however, that capital contributions you make, where no stock is received by you for such money, will not qualify for ordinary loss treatment.[10]

Note that the $50,000/$100,000 limit on the amount of loss that can qualify for ordinary loss treatment is an annual limitation. Thus, if you sell part of your stock for a loss in each of several years, you could theoretically claim up to $50,000 or $100,000 of your loss each year[11] as an ordinary deduction under Section 1244. See Section 11.9 as to whether state law also provides favorable tax treatment for losses on stock in a small business corporation.

9.7 SBA and Other Government Loans

If you need to borrow money for your business and cannot obtain regular bank financing, you should not overlook the possibility of obtaining a loan through the U.S. Small Business Administration (SBA). While many small business owners are under the impression that it is virtually impossible to obtain an SBA loan unless a member of a minority group, this is not the case. Although the SBA does make special efforts to provide financing for minority-owned businesses, only a relatively small percentage of SBA loans are made to minority firms. Furthermore, a very high percentage of applications for SBA loans are approved when applications are properly submitted.

To apply for an SBA or conventional loan, you will most likely need to include a complete, well-documented business plan in your financial request presentation. To take you step-by-step through the business plan writing process, get a copy of Rhonda M. Abrams' recent book, *The Successful Business Plan: Secrets & Strategies.* Not only will you learn to write a strong business plan, you will also gain special insight into the financing request process by reading the numerous tips and suggestions provided by venture capitalists, bankers, and various business leaders. The book also features easy-to-follow financial worksheets and samples. For more information, contact your local book source or:

The Oasis Press
(800) 228-2275

SBA Loan Programs

The SBA, an agency of the U.S. government, guarantees intermediate and long-term loans to small firms and, to a limited extent, also makes direct loans to some small businesses. The SBA is not allowed to grant such financial assistance unless the borrower is unable to obtain private-sector financing on reasonable terms. The SBA does not compete with banks or other lenders; instead, it works with private lenders to assure availability of capital to potentially profitable small firms.

For your firm to qualify for SBA financial assistance, it must come within the current definition of a "small business." In general, these are the types of small businesses eligible for SBA financing:

- Manufacturers with a maximum of 500 to 1,500 employees, depending upon the industry in which the applicant is engaged;
- Retailers with less than $3.5 million in annual sales — up to $13.5 million for some types of retailers;
- Wholesaling firms with not more than 100 employees;
- General construction firms, whose annual sales have averaged less than $9.5 million for the last three fiscal years; lower limits apply to various special trade construction firms;
- Service firms with annual receipts not in excess of $3.5 to $14.5 million, depending on the industry; and
- Other definitions apply for businesses engaged in activities, such as agriculture and transportation.

Private lenders that are eligible to make SBA-guaranteed loans or participate in SBA financing packages include banks, savings and loans, and certain other lenders. The SBA has several types of loan programs for small businesses.

Guaranteed Loans

Most SBA financing actually consists of loans by banks or other lenders that are guaranteed by the SBA. This enables the small business to obtain such loans at reasonable interest rates because the bank's risk is largely eliminated.

As the borrower, you must put up a reasonable amount of equity or collateral. These loans are usually secured by fixed assets, real estate, and inventory and are limited in term to seven years for working capital loans or 10 years for purchasing fixed assets. Construction loans can be for as long as 25 years.

Under this program, the bank or other private lender deals with the SBA, and you deal with the bank, not the SBA. You will, however, need to do the following in applying for such a loan or any other SBA financing:

- Define the amount you need to borrow and the purposes for which the funds will be used.
- Describe the collateral you will offer as security.
- Determine from a bank that a conventional loan is not available.
- Prepare current financial statements, preferably with your accountant's assistance. These would include, at a minimum, a relatively current balance sheet and an income statement for the previous full year and for the current year up to the date of the balance sheet.
- Prepare personal financial statements of the owners, partners, or stockholders owning more than 20% of the stock of the company.

Direct Loans

If you are unable to obtain sufficient conventional financing or SBA guaranteed loan funds, you may in some cases be able to obtain a direct loan from the SBA of up to $150,000; however, these direct loans are hard to get, and can only be made if the SBA has funds available.

In recent years, the funds available for lending by the SBA have been quite limited, so that eligible borrowers are frequently turned away because the SBA simply doesn't have any money to lend. When made, these loans are usually offered on a participation basis with a bank or other lender, where the bank oversees the loan payments and loan servicing on behalf of itself and the SBA.

Other SBA Programs

New legislation frequently adds to and modifies the number and scope of SBA loan programs. Other such programs include:

- Seasonal lines of credit;
- Economic opportunity loans for entrepreneurs who are physically handicapped or members of a minority group;
- Short-term contract loan guarantees;
- Energy loans to small firms to install, sell, service, develop, or manufacture solar energy or energy-saving devices; and
- Disaster recovery loans to firms harmed by natural disasters.

Since the nature, scope, and availability of funds under these numerous programs are constantly changing, you should consult your bank or local SBA offices, if you think your firm may qualify under one of these special financial assistance programs.

U.S. Department of Housing and Urban Development

The U.S. Department of Housing and Urban Development (HUD) makes Urban Development Action Grants (UDAG) to cities in economically distressed areas. The cities are then able to use these UDAG funds to make second-mortgage loans to private developers who are able to leverage these loans by borrowing at least five times such amounts — three times in small towns — from private sources. The purpose of such loans is to encourage new investment and development in depressed areas.

U.S. Department of Commerce

The Economic Development Administration (EDA) of the U.S. Department of Commerce makes direct loans and offers loan guarantees to businesses, in areas with low family incomes or suffering from high unemployment, to promote creation or retention of jobs for residents of such areas.

To qualify for this financing, your business must be located in an EDA redevelopment area and you need to demonstrate that the venture will directly benefit local residents and will not create local over-capacity for the industry in question. Application for EDA loan assistance is a long and complex process, taking much longer for processing than typical SBA loans.

Farmers Home Administration

The Farmers Home Administration (FmHA) can perhaps be thought of as an SBA for rural areas. It offers insured and guaranteed loans to develop business and industry in nonurban areas with populations of under 50,000. Like the SBA program, FmHA loan guarantees are for up to 90% of the total amount of the loan and are made for up to 30 years for financing real estate acquisition, 15 years for machinery and equipment, and 7 years for working capital. FmHA loan guarantees are not available for agricultural production.

Unlike SBA loan guarantees, there is no dollar limit on FmHA loan guarantees, nor does the FmHA make direct loans. Applicants for FmHA loan guarantees must not only have adequate collateral and good business histories, they must also demonstrate that the project will have a favorable economic impact and will create new jobs in the area — not merely shifting business activity and jobs from one area to another. Preference is given:

- To businesses who are expanding, rather than transferring into an area;
- To projects in open country areas or towns with populations of under 25,000; and
- To business owners who are military veterans.

Other Federal Loan Programs

Other major federal loan programs are provided through the Federal Land Bank Association, Production Credit Association, and the Federal Intermediate Credit Bank. These organizations offer loans to businesses that provide services to farmers. These loans can be for purchasing land and equipment and for obtaining start-up working capital.

SBICs and MESBICs

In addition to direct loans and guarantees from government agencies, don't overlook possible loans or equity financing from Small Business Investment Companies (SBICs) and Minority Enterprise Small Business Investment Companies (MESBICs) as possible sources of financing. Both are licensed and regulated by the SBA to provide equity capital, long-term loans, and management assistance to small businesses.

SBIC and MESBIC loans are usually subordinated to loans from other creditors and are typically made for five- to seven-year terms. Both types of investment companies are privately owned and thus tend to favor loans to established companies with significant net worth rather than new business start ups.

Be aware that you may have to give up a large part of the equity in your business if you obtain SBIC financing. An SBIC is not permitted to control a company (50% or greater ownership) it lends to, but typically an SBIC lender will insist on debt that is convertible into common stock, warrants, and options, which may give it up to 49% ownership in your company.

An SBIC will also want seats on your board of directors, will impose controls and restrictions on the way your business operates, and may insist upon salary limits for the principal owners. SBIC financing does not come without a price.

MESBICs serve only those small firms that are owned by members of economically or socially disadvantaged minority groups.

Business Development Corporations

Business Development Corporations are Local Development Companies (LDC), SBA Section 502, and Certified Development Companies (CDC), SBA Section 503, organized by local residents to promote economic development in their particular communities. These entities do not make working capital loans or loans to purchase free-standing equipment.

Instead, LDCs or CDCs will arrange for SBA-guaranteed bank loans and sale of SBA-guaranteed debentures for up to 90% financing for 25 years for land acquisition, building construction, or renovation and purchase of fixed assets such as machinery and equipment.

State Loan Programs

For information on what state business loan programs may be available in this state, refer to Section 11.9.

9.8 Mail Order Sales

If your business involves selling goods by mail order, you need to be aware of a regulation by the Federal Trade Commission that deals with mail order sales, Rule 435.1.[12] This federal regulation requires any business soliciting mail order sales to be prepared to ship the merchandise within 30 days after an order is received, unless it has clearly stated in its solicitation that orders will not be shipped for a longer period, such as 60 days. Otherwise, the solicitation will be considered as an unfair and deceptive trade practice.

In addition, if you receive an order and for some reason you cannot ship it within 30 days, or the period stated in your solicitation, you must:

- Immediately notify the customer and offer to either cancel the order and receive a refund or consent to the delay in shipment.
- Indicate when you will be able to ship or that you do not know when you will be able to ship the order.
- Provide other required information to the customer, which will vary in content depending upon when you expect to be able to ship.

Rule 435.1 is fairly complex and difficult to understand, but you need to understand and be familiar with it if you sell goods by mail order. If you are going into the mail order business and want a single source of information on state and federal mail order laws, obtain the *Mail Order Legal Manual*, by Erwin J. Keup, from your book source or:

The Oasis Press
(800) 228-2275

State Sales and Use Taxes

If you sell across state lines to customers in states where you have no offices, employees, or other presence, the sale is usually not subject to sales tax in either state, since it is an interstate sale; however, technically, such sales are subject to use tax in the customer's state. A use tax is sort of a shadow of the sales tax and, in most states, applies where the sales tax doesn't.

The U.S. Supreme Court and other courts generally have not supported attempts of the various states to force out-of-state retailers to collect use tax on mail order or other sales made to residents of the taxing state, so that most mail order firms tend to treat such interstate sales as being tax-free, or tell the customers that it is up to them to report the purchase and pay the use tax, which they rarely do.

Unfortunately, in the last few years, many states have enacted new and broader sales and use tax laws. Many of these laws require out-of-state retailers, who advertise in the local media or send substantial amounts of direct mail/catalog solicitations into the state, to register as retailers subject to sales or use tax in the state and to treat such direct sales as taxable.

Some states are aggressively enforcing these new laws, which will definitely cramp the style of many mail order firms if these laws stand up in court. On the other hand, some states, like Massachusetts, have passed such legislation; but, because of doubts as to its constitutionality, these states will not attempt enforcement until proposed federal legislation is enacted.

Even if these new state laws are held to be unconstitutional, a bill has been working its way through Congress in recent years that would specifically grant states the right to require out-of-state sellers to collect use tax on sales made into the state, with certain restrictions. The bill, as it currently stands, would provide exceptions for small businesses, since having to file and pay sales or use taxes to all 50 states would be extremely expensive and onerous for small firms, and would effectively put small mail order firms out of business if they were not exempted.

Note that, unlike the proposed federal legislation, the new state laws adopted in recent years do not generally make an exception for small firms.

To summarize, don't assume that in many states interstate sales are still free of sales tax. If the proposed federal legislation passes, you will probably be required to collect and pay sales or use tax in all 50 states fairly soon after any such enactment.

9.9 Environmental Laws Affecting Your Business

As the world becomes more crowded and as the damaging effects of two centuries of unrestrained industrial development becomes more apparent on the environment, political attempts to remedy these problems, particularly the problems of pollution and toxic emissions, have resulted in a flood of legislation, regulations, and litigation involving environmental matters. While this is probably all to the good in the larger sense, some of the immediate effects of these new environmental restrictions have been to create another whole layer of complex and often conflicting government regulations on business, plus a virtual minefield of legal exposure for companies of all sizes.

For small businesses, most of which do not have in-house legal staffs and can hardly afford the large legal fees needed for professional guidance through this maze of regulations, the effect of the growing body of environmental laws is especially harsh. Small businesses are also disproportionately affected by the heavy costs of complying with various mandated emissions requirements, which often require large capital expenditures for sophisticated new pollution control equipment.

While this section cannot do much more than scratch the surface of the environmental law exposure and increased operational complexities most firms are going to be faced with from now on, the outline below explains some of the main problem areas that you need to be at least passingly familiar with. This section also provides a capsule description of the major areas of federal environmental law that may currently apply to your business or which may apply at some time in the future.

Perhaps the most pervasive of the environmental laws, with the most devastating potential consequences for the unwary, are the environmental clean-up laws, and the legal liability that these laws attach to real estate that has been contaminated by hazardous substances. The main laws that apply in this area are the Comprehensive Environmental Response Compensation and Recovery Act[13] (CERCLA or the Superfund law) and the Resource Conservation and Recovery Act (RCRA).[14]

Environmental Clean-Up Laws

CERCLA and RCRA apply to virtually every real estate transaction. While RCRA applies primarily to currently generated hazardous waste, including limits on creation of waste and requirements for disposing of it, CERCLA is more focused on cleaning up hazardous substances that have been spilled or dumped in the past.

CERCLA deals with all kinds of pollution: air, surface water, groundwater, and soil. It covers virtually every type of hazardous substances as defined under CERCLA, the Clean Water Act, the Clean Air Act, or the Toxic Substances Control Act. There are, however, major exceptions for petroleum and certain petroleum derivatives. The main thrust of CERCLA is to impose liability on private owners of property to clean up hazardous wastes that they have created. CERCLA would also apply to owners of the inherited property, if the property in question was already contaminated when it was acquired.

CERCLA Liability

In short, even if you were not responsible for creating a contamination problem, if you acquire real estate that is already contaminated — and it later becomes apparent that there has been a spill or dumping that requires an environmental clean up, possibly at astronomical cost — you are liable for the costs of the clean up, if you are the current owner. You can't simply walk away from the property and let the government take it in lieu of paying the clean-up costs.

Once the owner, you are the responsible party and may be held liable for costs that exceed the value of the property many times over. You may even become liable somewhere down the road if you sell a business — an existing corporation, for instance — that has formerly owned contaminated property. The government could eventually institute environmental proceedings against the current property owner, who then sues all the prior legal owners of the property, including you, for indemnity or reimbursement.

Of course, you may be able to sue the prior owner or anyone in the chain of prior owners for indemnification, if they are still in existence and can be found. However, since that is a pretty slim thread upon which to hang your financial survival, you need to take precautions up front, before acquiring any real property, to protect yourself from possible environmental liability for clean up under CERCLA.

The following are some things you can and should do to reduce your risk in any real estate or existing business acquisition:

- Exercise considerable diligence concerning the current condition and past uses of any real estate involved in a transaction. Also, if buying an existing corporation, you need to find out what properties it owned in the past and be concerned whether any such properties may have been contaminated by hazardous substances.

- Be particularly wary of any sites that have been used as gas stations, landfill areas, locations of dry cleaners, chemical or other industrial production processes, battery production, recycling, or metal plating. Be extremely cautious if the site contains underground storage tanks.

- Consider retaining an environmental audit firm to do detailed site inspections and evaluations to determine if there may be a contamination problem.

- In a business or real estate purchase agreement, require written representations and warranties about the site from the seller and include provisions under which he or she will indemnify you if there is a problem. Be mindful of the seller's financial viability, in case you should be forced to seek indemnity from him or her. A promise isn't worth the paper it's written on, if the seller doesn't have the wherewithal to make good on it.

Even though under the Superfund law there is an innocent purchaser defense, you must be able to demonstrate that you made appropriate inquiry before acquiring the property to determine any pre-existing contamination problem. There is little guidance in the law at this point as to what constitutes an appropriate inquiry, so perhaps you should not expect to escape liability under that rule. The best defense is to avoid purchasing property that is contaminated by taking the steps outlined above. Even if such steps fail to discover a lurking environmental problem, at least you will have a much stronger argument to make under the innocent purchaser defense if you have done a due diligence survey and had an environmental audit performed by a reputable firm.

RCRA Requirements

RCRA contains a comprehensive set of rules for managing hazardous wastes, including petroleum-based substances, and regulating those who generate hazardous wastes, transport them, and store, treat, or dispose of them. Penalties for violations include monetary penalties of up to $25,000 a day, plus imprisonment.

One important focus of the RCRA law is on underground storage tanks (USTs), many of which are known to be leaking gasoline or other contaminants into the surrounding soil and groundwater. Under RCRA, much of the regulation of USTs is left to state governments. Thus, under federal regulations, the owner of a UST must notify the state of the tank's existence, including tanks that were taken out of service after January 1, 1974.[15] New USTs must satisfy federal performance standards, which generally require that they be constructed of fiberglass-reinforced plastic or steel that is cathodically protected from corrosion.[16] Furthermore, all existing USTs must be upgraded to federal standards by December 22, 1998,[17] which will result in some major expenditures for many small businesses, such as service stations.

Clean Water Act

Under the Clean Water Act,[18] the federal Environmental Protection Agency (EPA) and individual states are the watchdogs of water pollution standards. It also allows private citizens to sue to enforce the act. Penalties for violations can be as high as $50,000 a day, and even negligent, but unintentional, violations can result in imprisonment. For certain existing facilities, this law provides for a system of EPA permits for discharging certain amounts of water pollutants.

Wetlands Development

Portions of the Clean Water Act require that all proposed development activities, which involve the dredging or filling of wetlands, obtain permits from the U.S. Army Corps of Engineers.[19] Thus, before you acquire real property that you plan to develop in any way, you need to do a careful survey to determine if the property lies within an area that is considered to be a wetland. Otherwise, you may end up with a piece of property which is undevelopable and which can hardly be sold at all, even for a huge loss. This has been a trap for more than one unwitting buyer of land in wetlands districts, since wetlands include much more than swamps and marshes. Many dry-looking parcels may also fall within the regulatory definition. Furthermore, be aware that many states have adopted wetlands restrictions, which may require you to also obtain state development permits.

Clean Air Act

The Clean Air Act of 1970, which was substantially amended and strengthened by the Clean Air Act of 1991, among other things, restricts the ability of stationary sources of air pollutants to emit various pollutants into the atmosphere at new or modified facilities.[20] States are allowed to implement their own rules for controlling air pollution levels. Recent amendments to this law in 1991 have greatly expanded its impact on small businesses. As they go into effect, these new amendments will require a diverse number of air pollution controls. Some will include:

- Gasoline stations will need vapor-recovery devices on gasoline pumps.
- Furniture makers may need incinerators to burn off hydrocarbons released from spray-paint booths.
- Restaurants in smoggy areas will have to install containment units that collect hydrocarbon emissions from charcoal grills.

- Many bakeries will have to install oxidation devices or catalytic converters to neutralize the gases produced by fermenting yeast when dough is baked.
- Auto-body paint and repair shops will have to install extremely expensive equipment to catch hydrocarbon emissions from spray painting.
- Print shops will have to neutralize or eliminate use of chemicals that contribute to ozone formation.

As the foregoing examples indicate, the new requirements under the Clean Air Act of 1991 are very pervasive and will affect many nonindustrial types of businesses who would never have considered themselves to be polluters in the past. Companies that are sources of air pollutant emissions will have to obtain state-issued construction and operating permits under EPA rules. Small businesses will have to apply for permits at least every five years and file reports of their compliance with the law every six months, if they produce more than 100 tons per year of any ozone-forming pollutant. Ozone-forming pollutants are the main targets of the new legislation.

According to some experts, once these rules go into effect, a small business' main cost of complying with the clean air regulations is likely to be all the required paperwork. Penalties for violations are also very severe, with civil penalties as high as $25,000 a day for each violation, plus felony imprisonment and huge fines for willful or negligent releases of hazardous air pollutants. In addition, the EPA has set emissions fees of $25 a ton for every ton of regulated pollutants that a firm emits, up to $4,000 per year.

Toxic Substances Control Act

If your business is one that engages in the manufacturing, processing, or distribution of chemical substances, you may be required under the federal Toxic Substances Control Act (TSCA)[21] to report certain information to the EPA regarding the chemical substances and mixtures you use. The TSCA requires manufacturers to give a 90-day notification prior to producing a new chemical substance and, in some cases, for older chemicals. The EPA may require safety testing before approval of such a chemical. The TSCA also has extensive recordkeeping rules regarding use and disposal of toxic chemicals.

There are severe penalties for failing to make the required reports to the EPA, including civil and criminal penalties of $25,000 and up, plus up to a year's imprisonment for each violation. Each day the violation continues is considered a separate violation for purposes of the fines levied under the TSCA.

Pesticide Regulations

The Federal Insecticide, Fungicide and Rodenticide Act (FIFRA),[22] which amends the Federal Environmental Pesticides Control Act of 1972 (FEPCA), regulates both the manufacture and distribution of pesticides.

The National Environmental Policy Act of 1969 (NEPA)[23] requires an environmental impact statement (EIS) to be prepared with respect to major federal actions that significantly affect the quality of the human environment. While this would not, at first impression, seem to directly affect you, as a small business owner, the EIS requirement also applies in any situation where a federal agency approves some action by other persons, such as a private company. Also, many states have adopted similar EIS requirements, so that, for instance, when a local planning board approves a real estate development, an EIS may be required under state law, if not federal.

Environmental Impact Reports

In recent years, as the severe lung disease, cancer, and other health risks attributed to exposure to asbestos have come to light, a number of state and federal laws have been enacted to deal with this problem. In addition, huge numbers of individual damage suits for alleged harm to individuals, who were exposed to asbestos in the workplace and elsewhere, have resulted in enormous judgments against many companies, even forcing a giant building materials firm, Johns-Manville Corporation, into Chapter 11 bankruptcy to protect itself from a host of asbestos-related lawsuits.

Asbestos Regulation

Recent federal amendments to the TSCA and the Asbestos Hazard Emergency Response Act of 1986 (AHERA) have given the EPA power to issue regulations regarding asbestos in school buildings. In addition, Occupational Safety and Health Administration (OSHA) regulations[24] have been issued to limit asbestos exposure in the workplace and to set construction standards regarding use of asbestos.

Both OSHA and the EPA have issued regulations on noise emission standards, ranging from aircraft noise to protections of workers from hearing impairment in the workplace.

Noise Control

9.10 Consumer Credit Laws and Regulations

Many of the largest and most successful companies in America have gotten where they are, in part, by providing consumer credit to persons who buy their products. Classic examples would include such giant companies as Sears and General Motors, although countless smaller companies have also found that financing their customers' purchases can be a major boon to sales and that the interest earned on such credit can also become an important profit center in its own right.

The definition of consumer credit does not refer to the practice of allowing a client or customer to charge it and pay you at the end of the month, which is largely unregulated by the government. Instead, the following discussion deals with the situation where your business extends credit and charges interest during the period over which the loan amount (or amount financed) is being paid off by the customer.

The three main areas of the law regulating the extension of consumer credit, which affects nearly all businesses that grant such credit, are: the federal Equal Credit Opportunity Act, the federal Truth-in-Lending Act, and state laws that prohibit usury.

Equal Credit Opportunity Laws

If your business is engaged in providing consumer credit, note that you will most likely be subject to the provisions of the federal Equal Credit Opportunity Act (ECOA).[25] In general, the ECOA prohibits discrimination in credit transactions on the basis of race, color, religion, national origin, sex, age, or marital status.

The basic principle of this law is that each person applying for credit must be considered as an individual. This means, primarily, that there are very strict limits regarding what you may ask about marital status and about the spouse of the applicant. You may ask about marital status, but only to determine what rights and remedies you might have as a creditor — such as in a community property state — to refuse an applicant's credit.

The ECOA also forbids discrimination in providing credit because some or all of the applicant's income derives from public assistance programs, or because a person exercised a right, in good faith, under the Consumer Credit Protection Act.

Truth-in-Lending Requirements

If your business activities involve lending money, or if you sell to consumers on credit terms, you may have to comply with the federal Truth-in-Lending Act[26] and state laws such as those that prohibit the charging of usurious interest rates on loans or other credit transactions.

Regulations under the Truth-in-Lending Simplification and Reform Act provide that a business is not subject to the Truth-in-Lending rules unless it extended consumer credit at least 25 times in either the previous year or the current calendar year.[27] For loan transactions, required disclosures include:

- The annual percentage rate of interest;
- When the finance charge begins to accrue;
- The total amount of the finance charge;
- The number of payments to be made and the dollar amount of each payment;
- When payments are to be made;
- The total dollar amount of all payments;
- How any prepayment penalty and any late charges are to be computed;
- The amount of any prepaid finance charges and any deposit, plus the sum of the two;

- The amount financed;
- The existence of any balloon payment and its dollar amount;
- Annual statements of billing rights;
- Other information regarding security interests and rights to rescind; and
- Periodic billings to credit customers must include a number of disclosures regarding outstanding balances, how finance charges have been computed, and other items.

The rules regarding the Truth-in-Lending Act are far too complex to cover satisfactorily in a book of this nature; it can only alert you to the possibility that you may be required to comply with those rules and give you some sense of what will be required if the rules do apply to you. If you plan to extend credit to consumers — other than sending out bills requesting payment in full, without interest charge, after you have provided goods or services — you need to consult an attorney experienced in this area.

Fortunately, recent legislation has considerably simplified the truth-in-lending rules, and the Federal Reserve Board has published model disclosure statements and billing rights statements that can be used to satisfy the requirements of the truth-in-lending regulations.

Cash Discount Act

The Cash Discount Act (Public Law 97-25) permits sellers to offer a discount of any amount to customers who pay in cash or by check without running afoul of the truth-in-lending rules. The discount, in this case, has to be clearly disclosed and made available to all customers.[28] In the past, if you offered more than a 5% cash discount, you were considered to be imposing a finance charge on credit customers and had to give them all the required truth-in-lending disclosures.

Usury Laws

See Section 11.9 for a brief description of how this state's usury laws may apply to your business.

9.11 Employee or Independent Contractor?

As was pointed out in Section 5.2, there are some major advantages in hiring independent contractors rather than employees to work in your business. Not only do you gain considerable payroll tax savings by retaining independent contractors, but there are far fewer administrative headaches.

You don't have to withhold income and payroll taxes from payouts, provide workers' compensation coverage, or cover independent contractors in your retirement plan or other employee fringe benefit plans.

Unfortunately, just because you agree with someone you hire that they will be an independent contractor does not make it so for tax and legal purposes.

Thus, before you hire anyone to work for you as an independent contractor, you need to take a hard look at whether the IRS or a court of law would consider that person to be your employee rather than an independent contractor. While the IRS uses a 20-factor test to evaluate whether a person is or is not an employee, a few major warning flags will indicate to you whether the person is your employee or not. These include:

- The person works mostly or only for your firm. That is, the person is not like a lawyer, for example, who has a number of clients besides you that he or she works for.
- The worker is subject to your control, and you have the right to direct how the work is done, not just to demand a particular result.
- The person works in your office or establishment and does not have his or her own place of business, business cards, business name, etc.
- The kind of work the person does for you is normally done by employees, such as secretarial work.
- The person is not a licensed professional of any type.

Unless you are quite clear that the work relationship will not be considered that of employer/employee, be very careful about hiring someone as a so-called independent contractor. The consequences of being wrong can be quite severe. Here are just a few of the things that can happen if your independent contractor is held to be an employee:

- You are liable for not only the employer payroll taxes you failed to pay, but also for a portion of the employee taxes you failed to withhold (income taxes, FICA).

  If you treat someone as an independent contractor, you should report payments of $600 or more a year to that person on IRS *Form 1099-MISC*. If you do, and the IRS later determines that the person was really an employee, the back taxes you are liable for are limited to the employer payroll taxes, 20% of the employee's FICA tax you failed to withhold, and income tax withholding equal to only 1.5% of the wages you paid the person.

  If you do not file *Form 1099-MISC* and the person is reclassified as an employee, you are liable for 40% of the employee's FICA tax and income tax withholding equal to 3% of the wages — twice as much as if you would have filed *Form 1099-MISC*. Furthermore, there is now a $100 penalty for failure to file *Form 1099-MISC* and you will owe interest on the taxes due. It is no longer a bargain to "borrow" from the IRS.

  You may also be assessed other penalties if you did not have a reasonable basis for treating the person as a nonemployee and may be liable for up to 100% of the employee's FICA and income tax which you failed to withhold.

- If the person is hurt on the job and you have not provided workers' compensation insurance coverage, you will be liable for extensive legal damages.

- If your firm has a qualified retirement plan and you have not contributed to the plan on behalf of the person because he or she was not thought to be an employee at the time, the retirement plan could be disqualified for tax purposes for failing to cover the employee in question.

Thus, do not get stampeded into the independent contractor game by your friends and business associates who tell you how simple it is to avoid all those payroll taxes.

Note that the foregoing discussion of independent contractors summarizes federal rules only. Many states take an even more restrictive view than the IRS on the employee/independent contractor issue.

Independent Contractors Treated as Employees

There are a number of steps you may be able to take to make a stronger case for someone who works for you to be treated as an independent contractor. Obviously, not all of the following will necessarily be feasible in every case, and a number of these steps, if implemented, may require some significant changes in the way you do business. But if you can follow most of the suggestions below with regard to a given worker, you will improve your odds against having that worker reclassified as an employee by the IRS.

- Have a written agreement, signed by both parties, that makes it clear that the company doesn't have the right to control the methods or procedures for the worker to accomplish the work contracted for. Include language in the agreement that it is the worker's obligation to pay income and self-employment taxes on amounts earned, and that he or she will receive a 1099 reflecting amounts earned, if $600 or more.

- Try to avoid setting working hours by hour or week. It would be all right to specify starting and completion dates for the work.

- Make it clear that if additional workers are needed to help, the contractor will hire and pay them.

- The arrangement should make it clear that the contractor is not limited to working exclusively for you, but is free to take on other work from other customers.

- Compensation should be based on what work is performed rather than the time spent to do it. This may require careful estimates so that the worker is fairly paid, not overpaid, for the work done.

- Avoid providing office space to the contractor on a regular basis.

- Let the workers be responsible for their own training, if that is possible.

- Each worker should be advised, in writing, to provide for their own liability, workers compensation, health, and disability insurance coverage.

- Costs such as meals, transportation, and clothing should be built into the contract price of the job, rather than being billed directly to your account.
- It should be clear in your agreement with the worker that he or she can't be fired and can't quit. The worker's job is to fulfill a given work contract.
- Don't give the worker other work to fill in during downtime. This may mean, of course, that you will have to pay the worker somewhat more for the work done than you otherwise would, if you wish to keep him or her happy.
- Don't pay bonuses to a person you treat as an independent contractor.

9.12 Whether You Should Incorporate Outside Your State

For most small businesses, there is little reason to consider incorporating your business under the laws of some state other than where you live. In fact, there are a few very good reasons why you should not incorporate in a different state:

- Your corporation may have to pay a qualification fee to transact business in your home state as a foreign corporation. See Section 11.2 on this point.
- If your attorney is a local lawyer, he or she is likely to be much less familiar with the corporate law rules of some other state than those of your state. Thus, your attorney is likely to either charge you more for corporate law advice if he or she has to research the law of an unfamiliar jurisdiction or give you less accurate advice than he or she could about your state's corporation laws.
- In many states, your corporation will have to pay some sort of minimum annual franchise tax or capital tax to the state of incorporation, even if you do no business there.

Also, don't believe the newspaper ads that tell you to incorporate in wonderful, tax-free Nevada or some other state and avoid your state's corporation income or franchise taxes. It doesn't work. If your corporation does business in your state, it pays the same taxes on its taxable income regardless of whether it is incorporated in your state, Nevada, or in the Grand Duchy of Luxembourg.

Perhaps the only valid reason why you might want to incorporate elsewhere would be to take advantage of some particular provision or flexibility available under the corporate laws of a particular state. If you own all the stock of your company, it is unlikely you would ever need to take advantage of any such provisions, which are usually more important where different groups are struggling for control of a corporation's board of directors or the like.

9.13 Foreign Investment in U.S. Businesses

Under the Foreign Direct Investment and International Financial Data Improvements Act of 1990, foreign individuals owning or acquiring 10% or more voting interest in U.S. businesses, including interests in U.S. real estate, must report certain information, including annual financial and operating data, to the U.S. Department of Commerce. Failure to file can result in civil penalties of $2,500 to $25,000.[29]

Reporting requirements under this law may be summarized as follows:

- *Form BE-13*, *Form BE-13C*, and *Form BE-14* — These forms are initial investment reports representing the establishment or acquisition of a U.S. affiliate.

  A person is excused from filing these reports only in the case of purchases of U.S. real estate to be used exclusively for personal, non-business purposes.

- *Form BE-605* and *Form BE-606B* — These forms are used as quarterly reports for qualifying reporters.

- *Form BE-15* — This is an annual reporting form.

- *Form BE-12* — This form is for quinquennial (five-year) reporting in benchmark surveys.

For more information on this new law, write to:

Bureau of Economic Analysis
U.S. Department of Commerce
BE-50 (IN)
Washington, DC 20230
(202) 523-0547

9.14 Emerging Trends and Issues

Today, businesses of every size and type are being buffeted by the ever-accelerating rate of change in the business, economic, social, and political environment in which they must operate. Part of the reason, is that Congress, along with 50 state legislatures and countless government agencies, spew out reams of new laws and regulations all year long, in ever greater volume. As Benjamin Franklin once put it, "No man is safe in his bed when the Congress is in session."

To blame all of the disorienting changes that are occurring on lawmakers, however, is unfair since it seems that life in general is becoming more complex and unpredictable by the day. Accordingly, this section attempts to provide you, as a business owner, with a brief overview of developing and current trends in the business environment.

The Changing Economic Environment

Changes in the global economic structure in the wake of the collapse of communism throughout Eastern Europe and the break up of the Soviet Union, and the shift toward more efficient, free-market-oriented economies in places like Poland and Argentina, are creating a world that will soon look very different from the one you have become accustomed to since 1945.

While many applaud the changes taking place abroad, the net result seems to be the creation of a far more competitive world. U.S. businesses, even relatively small ones, are running up against increasingly severe international competition. Many firms that never gave a thought to export markets may have to get involved in doing business overseas if they wish to continue as viable operations in the global economy. Furthermore, even if your business is of a type or size that seems to make foreign competition seem irrelevant, you are still unlikely to completely elude its indirect effects, such as labor rates, increased automation, and downsizing.

Labor Rates

Low labor rates abroad are causing the permanent shutdown of many large and small U.S. manufacturers, who can no longer meet the competition from Japan, Mexico, and elsewhere, or from U.S. manufacturers who move their operations overseas to places like Indonesia or Thailand, where wages are lower. This trend seems likely to continue and will have a rippling effect throughout the U.S. economy, adversely affecting many of the small firms that are either suppliers to large U.S. manufacturers or whose service operations (restaurants, retail shops and the like) will be drastically affected as larger companies close plants and make massive and permanent layoffs of thousands of employees. This is a rude fact of modern life of which almost anyone doing business in the so-called "Rust Belt" is already acutely aware, and which the recession that began in 1991 is rapidly introducing to the parts of the country that have, up until now, escaped the brunt of the effects of increased foreign competition.

Automation

Increasing automation, both here and abroad, is also likely to have a dramatic effect on employment and competitiveness in this country and throughout the world. Automation has been a factor in replacing blue-collar labor for decades now. With the recent and continual explosion in computing power and sophistication, vast numbers of middle managers and other white-collar workers are beginning to be displaced. With the advent of expert systems and "artificial intelligence," which are still in their infancy, but rapidly coming into their own, it is difficult to say whose job, if anyone's, will be safe in a few years.

While the ability to replace workers with computers or computer-driven machinery may be very attractive, from a cost-savings standpoint to you as an employer, its societal effects are hard to predict and may prove to be very adverse to the overall business environment. The field of information processing is moving rapidly, and it is difficult to visualize how the world and the U.S. economy may look in as little as five or six years.

Downsizing

Largely in response to ever-fiercer foreign competition, employer down-sizing continued at a rapid pace in 1991, up sharply from 1990. According to an American Management Association (AMA) survey for the year ending in June 1991, 55.5% of the organizations polled engaged in downsizing and 60% of those firms had also made significant staff cut-backs in the previous year, suggesting that firms are now cutting even deeper and deeper. The survey revealed that the cuts were heaviest on the Pacific Coast, averaging 12.6% of the workforce among firms reporting downsizing. Middle management jobs, which are estimated to make up something like 5% to 8% of the total work force, accounted for more than 16% of the jobs cut in the 1991 survey period.

While much of this change seems frightening to business people, as well as to their employees — the hundreds of thousands, perhaps even millions, of skilled management and white-collar workers who are being given their pink slips and severance packages by downsizing corporations over the next few years — it may also give rise to fantastic new opportunities.

Many of these people are likely to start their own smaller businesses due to the permanent disappearance of so many middle management or automatable jobs. Many may even keep working for their former firms as independent contractors or consultants. In addition to enriching the over-all business environment by creating a major upsurge in the formation of new, small, and flexible business entities, firms that cater to the needs of other small businesses may find the coming decade to be one of explo-sive growth and unparalleled opportunity.

Telecommuting

One of the most predictable trends, which is already well under way, is the growth of telecommuting, where more and more people work out of their homes, communicating with their clients or employers by use of personal computers, modems, faxes, or multiple phone lines. Already, some employers, like certain government agencies in Washington, D.C., are tak-ing an intermediate step by setting up satellite telecommuting offices in suburban areas. By going to these nearby satellite offices, equipped with computer workstations, many workers can, on most days, avoid long and arduous commutes to downtown offices by piping their work product elec-tronically to the main office instead.

A 1991 survey by Link Resources Corporation, a research and consulting firm, showed telecommuting has become a major factor in the economy almost overnight. The survey estimated that company employees who work at home part- or full-time increased in 1991 by 38%, over 1989, to 38.4 million individuals, most of whom are believed to be telecommuting. The survey apparently did not even take into account home-based busi-nesses, which are also believed to be proliferating at truly startling rates.

The enormous changes in the workplace that are already taking place will obviously create tremendous new business opportunities, as well as problems, in the coming years. These should include the obvious ones such as sales of more fax machines and other equipment and supplies for home office use, as well as less obvious opportunities like restaurants that deliver meals to busy home workers, and doubtless many other novel kinds of services and products that no one has even conceived of yet.

Pending Law Changes

The election of a new administration in the 1992 presidential election is likely to lead to significant tax law changes in 1993. President Clinton has already promised that reviving the economy and attacking the deficit would be his first priorities. At the time of this printing, various tax law changes are being examined. Some of the major tax changes you should be looking out for, which may have already passed by the time you read this, would include:

- Mandatory health care coverage — This is likely to be the biggest item on the entire legislative agenda in Congress this year, as the battle over what to do about the increasing inaccessibility of medical care to large segments of the population gets fought out on Capitol Hill. Most of the legislative proposals that have been floating around Congress for the last year or two would involve a combination of:

  - Requiring that most, or all employers, provide some level of medical coverage for their full-time employees, and

  - Additional payroll taxes to finance the cost of government-provided health care for individuals outside of the work force. In some of the proposals, the employer would be given a choice of paying a hefty tax for national health insurance or providing coverage for employees; other proposals would require both, which could be a very difficult financial burden for many small businesses, even those that already provide medical insurance for their employees.

  In a related issue, close to the hearts of all self-employed individuals, some of the proposals would also put self-employed persons and S corporation shareholder/employees on the same footing as incorporated business owners, by increasing the deductible amount of medical insurance for such business owners from 25% of the amount incurred to 100%.

- Capital gains tax relief — The United States is one of the few countries that taxes capital gains at nearly the same rate as other income. Many of the fastest growing companies in the world don't tax capital gains at all, and much of the available evidence indicates that reducing capital gains in the late 1970s and early 1980s had a remarkable effect on stimulating capital investment and boosting economic growth in this country. Perhaps Congress will see this message this year and cut capital gains tax.

- Other incentives — Look for various other business tax incentives to be resurrected, such as restoring the investment tax credit, accelerated depreciation, or new jobs credits. Since the government has a history of taking such tax gifts back after a year or two, you may want to act fairly quickly to find out more about and take quick advantage of any such capital investment incentives that may be enacted.

The new federal Civil Rights Act of 1991 (CRA91), which became immediately effective upon enactment on November 29, 1991, is certain to make life a lot more complicated for all covered employers in the area of employment practices.

New Civil Rights Laws

The new law's most controversial aspect will be in the "disparate impact" cases, where a company's employment practices, although not shown to be intentionally discriminatory, have a disparate (unequal) impact on employment of protected groups.

For example, if a company is located in an area where 80% of the population consists of Native Americans, but only 5% of its employees are Native Americans, there may be grounds for a disparate impact claim against the employer, under prior civil rights law as well as the new CRA91 provisions, regardless of employer intent.

Under prior law, the U.S. Supreme Court held that the burden of proof was on the employee who alleged discrimination. The employee had to identify the particular business practice of the employer that resulted in the disparity. By contrast, under the new CRA91, the employee is relieved of this burden of proof if he or she can simply show that the employer failed to select an alternative employment practice (such as hiring quotas), that would not have had a disparate impact — that is, that would not have had a negative impact on the minority or other protected group. Instead, the burden of proof in these cases is now shifted to the employer, who must show that the challenged employment practice regarding hiring, promotions, pay, or other aspects of employment is job-related for the position in question and consistent with business necessity.

This vagueness regarding job-relatedness business necessity is what President Bush initially expressed concerns over, arguing that many firms would find it easier to simply adopt minority hiring quotas than to attempt to prove the "business necessity" defense in court. There are no easy answers as to what policy a company should adopt in this regard. It may seem that one safe way to avoid discrimination suits under the new law would be to adopt some sort of quota system; yet, using the quota system generates issues of unfairness and possible employee morale problems.

CRA91 also considerably expands the monetary damages that can be awarded in cases of intentional discrimination. Before, an employer who lost such a discrimination suit was usually liable only for back pay, front pay, lost benefits, attorney's fees, and court costs. Now, under CRA91 — which may even be retroactive in effect — compensatory damages may also be allowed in addition to other monetary damages. CRA91 also overrides a U.S. Supreme Court case that had limited fees — a flat $40 — recoverable by a claimant for expert witness fees.

In light of the foregoing changes in the Civil Rights Act of 1991, the odds, as well as the costs, of losing a discrimination action have increased significantly for employers. The new rules will make it much more attractive for plaintiffs to file such suits, both for claims of intentional discrimination and in disparate impact cases. Employers can now expect a great many more such claims to be filed. Thus, however fair you may feel your firm's employment practices are, if you are a large enough firm — generally 15 or more employees — to be subject to the Civil Rights Act, this may be a good time to consult an attorney who is familiar with employment discrimination matters to see what, if any, steps you may need to take to protect your business from liability in this area.

Sexual Harassment

The Clarence Thomas–Anita Hill hearings brought the issue of sexual harassment to a new and heightened level of awareness among the public. While sexual harassment, as such, is not mentioned anywhere in Title VII of the federal Civil Rights Act, the Equal Employment Opportunity Commission (EEOC) and the courts have long accepted such harassment as being illegal and discriminatory. In addition, many states have adopted specific laws banning sexual harassment.

Because this is now such a highly topical issue, many employment law experts expect an upsurge in litigation involving sexual harassment claims, so you should probably take a fresh look at your firm's policies regarding this subject. See Section 5.8 for a discussion of the federal sexual harassment law and steps you can take to protect your firm from being sued for failing to take proper steps to prevent such acts from occurring.

Other Legal Trends and New or Pending Legislation

Listed and discussed below are several other legal trends and new or pending legislation you should know about for future reference. This information provides possible tips for issues or rules which may affect your business.

Family Leave Legislation

Congress attempted in both 1990 and 1991 to pass a parental and family leave act. Both times, the legislation was vetoed; President Bush's veto, however, was barely sustained in 1991. The act was finally signed into law by President Clinton on February 5, 1993. The new Family and Medical Leave Act of 1993 will apply to all companies (as well as non-profit entities) that have 50 or more employees within a 75-mile radius. The law provides unpaid leaves of absence to employees for up to 12 weeks for family purposes such as:

- The birth or adoption of a child; or
- A serious health condition of the employee or a spouse, child, or parent.

As an employer, you would have to continue health insurance coverage during such a leave and hold the job, or a comparable position, open until the employee returns. In addition, a serious illness must be verified by a physician's certification, and you, as the employer, may require a second medical opinion if desired. The employee is also required to provide you with 30 days' notice for foreseeable leaves of absence for a birth, adoption, or planned medical treatment.

This new mandatory Family and Medical Leave Law will generally become effective August 5, 1993.

Shared Work Programs

Another program that has been adopted in a number of states and appears to be growing in acceptance is a shared work program under state unemployment insurance laws. Essentially, what the shared work programs do is allow employees to collect full unemployment benefits while still working a minimal number of hours per week. This not only benefits the employee, but can also be very helpful in the case of an employer who, due to the recession or other business difficulties, has to temporarily cut back the hours it can employ workers for a period of time until business conditions improve. In states where there is no such program, it is often necessary to lay a worker off entirely for him or her to collect unemployment benefits.

Under shared work programs, you, the employer, can often retain a good employee during a temporary slow period, while the employee supplements his or her unemployment benefits with a modest amount of wages from working part-time. Together, this may be sufficient to keep the employee in question from taking a permanent position elsewhere. Then, if things improve in a few months, you may be able to restore the cutback employee to full-time status again.

These shared work programs make a lot of sense for everyone, so if your firm is getting to a point where you are considering having to lay off good employees whom you don't want to lose, be sure to contact your local state unemployment office to find out if your state has adopted such a program. If so, you may be able to keep personnel on a part-time basis until business picks up again. Good people are hard to find, and you don't want to lose them.

Wrongful Termination of Employees

Wrongful termination of employees is another area of growing importance in terms of employer/employee relations. For a great many years, it was generally the rule that an employer was free to fire employees "at will," without needing any good reason to do so, unless there was some sort of formal contractual arrangement or collective bargaining agreement.

This situation has begun to change in recent years, mainly as a result of a number of revolutionary court decisions in California, which hold employers liable for damages for wrongfully discharging employees. Initially, such cases tended to involve extreme and egregious situations, where employees fired whistle-blowing employees who threatened to report fraudulent activities of their employer.

However, as the legal concept of wrongful termination has become more accepted and spread to courts in states other than California, the scope of what constitutes "wrongful termination" has begun to expand, and at this point, it is difficult to say how far this new right will be extended in the future.

Suffice it to say that in the future, employers are going to have to become increasingly careful about documenting their reasons for firing any employee. The days when you, as an employer, could choose to fire an employee just because you got up on the wrong side of the bed that morning may be coming to an end, soon — at least in a number of states.

Striker Replacement Law

Another piece of legislation that was introduced in Congress in 1991 but which didn't pass was the Worker Replacement Act. Since it has strong American Federation of Labor & Congress of Industrial Organizations (AFL-CIO) backing, it is by no means dead, and its passage could be extremely damaging to small employers.

This is a hot issue and one you may want to write or call your Congressperson about before it is too late. The legislation, as it was proposed in 1991, would prohibit employers from permanently replacing workers who go on strike. This would fundamentally alter the balance between unions and employers that has been in effect since the New Deal days, tilting the balance strongly in favor of unions.

The law, if passed, would require that you refrain from hiring permanent replacement employees during a strike, and you would have to give the strikers their jobs back when they are ready to return to work after the strike is over.

At present, companies can fire workers who go on strike over economic issues, such as wages, but not if the company refuses to bargain in good faith with the union, or if the walkout stems from other acts of the employer.

The proposed law would extend the firing ban to strikes over economic issues, which are usually the reason for labor walkouts. By extending this protection only to unionized workers — as the House version of the bill, H.R. 55 would do — such a law would give unions tremendous clout in organizing the workers of small companies, since they would be able to offer a major advantage that is not available to nonunion workers.

Finally, the proposed legislation would permit any two workers of a nonunionized small business to walk off a job in protest of working conditions, in effect giving them the benefits of a union without their having to go through the process of a certification election to establish a collective bargaining unit. This provision could also prove to be a major burden on small, nonunion employers.

Although this bill didn't get enacted in 1992, it is expected to be given high priority under the new Democratic administration.

An article in the January 1992 issue of *California Lawyer* reported that, despite hard economic times, the demand for lawyers in the field of environmental law is expanding beyond the capacity of many law firms and companies. While this may be wonderful news for the legal profession, at a time when even law firms have been making significant layoffs, it is decidedly not good news for the typical small business.

The reason for all the new demand for environmental lawyers is that this is an area of the law that is already beginning to have a huge impact on the way many companies do business, and it seems clearly destined to exert an even greater impact in coming years.

The Clean Air Act of 1991, for example, will have a disproportionately large effect on small businesses, particularly because they are small and their economies of scale are not as great; thus, they will tend to be hit much harder by the costs of the new environmental restrictions. All sorts of small firms, such as bakers, dry cleaners, body shops, painters, service stations, and printers, are going to be required to purchase expensive new technology and machinery to reduce emissions of air pollutants, if they wish to remain in business.

For example, gas stations will have to install expensive vapor-recovery devices on each gas pump. This can cost about $30,000 for a typical gas station, plus significant ongoing maintenance costs. Also, businesses operating in extremely smoggy areas — such as parts of California, Houston, and elsewhere — will soon be subject to environmental rules imposed by local government, as well. If those areas are to achieve compliance with federal clean air standards in the next few years, as federal law requires they must, local governments will have to start imposing environmental rules.

While it is beyond the scope of this book to go into great detail on increasing environmental restrictions, you should be aware that almost every business in urban areas of America may need to consult an environmental law specialist at some time in the next few years. Penalties for violations tend to start at levels like $25,000 a day under many of the environmental statutes, so this is an area where you can't afford even a brief slip up.

See Section 9.9 for a general overview of some of the major federal environmental laws your business may be subject to already, in addition to the latest Clean Air Act amendments mentioned here, some of which won't go into effect for up to 20 years.

Environmental Legislation

State Unitary Taxation of Worldwide Income

If your firm does business overseas as well as in certain states (particularly California), you are undoubtedly already well aware of the worldwide unitary method of taxing your firm's worldwide profits. What you may not be aware of is that legislation is pending in Congress that would ban such worldwide unitary taxation by the states.

If such legislation passes, it may reduce state income and franchise taxes on a number of international companies doing business in the states with such laws. If yours is such a company, keep an eye out for news of any such legislation passing, because it is possible that you may be able to file for refunds of state taxes paid in prior years, if the statutes of limitations for those years have not yet expired. In short, you may need to move quickly to take full benefit of such legislation enacted in the Congress.

Video Display Terminals

Until recently, white-collar workplaces or offices generally created very little liability exposure for employers, with regard to hazardous working conditions. This, too, is beginning to change.

In recent years, there have been an increasing number of lawsuits filed by employees in connection with hazards of working long hours on computers; and in late 1990, the city of San Francisco adopted an ordinance that provides regulatory safeguards for workers using video display terminals (VDTs) for four or more hours per shift. Apparently, Los Angeles and a number of other city and state governments around the nation are now considering similar laws or ordinances, since use of computers in the workplace is now a universal phenomenon and because a number of threats of employees' health have arisen in connection with the heavy use of computers.

These range from excessive exposure to radiation emitted by VDTs to carpal tunnel syndrome, a now common and debilitating nerve entrapment disorder that can cause severe pain and weakness in the wrist. Carpal tunnel syndrome can a result from too many hours spent typing on a computer keyboard — as well as from many other tasks requiring repetitive flexing and extensions of the wrist.

Laws regulating VDTs are likely to begin appearing all over the country in the near future, and offices that don't pay attention to ergonomics — the study of equipment design to reduce workplace injury — may well become sitting ducks for lawsuits or fines. While most legal claims by employees regarding VDT usage have been imposed on workers' compensation insurers thus far, employers may become directly liable:

- If they participate actively in the design of computer systems or workstations that allegedly caused the injury to an employee, or
- If new state legislation removes such claims from the workers' compensation system and places financial responsibility directly upon employers.

National Federation of Independent Business

Communicate your thoughts on government policy and pending legislation to groups like the National Federation of Independent Business (NFIB), the U.S. Chamber of Commerce, your local chamber of commerce, or a trade association for your industry. It also can be helpful to call or write your senator, U.S. representative, or the state legislator to voice your opinion in favor of or opposition to pending legislation or regulations that will affect your business.

Small business has been hit very hard by the government at all levels in recent years, and the more small business owners join and work together through organizations like the NFIB, the better the chances of shaping the future.

Footnotes

1. I.R.C. §168.
2. I.R.C. §168(i).
3. I.R.C. §179(b)(1).
4. I.R.C. §6425.
5. 15 U.S.C. §§1051–1127.
6. I.R.C. §1244(c). The Tax Reform Act of 1984 §481(a).
7. I.R.C. §1211(b).
8. I.R.C. §1244(c)(1)(C).
9. I.R.C. §1244(c)(3).
10. I.R.C. §1244(d)(1)(B).
11. I.R.C. §1244(b).
12. 16 C.F.R. §435.
13. 42 U.S.C.A. §9601 *et seq.*
14. 42 U.S.C.A. §6901 *et seq.*
15. 40 C.F.R. §280.3(a) and (b).
16. 40 C.F.R. §280.20.
17. 40 C.F.R. §280.21.
18. 33 U.S.C.A. §§1251–1376.
19. 33 U.S.C.A. §1344(a).
20. 42 U.S.C.A. §§7401–7626.
21. 15 U.S.C.A. §§2601–2629.
22. 7 U.S.C.A. §135 *et seq.*
23. 42 U.S.C.A. §§4321–4347.
24. 29 C.F.R. §§1910 and 1926.58.
25. 15 U.S.C. §1691.
26. 15 U.S.C. §1601 *et seq.*
27. 12 C.F.R. §226.2(a)(17).
28. 12 C.F.R. §226.4(c)(8).
29. 15 C.F.R. §806.

Chapter 10

Sources of Help and Information

If you're going to sin, sin against God, not the bureaucracy.
God will forgive you, but the bureaucracy won't.

— Admiral Hyman G. Rickover

10.1 General Considerations

Many government and private organizations provide free or low-cost services and publications to small business. Unfortunately, most small business owners only find out about a few of these sources and then only on
a haphazard basis. This chapter summarizes many of the services and
publications that you may need to draw on as an owner or operator of a
small business.

10.2 Professional Services

Select your accountant carefully, for this is the one person outside your
business who is most likely to be closely in touch with almost everything
going on in your operation. Besides helping to set up your books and to
establish systems for handling cash receipts and disbursements, a good
accountant can provide a wealth of practical advice on a wide range of
subjects that are important to your business, including planning for taxes,
managing your money, obtaining financing, and evaluating business
opportunities. Attorneys and bankers are often in a good position to recommend accountants whom they know.

Accountants

Attorneys

Unless you are starting out as a sole proprietor, you will usually need an attorney to prepare a partnership agreement or to set up a corporation. You will probably do well to consult an attorney anyway to make sure you are obtaining necessary licenses and permits or to help you obtain them in some cases. In most parts of the country, local bar associations have lawyer referral services that can put you in touch with attorneys in your area practicing in various fields. In most cases, however, you will do better to ask an accountant or banker to recommend a good business lawyer. If you need highly specialized legal advice or representation, ask an attorney you know to recommend a specialist.

Bankers

Establishing a good relationship with officers of the bank branch where you open an account for your business is strongly recommended. While you may find it tough to borrow from your friendly banker when you first go into business, he or she will be interested in keeping an eye on your business to see how it develops. It pays to cultivate the relationship to create a good impression before you want to apply for a business loan from the bank. Ask around before opening an account; find out if there is a bank in your area that is well known for lending to small businesses. Many of the large banks tend to be more interested in larger accounts, although different branch managers of the same bank may have very different ideas about working with small businesses.

Your banker can be a useful source of free financial advice and a good connection when wanting to meeting other business owners in your community.

Benefit Consultants

If you intend to establish a corporate pension or profit-sharing plan — or Keogh plan, if you have a number of employees — you may want to seek out a benefit consulting firm and obtain their proposals as to the type of benefit plan you need and how it should be structured. Since many such firms are primarily engaged in selling insurance products, such as life insurance, annuities, and investment contracts, designed for pension plans, the plan those firms design for you will almost invariably involve building in their products. Since an insured retirement plan may not necessarily make sense in your particular situation, you should ask your attorney or accountant to recommend a benefit consulting firm that does not have products to sell other than their consulting and plan administration services.

10.3 U.S. Small Business Administration and Other Helpful Agencies

The federal Small Business Administration (SBA) is one government agency that is genuinely helpful to small businesses. The SBA not only guarantees financing for many small businesses (see Section 9.7) but it also provides a number of valuable services.

One service you might find helpful is the Service Corps of Retired Executives (SCORE). SCORE is a program in which retired executives with many years of business experience volunteer their services as consultants to small businesses and charge only for their out-of-pocket expenses.

Other SBA programs designed to provide assistance to small businesses include:

- Small Business Development Centers (SBDCs) — SBDCs are local centers operated by the state or community, with SBA assistance, to provide a wide range of business counseling and training. To see if your state has an SBDC network, refer to Section 11.10.
- Small Business Institutes (SBIs) — SBIs provide in-depth business counseling at hundreds of universities across the country.

In addition, SBA offices perform a variety of seminars and workshops on topics of interest to people who are starting or operating small businesses. Here are some of the seminars recently offered by the SBA.

- *Small Business Seminar with the IRS*
- *Pre-Business Workshop*
- *Starting Your Own Business: A Seminar for Women*
- *Export Workshop*

Contact your local SBA office for more information.

Telephone Hotlines

The SBA and several other government agencies maintain toll-free telephone hotline information services to assist businesses and taxpayers. Some of the more important ones to know about are listed below.

SBA Answer Desk

The SBA Answer Desk has a toll-free number of a small business information and referral service offered by the SBA, which you can call from anywhere in the continental United States, except Washington, D.C. In the District of Columbia, call 653-7561. The telephone Answer Desk offers a wide range of prerecorded informational messages, any of which you may access if you have a touch-tone phone.

SBA Answer Desk
(800) U-ASK-SBA or 827-5722

Small Business Hotline

The Small Business Hotline is a specialized free service offered by the Export-Import Bank to small exporters needing general information or problem-solving assistance relating to doing business abroad. It provides information on export credit and on assistance available from other government agencies and the private sector.

Small Business Hotline
(800) 424-5201

Internal Revenue Service

The IRS has created a new assistance program called Tele-Tax, which went into effect January 1992. The program allows you to call a toll-free number in your state to listen to pre-recorded tax information that will answer many federal tax questions.

About 140 topics are available, including information on the Small Business Tax Education Program (STEP), business income, sole proprietorships, and the self-employment tax.

For more information on Tele-Tax, call the IRS' toll-free number to request *Publication 910, Guide to Free Tax Services*. This publication not only lists the many tax publications you can order, but it also lists the Tele-Tax phone numbers and topic numbers in your state.

Internal Revenue Service
(800) 829-3676

Trade Information Center

The Trade Information Center has a hotline where you can receive general information on exporting that is provided by various U.S. government agencies.

Trade Information Center
(800) USA-TRADE or 872-8723

Or, for information on doing business in the unified European Market after 1992, call for written information and a quarterly newsletter from:

U.S. Department of Commerce's Single Internal Market – 1992 Information Service
(202) 377-5276

European Center – Washington, D.C. Office
(202) 862-9500

Ernst & Young

Ernst & Young, one of the Big Six accounting firms, publishes some helpful guides for anyone interested in expanding their business into the global markets. They are:

- *The Ernst & Young Guide to Expanding in the Global Market* — This guide is for those managers who want to succeed in complex international ventures; book includes step-by-step programs and helpful examples.
- *The Ernst & Young Resource Guide to Global Markets 1991* — This guide is an up-to-date resource to global market trends and regional county data.

For more information, contact:

John Wiley & Sons, Inc. – Sales Department
605 Third Avenue
New York, NY 10158-0012
(212) 850-6000

Like certain Scandinavian countries, the Environmental Protection Agency (EPA) now has a small business ombudsman to give easier access to the EPA, help you comply with EPA regulations, and make sure you are treated fairly in any EPA disputes.

EPA Ombudsman

EPA Small Business Ombudsman
(703) 305-5938
(800) 368-5888

If you want to find out what records the Social Security Administration (SSA) has on your earnings and your projected benefits at retirement age, you can file a simple form requesting a detailed printout of this information.

Social Security Administration

This is something everyone should do once every few years because if the SSA has made a serious mistake in your earnings record, you have only a limited number of years in which you can contact them and have your record corrected. To obtain the request form, call the SSA's toll-free number or write the SSA for this form at the Consumer Information Center address below.

Social Security Administration
(800) 772-1213

Consumer Information Center
Department 72
Pueblo, CO 81009

There are also companies who can assist in the incorporation process, providing a variety of incorporation kits and services. One such company, Corporate Agents, Inc., can help you form your corporation in any state for as little as $99 (plus state fees), depending on the state. Some examples of complete costs for other states are $115 for Delaware, $169 for Florida, $269 for New York, and $1,014 for California.

Corporate Agents, Inc.

The fees cover all costs, including all state filing fees and recording costs, preparing and filing articles of incorporation, and registered agents fee service for the first year. Also available for a nominal additional cost are the corporate kits, which include the corporate seal, minute book, stock certificates, and sample forms and bylaws.

For more information on this company, you can send the preaddressed post card located at the back of this book or call Corporate Agents at the toll-free number below:

Corporate Agents, Inc.
1013 Centre Road
P.O. Box 1281
Wilmington, DE 19899
(800) 877-4224
FAX (302) 998-7078

10.4 Publications Regarding Small Business Operations

U.S. Small Business Administration

The U.S. Small Business Administration (SBA) has more than 50 helpful booklets and other publications on subjects of importance to new and existing small businesses. The publications, which sell for a nominal fee — usually about $0.50 (50 cents) to $1.00 each, and never more than $2.00 — can be obtained through your nearest SBA office or by calling the SBA Answer Desk and asking for a list of publications.

SBA Answer Desk
(800) U-ASK-SBA or 827-5722

You can also use the preaddressed post card in the back of this book to request lists of SBA publications.

Small Business Institutes

Small Business Institutes (SBIs) are located on university campuses throughout the United States. Part of a cooperative program with the SBA, SBIs offer you business assistance while furthering the education of college students. Students, supervised by faculty members, provide your business with:

- Free confidential consulting;
- In-depth analysis of your firm's business situation;
- Alternatives and recommendations to business problems; and
- Written and oral reports.

Headquartered at the University of Central Arkansas, the Small Business Institute Directors' Association (SBIDA) National Center and the Small Business Advancement Network perform research and gather information on small business. The SBIDA National Center is the link between all SBI universities and the government. The SBIDA also:

- Is the center of correspondence for SBI schools;
- Keeps records on all SBI schools;
- Publishes the *SBIDA News*;
- Processes SBIDA membership; and
- Is a center for advocacy.

The Small Business Advancement Network is an electronic bulletin board which provides information on grant opportunities, cooperative ventures between the SBA and SBI, and small business research. The network is available during regular business hours and is updated daily. For information on the SBI nearest you, contact:

SBIDA National Center
University of Central Arkansas
College of Business
UCA P.O. Box 4983
Conway, AR 72035-5002
(501) 450-5300

For more on the Small Business Advancement Network, contact:

Small Business Advancement National Center
University of Arkansas
College of Business
UCA P.O. Box 5018
Conway, AR 72035-5002
(501) 450-5377

The publisher of this book, The Oasis Press, also has a number of how-to business guides targeted toward small businesses. A free list of these related resources can be obtained by calling:

The Oasis Press

The Oasis Press
(800) 228-2275

Here are some magazines that provide continuing information for businesses in general and small businesses in particular. There are also a number of specialized publications you may find helpful. Most of these publications can be located through your local library, or you can contact them at the addresses below.

Magazines

The Wall Street Journal
84 Second Avenue
Chicopee, MA 01220
(413) 592-7761

D&B Reports
299 Park Avenue
New York, NY 10171
(212) 593-6728

In Business
419 State Avenue
Emmaus, PA 18049
(215) 967-4135

Success Magazine
230 Park Avenue
New York, NY 10169
(800) 234-7324

Entrepreneur Magazine
Subscriber Service
2392 Morse Avenue
P.O. Box 19787
Irvine, CA 92713-9441
(800) 421-2300
(800) 352-7449 (in CA)

Family Business Magazine
Subscriber Service
One Heritage Way
P.O. Box 420265
Palm Coast, FL 32142-0265
(800) 423-1780
(800) 858-0095 (in FL)

Business Week
Subscriber Service
P.O. Box 506
Hightstown, NJ 08520
(800) 635-1200

Nation's Business
1615 H. Street, NW
Washington, DC 20062
(202) 463-5650

INC.
Subscriber Service
P.O. Box 54129
Boulder, CO 80322-4129
(800) 525-0643

Small Business Opportunities
1115 Broadway, 8th Floor
New York, NY 10010
(212) 807-7100

Small Business Reports
Subscriber Services
P.O. Box 53140
Boulder, CO 80322-3140
(800) 234-1094

Independent Business
National Federation of Independent Business
Membership Development Office
600 Maryland Avenue, SW
Suite 700
Washington, DC 20024
(202) 554-9000

Statistical Information

Some of the more important sources of statistical information that you will need if you do your own marketing research are:

Title	Publisher
Survey of Buying Power *Sales and Marketing Management Magazine* Comprehensive data on population, retail sales, and consumer buying income for states, counties, and cities.	**Bill Communications, Inc.** 633 Third Avenue New York, NY 10017-6706 (212) 986-4800
Publication Price List Titles on corporate relations, human resources, management, economic and business environments, and consumer research.	**Conference Board** 845 Third Avenue New York, NY 10022 (800) 872-6273
Survey of Current Business U.S. Department of Commerce's monthly survey of business trends and conditions.	**Superintendent of Documents** **U.S. Government Printing Office** Washington, DC 20402 (202) 783-3238
The Complete Information Bank for Entrepreneurs & Small Business Managers, Second Edition An excellent sourcebook which lists and describes hundreds of leading business books and other sources of help and information for small businesses.	**Center for Entrepreneurship and** **Small Business Management** Wichita State University Campus Box 147 1845 Fairmont Wichita, KS 67208 (316) 689-3000

10.5 Do-It-Yourself Incorporation

If you want to form your own corporation and save several hundred dollars in legal fees, there are books that tell you how to do it and provide the forms you need; however, you should think carefully before you attempt to do this on your own. In some cases, setting up a corporation is not that complicated, and if you follow the instructions in a self-incorporation book precisely — if one is available for your state — you should be able to do it properly. But you will have to spend many hours carefully figuring out and then doing all that is required. Your time might be worth much more than the money you would save in legal fees because you could concentrate more on getting the business off to a good start. Check Section 11.10 to see if there is an incorporation book for your state.

Regardless of whether or not you decide to incorporate your business yourself or work with an attorney, you may find a new publication on incorporation extremely helpful. *The Essential Corporation Handbook,* written by attorney Carl R.J. Sniffen, is an easy-to-read introduction into what you will need to know if you incorporate your business. This handbook could supplement any state do-it-yourself incorporation guide by filling you in on the specifics of bylaws, articles of incorporation, shareholder agreements, required meetings, stocks, and other corporate formalities. If you decide to work with an attorney when incorporating, this book will help you make the best use of your attorney's time because you'll understand the issues and terminology, and you'll know what questions to ask. *The Essential Corporation Handbook* arms you with knowledge so you can avoid common mistakes. To find out more, contact your local book source or contact:

The Oasis Press
(800) 228-2275

10.6 Information Regarding Payroll Taxes and Withholding

Major offices of the Internal Revenue Service (IRS) frequently put on seminars for new employers regarding payroll tax requirements. Call your local IRS office for information as to when such seminars will be held in your area. In addition, you may want to obtain *Circular E*, *Employer's Tax Guide,* and *Notice 109, Information About Depositing Employment and Excise Taxes.* Both can be obtained from the IRS office nearest you.

In addition, the Matthew Bender publishing company puts out an excellent book called the *Payroll Tax Guide*, which covers almost every aspect of federal payroll tax returns.

10.7 Other Useful Tax Publications

The publications below can also be obtained from your local IRS office:

Publication	Subject
Publication 334	*Tax Guide For Small Business Income and other Federal Taxes*
Publication 349	*Federal Highway Use Taxes on Heavy Vehicles*
Publication 378	*Fuel Tax Credits and Refunds*
Publication 463	*Travel, Entertainment, and Gift Expenses*
Publication 510	*Federal Excise Taxes*
Publication 541	*Tax Information on Partnerships*
Publication 542	*Tax Information on Corporations*
Publication 544	*Sales and Other Dispositions of Assets*
Publication 552	*Recordkeeping Requirements*
Publication 583	*Taxpayers Starting a Business*
Publication 587	*Business Use of Your Home*
Publication 589	*Tax Information on S Corporations*
Publication 910	*Guide to Free Tax Services*
Publication 937	*Business Reporting*

To order these free tax publications or other tax forms, call:

Internal Revenue Service
(800) 829-3676

10.8 ERISA Compliance

If your business has a pension or profit-sharing plan and you wish to handle your own Employee Retirement Income Security Act (ERISA) filings for the plan, you should obtain a copy of Charles D. Spencer & Associates' publication, *5500 Annual Reports for Employee Benefit Plans*.

This publication will help you prepare the necessary *Form 5500* series through its easy-to-understand, step-by-step instructions. For ordering information, contact:

Charles D. Spencer & Associates, Inc.
250 South Wacker Drive, Suite 600
Chicago, IL 60606
(312) 993-7900

10.9 Managing Your Own Keogh or IRA Investments

If you want to set up a canned Keogh plan or an individual retirement account (IRA) and have the ability to manage the plan or account's investments for yourself, you can do so through certain stockbrokers. Check with your local bank or stockbroker to compare services and prices. Discount brokers, such as Charles Schwab & Co. and Fidelity Brokerage Services, provide such accounts at competitive rates.

10.10 Information on Franchising

Title and Author	Publisher
Franchise Bible Erwin J. Keup	**The Oasis Press** 300 North Valley Drive Grants Pass, OR 97526
Miscellaneous titles on franchise topics. Write for a catalog.	**International Franchise Association** 1350 New York Avenue, NW, Suite 900 Washington, DC 20005

Title and Author	Publisher
Business Franchise Guide	**Commerce Clearing House, Inc.** 4025 West Peterson Avenue Chicago, IL 60646
The Complete Handbook of Franchising David D. Seltz	**Addison-Wesley** General Books Division Reading, MA 01867
Miscellaneous titles on franchise topics. Write for a catalog.	**Pilot Books** 103 Cooper Street Babylon, NY 11702
Franchise Opportunities Handbook	**U.S. Department of Commerce** U.S. Government Printing Office Washington, DC 20402
Franchising in the U.S. Michael M. Coltman	**Self-Counsel Press Inc.** 1704 North State Street Bellingham, WA 98225 (800) 663-3007
Franchisee Rights — A Self-Defense Manual for The Franchisee Alex Hammond	**Hammond & Morton** 1185 Avenue of the Americas New York, NY 10036
Franchising: Regulation of Buying and Selling A Franchise Philip F. Zeidman, Perry C. Ausbrook & H. Bret Lowell	**Bureau of National Affairs, Inc.** 9435 Key West Avenue Rockville, MD 20850 (800) 372-1033
The Info Franchise Newsletter *The Franchise Annual*	**Info Press** 728 Center Street Lewiston, NY 14092-0550 (716) 754-4669
Survey of Foreign Laws and Regulations Affecting International Franchising Compiled by the Franchising Committee of the Section of Antitrust Law of the American Bar Association	**Publications Planning and Marketing American Bar Association** 705 North Lake Shore Drive Chicago, IL 60611

10.11 Estate Planning

To help you develop a retirement plan, you may want to obtain a copy of *Retirement & Estate Planning Handbook* by Chuck Tellalian and Walter Rosen. This do-it-yourself workbook comes complete with step-by-step instructions, worksheets, samples, and forms. For more information, contact your local book source or:

The Oasis Press
(800) 228-2275

10.12 OSHA Publications

If your business will be subject to OSHA laws (see Section 5.6), you should obtain the following free booklet on OSHA requirements from your local office of the U.S. Department of Labor, Occupational Safety and Health Administration:

- *Recordkeeping Requirements for Occupational Injuries and Illnesses*

10.13 Mail Order Sales Regulations

If you intend to sell goods by mail order, you need to be familiar with Federal Trade Commission Rule 435.1 (see Section 9.7). For a complete treatment of federal and state laws (all 50 states) affecting mail order businesses, you can obtain the *Mail Order Legal Manual*, by Erwin J. Keup, from:

The Oasis Press
(800) 228-2275

10.14 "Expert" Software for Small Businesses

As a business owner or prospective owner, you may be interested in a computer software program designed to aid and advise small- to medium-sized businesses with respect to tax, legal, and other business questions. *The Small Business Expert*, developed by Michael D. Jenkins, the principal author of this book, is a "smart" or "expert" program that provides such a capability.

This easy-to-use software is a bit like having a high-powered business, tax, and legal consultant on retainer, available day or night. The program allows you to simply type in a question or a key word or two about various business-related subjects and immediately responds by giving you textual information on that subject. Or you may quickly scan through a lengthy subject index and simply hit one key to view information on any item in the index. The software covers a wide range of subjects applicable to small businesses, with a primary emphasis on tax and legal information relevant to the state you do business in.

The program will first prompt you for numerous details about your business or proposed business. It will then create — and you may print out — detailed checklists of state and federal government regulations and other items your particular business must deal with. The program will also give you specific tax planning suggestions, all tailored specifically to your business. The program does quick calculations of both personal and corporate income taxes — allowing you to do instant "what if" projections — and will also compute federal estate taxes to assist you in income and estate tax planning.

The Small Business Expert also provides a number of consulting session topics, where you engage in a question-and-answer sequence with the program, regarding such subjects as whether or not you should incorporate your business, what accounting method can or should your new business adopt, and other topics. After you answer a series of questions, the program will offer you recommendations or advice regarding your specific situation, as well as its reasons for such advice.

Among other useful features, built-in worksheets are also provided for you to simply fill in the blanks on screen and print out a business plan outline, marketing feasibility study, or personnel policies summary for your business. *The Small Business Expert* is available from The Oasis Press which also publishes other economical software to streamline business activities. See the Related Resources section at the back of this book for more information. These and other related resources can be purchased through your book or software source or by calling:

The Oasis Press
(800) 228-2275

State Laws & Related Resources

Notes to Colorado State Chapter

What's New

This update of the Colorado state chapter features new information and additions in several areas. The list below will help you locate the most significant changes by chapter–section number.

- Information on a new legal entity called a limited liability company which can be formed in Colorado – 11.2

- A change in graduated income tax rates for corporations – 11.2

- A change in due dates for property taxes – 11.4

- A change in unemployment insurance rates – 11.4

- An update of phone numbers and addresses of helpful agencies – throughout the chapter

- Information on new excise taxes on alcoholic beverages – 11.7

If changes have occurred since publication of this update, you are advised to contact the state office listed below for assistance or referral to the appropriate agency.

Small Business Hotline
1560 Broadway, Suite 1530
Denver, CO 80202
(303) 592-5920
(800) 333-7798 (Nationwide)

About the Author

The state co-authors of *Starting and Operating a Business in Colorado* are Greg Romberg and Joan D. Ringel, who have updated this chapter through October 1991.

Greg Romberg is the director of the newly-established Denver Office of Regulatory Reform and a member of Mayor Wellington Webb's cabinet. He is the former Director of the Colorado Office of Regulatory Reform and has more than 10 years experience representing the interests of small businesses.

Mr. Romberg received a B.A. in Political Science from Colorado State University in Fort Collins and a Master of Public Administration degree from the Maxwell School of Citizenship and Public Affairs at Syracuse University.

Joan D. Ringel, a partner in the public policy research and management consulting firm, The KR Group, has represented business interests before the Colorado General Assembly for 13 years.

Formerly the Senior Vice President of the Colorado Association of Commerce and Industry and Director of the Colorado Office of Regulatory Reform, Ms. Ringel was also a sunset analyst at the Colorado Department of Regulatory Agencies.

Ms. Ringel received an A.B. in English from the University of Michigan in Ann Arbor and a Master of Public Administration degree from the University of Colorado.

Chapter 11

State Laws and Taxes

11.1 Introduction

Colorado is a state full of opportunity for entrepreneurs who want to start their own business. The state's unparalleled beauty is a frequently cited reason why many companies organize and operate in Colorado. In addition to Colorado's natural attributes, the state has many other reasons why the business climate is conducive to success.

Colorado is a transportation hub with major highways running through the state. Denver's Stapleton International Airport, which will be replaced by a new international airport in 1993, is the sixth busiest in the world. Colorado also has a favorable tax climate with a low graduated corporate income tax.

Colorado's people may be her greatest asset. In addition to their western hospitality, Coloradans are among the best-educated people in the country with the state boasting the most college graduates per capita in the United States.

Although there are more retail stores and restaurants in Colorado than other types of businesses, the state is also a leader in the field of high technology. Most Colorado businesses are small with more than 95% having fewer than 50 employees.

Whatever your business, many programs are provided throughout Colorado state government to help you succeed, some of which are detailed in Section 11.10.

Good luck in your business endeavors!

11.2 Choosing the Legal Form of the Business

As discussed in Chapter 2, the choice you make on the legal form of your business will dictate a range of state requirements you must fulfill. In Colorado, you can choose among four legal forms when starting your business: the sole proprietorship, the partnership, the corporation, and the most recent form, the limited liability company.

Sole Proprietorships

Sole proprietorships in Colorado are not taxable entities. The state requires no registration or official recognition for the business. If you plan to conduct your business under your full legal name, you do not have to register your trade name; however, you will have to register your trade name, if you are operating your business under a name other than your own, or if your business name includes other words such as "Co.," "Son," or "Company." See Section 11.4.

You, as the owner, will also be responsible for various state and local taxes, licenses, and permits which may be specific to a type of business as well as payroll responsibilities to employees such as unemployment insurance and workers' compensation. Income is taxed to the individual.

Partnerships

Partnerships, like sole proprietorships, are also not taxable entities. You will, however, be subject to trade name registration requirements, payroll taxes, business-specific licenses and permits, and anti-discrimination statutes. Income is taxable to the partners.

Limited partnerships are treated differently from general partnerships. A limited partnership is one formed by two or more people under Colorado law — or the law of other jurisdictions — with one or more general partners and one or more limited partners. The contribution of a partner may be in cash, property, or services rendered, or obligations to contribute cash or property to perform services.

Limited partnerships must file a *Certificate of Limited Partnership* with the secretary of state's office.

Colorado Secretary of State
1560 Broadway, Suite 200
Denver, CO 80202
(303) 894-2251

You will need to file two signed copies of the *Certificate of Limited Partnership*.[1] Amendments to the *Certificate of Limited Partnership* and the certificate of cancellation can be filed in the same office.

If you are required to file a federal partnership return of income form, you are also required to file Colorado *Form 106:5*, available from the Colorado Department of Revenue.

Limited Liability Companies

Colorado now allows businesses to organize as limited liability companies by filing articles of organization with the secretary of state. Such an entity is treated as a partnership for federal and state income tax purposes while retaining the limited liability of a corporation. If you choose to organize in this manner, the official name of your organization must contain "limited liability company." As a limited liability company, you must file a certificate with the secretary of state's office.

Because limited liability companies are new and not recognized in all jurisdictions, you should consult your legal adviser before forming one.

Corporations

Corporations are somewhat more complicated legal entities because they are legal structures which exist separately from the people who create them. If you choose to incorporate, you must file duplicate articles of incorporation with the secretary of state and pay a $50 filing fee.[2]

If you wish, you may reserve a corporate name before you are ready to file your articles.[3] After you file your articles of incorporation, you will receive a certificate of incorporation, at which point the corporation becomes a legal entity, just like a person. The articles must include the corporate name, duration of corporation, corporate purpose, number of shares, whether cumulative voting is authorized, provisions regarding preemptive rights of shareholders, address and name of registered agent, initial board of directors, and incorporator's name and address.

Typically, officers of the corporation who work there day-to-day are employees of the corporation, even if they own the corporation's stock. Therefore, they are liable for employee-related obligations such as withholding tax, unemployment insurance, workers' compensation, and Social Security. In some instances, a corporate officer may choose not to be covered by workers' compensation.

As a legal entity, the corporation is subject to income based on its profits — see the table below. Colorado has graduated income tax for corporations.

Corporation Income	Tax Rate
$50,000 or less per year	5.0%
A balance over $50,000	5.2%

Colorado uses the water's edge method of taxation for multi-national corporations.

A nonprofit corporation is one whose income or profit is not distributed to its members, directors, or officers. All of the income from the corporation's activities must be used for the nonprofit activities of the organization. Nonprofit corporations file similar articles of incorporation with the secretary of state.[4] Once incorporated, you will have to comply with additional reporting requirements: articles of amendment, mergers, consolidation, dissolution, changes of registered office and agent, and corporate reports which are filed every two years.

Foreign Corporation

A corporation incorporated under the laws of another state that wants to do business in Colorado must register as a foreign corporation doing business in the state.[5]

To operate a foreign corporation, you must submit the following information to the secretary of state: duplicate original applications for authority and a certificate of good standing from the state in which it was incorporated.

The certificate of good standing must be dated within 90 days of when the application is made. Foreign corporations are required to maintain a registered agent and a registered office in Colorado. For more information about operating as a foreign corporation in Colorado, contact:

Commercial Recordings Division
Colorado Secretary of State
1560 Broadway, Suite 200
Denver, CO 80202
(303) 894-2251

Foreign corporations are required to pay corporate income tax in Colorado based on the percentage of their corporate activity that takes place in Colorado. The corporate income tax rate in Colorado is explained in Section 11.2.

Corporate Income Tax

Every domestic or foreign corporation located or doing business in Colorado is subject to the corporate income tax. For tax purposes, you will be considered doing business in Colorado if you have employees or business property in the state.

Every corporation subject to Colorado income tax must file a declaration of estimated income tax if its estimated tax is greater than $5,000, plus estimated credits. If your Colorado activities consist only of making sales, you may elect to pay a tax of 1/2 of 1% of your annual gross receipts from sales in or into Colorado, instead of paying income tax, provided you meet the following requirements:

- Your annual gross sales in Colorado are not more than $100,000; and
- You do not own, lease, or rent real estate within Colorado.

The Colorado Department of Revenue provides necessary forms, such as:

- *Corporate Income Tax, Form 112*
- *Multi-state Compact Apportionment Schedule, Form AS-4*
- *Corporation Credit Schedule, Form 112-CR*
- *Extension, Form DR-158C*
- *Affiliation Schedule, Form 112-AS*
- *Tax Corporation Schedule, Form 112-TC*

Investment Tax Credits

If the federal government reinstates its investment tax credits, Colorado businesses may then take a credit against state income taxes of 10% of the federal investment tax credit. The credit is limited to your local business' state tax liability less the Job Expansion Tax Credit up to $5,000 and 25% of the tax liability over $5,000. Any excess investment tax credit may be carried back three years or forward seven years. For taxable years beginning on or after January 1, 1987, the regular investment credit is only available to corporations, and the triple investment tax credit for businesses located within an enterprise zone will be available to individuals as well as corporations.

Impact Assistance Credit

If your company contributes to a local government to solve problems which arise from the impact of new or expanded milling operations, you may take a credit against severance taxes due. For additional information, contact:

Colorado Department of Revenue
1375 Sherman Street, Room 286
Denver, CO 80261
(303) 534-1209
(800) 332-2085 (in Colorado)

Securities Laws

Colorado law does not distinguish between closely held corporations and corporations in general, except in judicial proceedings. State law does provide for exemptions from registering with the Division of Securities. These exemptions include:

- Any security, including a revenue obligation issued or guaranteed by the United States, any state, or political subdivision — or any agency, corporation, or instrumentality of these entities;
- Any Canadian or foreign government security, if the security is "recognized as a valid obligation";
- Any security issued by a bank, savings institution, trust company, federal credit union, or industrial concern in business in Colorado for more than 20 years with first mortgages on Colorado real estate, a combination of securities of the United States, and cash equal to 100% of the amount of issued securities;
- Any security issued or guaranteed by a railroad, common carrier, or public utility subject to the Public Utility Holding Company Act of 1935;
- Any security approved for listing by the New York, American, Pacific, or Midwest stock exchanges;
- Any security issued by a person organized as a not-for-profit, private organization, but for exclusively religious, educational, benevolent, charitable, fraternal, social, athletic, or reformatory purposes;
- Commercial paper which arises from current transactions and investment contracts related to employee programs;
- Securities registered under the Securities Exchange Act of 1934; and
- Transactions in a bond secured by mortgage, security agreement, deed of trust, real estate or chattels, and offerings which are defined in the Investment Company Act of 1940.

Colorado law also excludes from registration any Colorado transaction which is not a public offering, preorganization subscriptions without commissions, or transactions involving existing security holders.

For additional information, contact:

Division of Securities
Colorado Department of Regulatory Agencies
1580 Lincoln, Suite 420
Denver, CO 80203
(303) 894-2320

Dividends Received Deduction

The Colorado tax code treats dividend received deductions as the federal government does.

S Corporations

Colorado accepts the federal distinction for S corporations and requires them to file according to a shareholder schedule.

For more information on corporations, contact:

Corporations Office
Colorado Secretary of State
1560 Broadway, Suite 200
Denver, CO 80202
(303) 894-2251

11.3 Buying an Existing Business — State Legal Requirements

When you purchase an existing business, you should ensure that no one else has a prior claim on the goods or products you are purchasing as part of the business — and that you are not inheriting debts about which you are unaware.

Bulk Sales Law

Colorado adopted the Uniform Commercial Code Bulk Transfer Act in 1965.[6] When you purchase an existing business, you must require the seller to provide a list of all his or her creditors. All creditors must then be notified that the business is about to be sold along with disclosure of when and by whom any existing debts will be settled.

Recorded Security Interests

When you buy an existing business, you should try to find out if there are prior liens against property that you are purchasing.

Ask the seller if there are liens, and then check the records of the county clerk in the county in which the seller is located or where the property — that may have a lien filed against it — is located. Also check with the Uniform Commercial Code section at the secretary of state's office.

Colorado Secretary of State
1560 Broadway, Suite 200
Denver, CO 80202
(303) 894-2200

Employment Tax Release

With proof that you are purchasing an existing business, the Division of Employment and Training will allow you to find the employment tax rate of the business and if it has any outstanding debts in unemployment insurance. If you purchase an existing business, you will assume the corporation's account number and experience rating. For more information, contact:

Unemployment Insurance Tax
Division of Employment and Training
Colorado Department of Labor and Employment
639 East 18th Avenue, 1st Floor
Denver, CO 80203-1483
(303) 839-4922

Sales Tax Release

If you are purchasing the stock of a corporation, you also acquire any corporation's debts for sales tax. If you acquire a sole proprietorship or partnership, the liabilities belong to the owner, not the business, and you will not be liable for them. On company letterhead, write to the Colorado Department of Revenue to explain your situation and to find out if there is sales tax liability.

Also, request a taxpayer clearance letter. This letter will clarify if taxes are owed by the business. If you are purchasing a sole proprietorship or general partnership, you should obtain a new sales tax account number. If you buy the stock of a corporation, you can continue to use the existing account number.

Taxpayer Service Division
Colorado Department of Revenue
1375 Sherman Street, Room 186
Denver, CO 80261
(303) 534-1209
(800) 332-2085 (in Colorado)

Other Tax Provisions

When you purchase an existing business, you are liable to pay sales tax for any tangible property you buy as part of the business. This type of property may include things like furniture or fixtures. It may be in your best interest to clearly define in your sales contract how much of the purchase price is for the equipment included with the business.

Similarly, the county in which you are located may assess personal property tax on the equipment you use in the business. To clarify tax liability, you should detail the value of the equipment purchased as part of the business.

11.4 State Requirements that Apply to Nearly All New Businesses

Colorado's favorable business climate is enhanced by the existence of the Small Business Hotline, a one-stop permit assistance agency. This office provides the *Colorado Business Start-up Kit*, a 40-page kit for persons interested in starting or purchasing a business in Colorado.

The hotline is the only place in Colorado where you can get federal, state, and local permit and tax information in one place. For details, contact:

Small Business Hotline
1560 Broadway, Suite 1530
Denver, CO 80202
(303) 592-5920
(800) 333-7798 (Nationwide)

State Licenses

When you are ready to begin a new venture — whether you decide to form a sole proprietorship, partnership, limited liability company, or corporation — you need to determine if your particular type of business requires licenses or permits. Section 11.6 lists all state licenses and the state's regulatory agencies.

The Small Business Hotline has federal, state, and county licensing information as well as municipal information for all cities and towns in Colorado. A general business license is not available for all businesses in Colorado.

For more information, contact:

Small Business Hotline
Office of Regulatory Reform
Colorado Department of Regulatory Agencies
1560 Broadway, Suite 1530
Denver, CO 80202
(303) 592-5920
(800) 333-7798

Estimated Income Tax

If a Colorado corporation expects its tax liability for the year to exceed $5,000 plus estimated credits, its officers must file a declaration of estimated tax, *Form 112-ES*. Individuals not subject to withholding tax must file a similar declaration, *Form 104-E*, if their estimated income tax net of anticipated credits exceeds $1,000. Colorado has no franchise tax.

For more information, contact:

Income Tax Section
Taxpayer Service Division
1375 Sherman
Denver, CO 80261
(303) 534-1209
(800) 332-2087 (in Colorado)

If you sell tangible personal property to anyone in Colorado, you need to collect retail sales tax. A retail sale is taxable, unless what is bought is to be resold or used to manufacture something that will be sold.

Sales and Use Tax

If, however, a manufacturer or wholesaler sells products that are not to be resold, those sales are also subject to sales tax. Sales tax must be shown separately on your invoice. Sales tax is not imposed upon the sale of real property. Colorado sales and use tax is 3%.[7]

To obtain a Colorado sales tax license, apply at the Colorado Department of Revenue or any of the department's seven district offices in Alamosa, Colorado Springs, Denver, Durango, Fort Collins, Grand Junction, and Pueblo. Licenses cost $16 for a two-year period, plus $50 for a deposit for new businesses. After you remit $50 in state sales tax, your deposit will be refunded.

As a retailer, you must also file the *Combined Sales Tax Return, Form DR 100,* by the 20th day of the month of your reporting period. Your reporting period is based on the amount of tax remitted. You will file your reports annually or quarterly until your monthly tax reaches $300, at which point, you will file monthly.

Staff from the Taxpayer Service Division offer weekly seminars, which describe where and how to collect and file sales and use tax, every Friday from 9:00 A.M. to 12:00 A.M. at 1560 Broadway in Denver. No reservations are necessary, and there is no cost. At the seminar, you can apply for your sales tax license and learn how to fill out required forms. Classes are also held at other district offices. Call the district office in your area for details.

Tax Seminars

Many Colorado cities and counties also have sales and use tax. The Colorado Department of Revenue collects tax for 186 of these local governments; however, 41 cities collect their own tax.

Local Sales Tax

If you do business in any of the following cities, you will need to apply for licenses and file sales taxes directly with the city.

Alamosa	Durango	Larkspur
Aurora	Edgewater	Littleton
Arvada	Englewood	Longmont
Avon	Fort Collins	Montrose
Breckenridge	Glendale	Mt. Crested Butte
Boulder	Glenwood Springs	Northglenn
Canon City	Golden	Pueblo
Central City	Grand Junction	Rifle
Cherry Hills Village	Greeley	Steamboat Springs
Colorado Springs	Greenwood Village	Thornton
Commerce City	Lafayette	Vail
Cortez	La Junta	Westminster
Delta	Lakewood	Wheat Ridge
Denver	Lamar	

While special districts — such as sanitation, water, and school districts — could be authorized to collect sales tax, only the Regional Transportation District (RTD), the Cultural Facilities District, and the Stadium District do. If you are doing business in Adams, Arapahoe, Denver, Douglas, Boulder, or Jefferson counties, you will have to charge a 0.6% sales tax for RTD, 0.1% sales tax for the Cultural Facilities District, and 0.1% sales tax for the Stadium District.

Tourism Promotion Tax

Colorado and some counties also levy a Tourism Promotion Tax[8] on all lodging that is subject to sales tax (including condominium rentals of less than 30 days), nongrocery food and drinks, ski lift tickets, private tourism attraction admissions, short-term automobile rentals, and tour bus and sightseeing carrier tickets. If you are in any one of these tourist-related businesses, you must collect the 0.2% tax. The Tourism Promotion Tax may be either shown separately on your sales ticket or included in the total charge. Counties are now authorized to levy sales taxes to support mass transportation.

Use Tax

Use tax, a complement to sales tax, can be collected by the state, a city, a county or RTD or both. It is imposed on the storage, use, or consumption of tangible personal property in Colorado upon which sales tax has not been paid.[9]

The amount of tax is computed on the purchase price or fair market value. Sales tax is due if you purchased tangible personal property when buying a business and did not pay sales tax. If you buy things from an out-of-state business that is not required to collect Colorado sales tax and tax is due, you are liable for retailer's use tax.

Underground Storage Tank Law

Colorado has a regulatory system for underground storage tanks which substantially mirrors federal regulation as to definitions and regulatory authority. Businesses that have underground storage tanks are responsible to the state's oil and gas inspector for the design, performance, operation, release detection and reporting, closure, and financial responsibility for underground tanks that contain regulated substances. For more information, call:

State Oil and Gas Inspector
1001 East 62nd Avenue
Denver, CO 80216
(303) 284-5643

In addition, owners of such tanks must annually register their tanks and pay a registration fee. You will be assessed a penalty for failing to register. You must also establish that you are capable of self-insurance for tanks that contain regulated substances; furthermore, you must establish and maintain evidence of financial responsibility for taking corrective action and for compensating third parties for bodily injury and property damage due to problems with the tanks. The law establishes a fund from which the state can draw upon for mitigation beyond the limits of the owner's financial responsibility. This fund is maintained from a surcharge on the shipment of fuel products.

The state health department has authority to oversee the mitigation of releases from underground storage tanks. For more information, call:

Hazardous Materials and Waste Management Division
Colorado Department of Health
4300 Cherry Creek Drive South
Denver, CO 80222-1530
(303) 692-3300

Finally, the new law establishes a licensure system for installers of tanks, other than those who install tanks for their own companies, under the purview of the state oil and gas inspector.

Property Taxes

All property in Colorado with certain statutory exemptions is subject to ad valorem or property tax levied by local political subdivisions.[10] While the state government does not levy the property tax, state statutory guidelines prescribe the assessed valuation of each class of property.

By constitution, assessed valuation is based on a base year concept. The value of property is set to its June 30, 1990 value. A property's assessed value is determined by considering a cost, market, and income approach, while agricultural property is assessed by determining its productive capacity.

Residential property — including mobile home parks, but not hotels and motels — is valued at 14.34% of actual value. All other property is assessed at 29% of actual value.

Several classes of personal property are exempt from property taxation:

- Household furnishings;
- Personal effects not used for the production of income at any time;
- Inventories of merchandise, materials, and supplies used by a business or to be sold;
- Livestock;
- Agricultural and livestock products; and
- Agricultural equipment used on a farm or ranch to produce agricultural products.

The amount of tax is determined by multiplying a mill levy — set by local governing bodies including school boards, county commissioners, and special districts — by the assessed valuation of the property. A mill levy is the dollars of tax per $1,000 of assessed valuation.

Personal Property

If you own personal property, you need to file a personal property declaration with the county assessor by April 15. By law, the county assessor is required to mail two copies of the personal property declaration schedule to businesses known or believed to own taxable personal property.

Failure to receive a schedule does not negate the responsibility to file. A declaration schedule is confidential.

If personal property is brought into or removed from the state, demolished, or becomes exempt, you need to notify the assessor. The value of the property will be prorated over the part of the year in which it is taxable.

Tax bills are mailed each January by the county treasurer. Half of the payment is due February 28, the second half by June 15, or the full payment can be made by April 30. If you disagree with the assessor's valuation, you may file an objection with the assessor and may appeal, if necessary, to the County Board of Equalization, the State Board of Assessment Appeals, and the district court.

The Division of Property Taxation offers taxpayers two helpful publications:

- *Understanding Property Taxes*; and
- *Property Valuation and Taxation for Business and Industry.*

To order the publications, contact the office listed below or mail the preaddressed post card that is provided for your use at the end of this book.

Division of Property Taxation
Colorado Department of Local Affairs
1313 Sherman Street, Suite 419
Denver, CO 80203
(303) 866-2371

The county assessor in the county where the property is located may also be contacted.

Fictitious or Assumed Business Name

In Colorado, if you do business under your own name, you are not required to register a fictitious name statement; however, if the name of your business includes the words "Co.," "Son," or "Company," or if you use a name other than your own, you will need to register your business or trade name.

To register, you must complete *Form DR590, Tax Application and Trade Name Registration* or *Form CR100, Colorado Employer Registration Form*, and return it to the Colorado Department of Revenue.

When a corporation does business only under its true corporate name, it is not required to register a trade name except to file articles of incorporation with the secretary of state. Corporations that so file have the exclusive corporate right to the use of that name.

If a corporation does business under an assumed name — a name different from the one filed in its articles of incorporation — it has to file the assumed name with the secretary of state.[11] The secretary of state's fee is $10.

Sole proprietorships and general partnerships register trade names with the Colorado Department of Revenue. Corporations and limited partnerships register their assumed names with the secretary of state.[12] For more information, contact:

Taxpayer Service Division
Colorado Department of Revenue

1375 Sherman Street, Room 186 (by mail)	1560 Broadway, Suite 1530 (in person)
Denver, CO 80261	Denver, CO 80202
(303) 534-1810	
(800) 332-2085 (in Colorado)	

Trade name registration has been enacted to allow consumers to know who owns a particular business. The registration does not grant exclusive use of the name to the owner nor can the owner be assured that a name is not already in use in Colorado.

Courts rely on common law evidence — possibly an advertisement from a telephone directory or newspaper — when determining which of several businesses may have the right to use a name. Typically, the court will want to know which business used the name first, and if another business using the same or a similar name is deceptive to the public or damages the business which initially used the name.

Failure to register a trade name may be punished by a fine of up to $500. Businesses which fail to register their trade names may be denied standing in court.

Other State Requirements

Colorado income tax law has adopted almost all provisions of the federal Internal Revenue Code in the definition of gross income, deductions, and the criteria for the determination of allowable exemptions.

The Colorado income tax rate is a flat 5% of federal taxable income with a very few modifications. An alternative minimum tax of 3.75% of the federal alternative taxable income, with a few modifications, was also enacted.[13]

- All individual taxpayers are expected to file *Form 104-AMT* or *Form 104-CR* or both with the return, if applicable. A copy of the federal return and schedules must be provided on request.
- Forms for partnerships and corporations are explained in Section 11.2.

11.5 Additional Requirements for Businesses with Employees

If your business has employees, you will need to withhold taxes, pay premiums for unemployment and workers' compensation insurance, and post posters from the divisions of Labor and Civil Rights. Information about these requirements and the state and federal forms that you will need have all been compiled in the *Colorado Business Start-up Kit*, which is available from the Small Business Hotline.

Withholding Taxes

As an employer, you will be required to withhold state income taxes from your employee's paychecks. Depending upon how much tax you withhold, you will be required to pay it to the Colorado Department of Revenue either monthly or quarterly.[14] You must withhold taxes for your employees so that at the end of the year, they will not need to come up with all the taxes they owe at one time. Colorado taxes personal earnings at a flat rate of 5%. You will also be required to pay unemployment insurance on each employee, so if he or she becomes unemployed through no fault of his or her own, money will be in the unemployment insurance trust fund to cover it.

Register for withholding by using *Form CR100* which is the *Colorado Employer Registration* form in the *Colorado Business Start-up Kit.*

State Unemployment Tax

All for-profit businesses in Colorado with at least one employee must pay unemployment insurance.[15]

Unemployment insurance rates vary based on a number of factors. Your initial rate will be established based on the kind of business you operate and the amount of money in the state's unemployment insurance trust fund.

After three years, your rate will be adjusted based on your actual experience and the trust fund balance. Your rate may vary between zero and 5.4% and will be assessed on the first $10,000 of wages paid to each employee, as well as a 0.2% surcharge for administration.

Unemployment insurance is an expense to be borne by the employer and cannot be passed on to the employee. You will open your unemployment insurance account by filing *Form CR100,* the *Colorado Employer Registration* form in the *Colorado Business Start-up Kit.*

After you open your account, the Division of Employment and Training will send you *Form CUC-1* with which you may make payments quarterly.

Nonprofit corporations and political subdivisions may choose to pay unemployment insurance quarterly as other businesses do or may reimburse the Unemployment Insurance Trust Fund for benefits paid to workers.

The Division of Employment and Training publishes the *Employer's Handbook*, which is a guide to the state's unemployment insurance tax rules and regulations.

To request this booklet or additional information, contact:

Unemployment Insurance Tax
Division of Employment and Training
Colorado Department of Labor and Employment
639 East 18th Avenue, 1st Floor
Denver, CO 80203-1483
(303) 839-4922

Workers' Compensation Insurance

With few exceptions, all Colorado employers are required to insure their employees with workers' compensation insurance for job-related injuries.[16] Some real estate brokers, salespersons, and truckers who are independent contractors are exempt.

In addition, a contractor who is a sole proprietor may waive workers' compensation but his or her employees must be covered; however, a prime contractor who hires such a contractor/sole proprietor is liable for any risk incurred. This insurance may be purchased through any private insurance company or through the State Compensation Insurance Authority.

Workers' compensation insurance rates are based on how hazardous the employee's job is and how much money he or she earns. Rates are filed with the insurance commissioner, but individual companies and the State Compensation Insurance Authority may discount those rates.

Owners of sole proprietorships and general partnerships are not required to cover themselves with workers' compensation, but they may choose to do so. The working officers of a corporation are required to cover themselves, unless they formally reject coverage.

Notice to Employees of Coverage

When you purchase workers' compensation insurance, your carrier will give you a poster to display prominently in your business where employees will see it. This poster will notify employees that coverage is in effect and explain what the coverage includes.

Notice to Injured Employee

If one of your employees is injured while on the job, you are required to file a *First Report of Accident Form* with your insurance company. For more information about workers' compensation, contact:

Workers' Compensation Section
Colorado Division of Labor
1120 Lincoln Street, 14th Floor
Denver, CO 80203
(303) 764-2929

Employee Safety and Health Regulations

Colorado defers to the federal government for the promulgation and enforcement of occupational safety and health regulations. These regulations are set forth in the Occupational Safety and Health Act of 1970. The federal agency that administers this act is the Occupational Safety and Health Administration (OSHA). Some of the OSHA requirements include posting specific notices to employees; keeping accurate records of all job-related injuries or illnesses; and reporting these injuries or illnesses to the appropriate agencies in a timely manner. For a more detailed discussion of OSHA requirements and law, refer to Section 5.6.

The Occupational Safety and Health Administration has an office in Denver. If you are interested in learning more about OSHA requirements, this office will be able to answer your questions as well as send you some helpful OSHA-related publications at no charge. Some publications you may wish to request are listed below.

- *Your Workplace Rights in Action, OSHA 3035*
- *All About OSHA, OSHA 2056*
- *OSHA Handbook for Small Businesses, OSHA 2209*

U.S. Department of Labor – OSHA
1961 Stout Street, Room 1576
Denver, CO 80294
(303) 844-3061
(800) 332-5858 (in Colorado)

Labor Laws

Colorado has labor laws and standards for employers operating only in intrastate commerce. The federal standards apply to businesses that are involved in interstate commerce.

Wage-Hour Laws

For certain industries, Colorado's minimum wage is currently $3 per hour; otherwise, the federal minimum wage of $4.25 per hour is applicable. If workers work more than 40 hours per week or 12 hours per day, they are entitled to time and a half for the excess time.[17] For more information, call:

Division of Labor – Labor Standards Unit
1120 Lincoln Street
Denver, CO 80203
(303) 894-7541

Breaks, Holidays, and Sick Leave

Employees are entitled to breaks for meals and rest. At least 30 minutes to eat must be made available for every five hours worked. Similarly, at least a 10-minute break shall be provided for rest for every four hours worked.[18]

Colorado law does not require holiday or sick pay, time off for holidays or vacations, or any particular frequency of paydays. You are, however, required to provide whatever you promise employees in these areas.

Child Labor Laws

There are additional labor standards for employment of unemancipated minors under 18 years of age.[19] The minimum wage for these employees is $2.55 per hour.

They are entitled to time and a half for work over 40 hours per week or 12 hours per day and shall not work overtime, unless it is an emergency. Minors must have certification from their schools before they begin working. Certain kinds of work, as spelled out in the Child Labor Law, may not be done by minors on a tiered schedule.

Specific occupations are allowed for children once they reach age 9. They include delivery of handbills; shoe-shining; gardening (and lawn care that does not involve the use of power-driven vehicles); snow removal (that does not involve the use of power-driven vehicles); casual work in the home; and golf caddying.

Children 12 years of age and older may additionally be involved with door-to-door sales, baby-sitting, gardening, lawn care and snow removal with approved power-driven vehicles, and nonhazardous agricultural work.

Those 14 years of age and older may work in nonhazardous manufacturing, messenger services, elevator operation, janitorial work, warehousing and storage, nonhazardous construction and repair work, retail food service, retail store and hotel work, gas station work, and any other nonhazardous work.

Work that has been defined as hazardous and which may not be engaged in by minors, unless it is part of an approved training program, includes:

- Operation of high pressure steam or high temperature water boilers;
- Work that requires the minor to be more than 10 feet off the ground and involves the risk of falling;
- Work requiring exposure to or use with explosives, radioactive substances, or ionizing radiation;
- Operation of dangerous power-driven machinery;
- Slaughter of livestock;
- Manufacturing of brick or roofing; or
- Excavation.

Copies of the Colorado Child Labor Law are available from the Division of Labor. For a list of other Division of Labor publications, contact the Labor Standards Unit at the address below or use the preaddressed post card located at the back of this book.

Labor publications and Posters

Division of Labor – Labor Standards Unit
1120 Lincoln Street, 14th Floor
Denver, CO 80203
(303) 894-7541

Colorado law also requires employers to display the poster from the Division of Labor informing employees of minimum wage laws and similar rights they have. You can obtain this poster from the above office in Denver.

Copies of the federal Fair Labor Standards Act (FLSA) can be obtained from the U.S. Department of Labor.

Wage and Hour Division
U.S. Department of Labor
P.O. Drawer 3505
Denver, CO 80294
(303) 844-4405

Anti-Discrimination Laws

Equal opportunity in employment is guaranteed under Colorado law.[20] It is unlawful to discriminate in employment based on mental or physical handicap, race, creed, color, sex, age, national ancestry, or origin.

For more information, contact:

Civil Rights Division
1560 Broadway, Room 1050
Denver, CO 80202
(303) 894-2997

Colorado law requires all employers to prominently display posters from the division of Civil Rights informing employees of state laws regarding illegal discrimination. To obtain this poster, contact the Denver office of the Civil Rights Division.

City Requirements for Employers

Three Colorado cities — Aurora, Denver, and Greenwood Village — have occupational privilege taxes. In Aurora and Greenwood Village, employers are required to withhold $2.00 per month for each employee that works in the city and match it with $2.00 more. Denver employers are required to withhold $5.75 per month and also contribute $4.00 per employee per month.

Contact the appropriate office listed below for registration.

Aurora Employers:

Finance Department
1470 South Havana Street
Aurora, CO 80012
(303) 695-7057

Greenwood Village Employers:

Finance Department
6060 South Quebec Street
Greenwood Village, CO 80111-4591
(303) 773-0252

Denver Employers:

Occupational Privilege Tax Office
P.O. Box 17430
Denver, CO 80217-0430
(303) 640-2644

11.6 State Licenses

Certain professions and occupations in Colorado require licenses. The Occupation – Agency Key listed on the opposite page tells you which state agency to contact for licensing information on a particular occupation. The number preceding the occupation or business corresponds to the Agency Addresses list which follows the Occupation – Agency Key.

Occupation – Agency Key

1 – Accountants
1 – Acupuncturists
1 – Architects
12 – Asbestos removal
2 – Attorneys
3 – Banking
1 – Barbers and cosmetologists
13 – Bingo and raffles
4 – Butchers and slaughterers
6 – Carnivals and amusement parks
7 – Cemeteries
8 – Child care
1 – Chiropractors
5 – Cigarette wholesalers
9 – Coal mine officials
10 – Collection agencies
6 – Construction of school buildings
10 – Consumer lenders
26 – Credit unions
12 – Dairy products handling
1 – Dental hygienists
1 – Dentists
14 – Driving schools (commercial)
15 – Egg dealers
16 – Electrical contractors
16 – Electricians
12 – Emergency medical technician
6 – Explosives
17 – Farm product and feed dealers

17 – Fertilizer applicators
13 – Fireworks
4 – Frozen food and wild game processors and provisioners
13 – Games of chance
7 – Insurance
12 – Kennel
1 – Land surveyors
7 – Life care institutions
18 – Liquor sales
13 – Lobbyist
1 – Marriage and family therapist
1 – Medical doctors
19 – Messengers and delivery service
12 – Milk handling
1 – Mobile home dealers
3 – Money orders
20 – Motor vehicle (auto) dealers
20 – Motor vehicle (emissions) inspection stations and mechanics
13 – Notary Public
11 – Nursery and greenhouses
1 – Nurses/nurse's aides
1 – Nursing home administrators
21 – Occupational schools
1 – Optometrists
22 – Outdoor advertising
1 – Outfitters
1 – Passenger tramway safety

11 – Pesticide applicators
1 – Pharmacists
1 – Physical therapists
1 – Physicians
1 – Physician assistants
16 – Plumbers
1 – Podiatrists
15 – Poultry processors
1 – Professional counselors
1 – Professional engineers
1 – Psychologists
23 – Racing events
24 – Real estate brokers, salespersons, and appraisers
25 – River rafters
26 – Savings and loan
27 – Scale license
28 – Securities
1 – Social workers
19 – Taxis
29 – Teacher education and certification
19 – Trucking, intrastate for hire
3 – Trust companies
1 – Veterinary medicine
12 – Wastewater operators
30 – Water well drilling
31 – Wildlife, fishing, and hunting

Agency Addresses

1. **Division of Registrations**
   Colorado Department of Regulatory Agencies
   1560 Broadway, Suite 1550
   Denver, CO 80202
   (303) 894-7855

2. **Colorado Supreme Court**
   2 East 14th Avenue, Room 415
   Denver, CO 80203
   (303) 861-1111

3. **Division of Banking**
   Colorado Department of Regulatory Agencies
   1560 Broadway, #1550
   Denver, CO 80202
   (303) 894-7855

4. **Colorado State Veterinary Office**
   Colorado Department of Agriculture
   700 Kipling, #4000
   Lakewood, CO 80215-5894
   (303) 239-4161

5. **Colorado Department of Revenue**
   1375 Sherman Street
   Denver, CO 80261
   (303) 534-1208

6. **Public Safety Section**
   Division of Labor
   Colorado Department of Labor and Employment
   8471 Turnpike Road
   Westminster, CO 80030
   (303) 427-2720

7. **Division of Insurance**
   Colorado Department of Regulatory Agencies
   1560 Broadway
   Denver, CO 80202
   (303) 894-7855

8. **Colorado Department of Social Services**
   1575 Sherman Street
   Denver, CO 80203
   (303) 866-5700

9. **Division of Mines**
   Colorado Department of Natural Resources
   1313 Sherman Street, Room 215
   Denver, CO 80203
   (303) 866-3401

10. **Colorado Attorney General**
    110 16th Street
    Denver, CO 80202
    (303) 620-4500

11. **Colorado Department of Agriculture**
    700 Kipling, #4000
    Lakewood, CO 80215-5894
    (303) 239-4100

12. **Colorado Department of Health**
    4210 East 11th Avenue
    Denver, CO 80220
    (303) 320-8333

13. **Colorado Secretary of State**
    1560 Broadway, Suite 200
    Denver, CO 80202
    (303) 894-2214
    (for bingo and raffles)

    Department of Revenue
    1375 Sherman Street
    Denver, CO 80261
    (for limited casino gambling)

14. **Motor Vehicle Division**
    Colorado Department of Revenue
    516 Acoma
    Denver, CO 80204
    (303) 572-5601

15. **Inspections and Consumer Services**
    Colorado Department of Agriculture
    2331 West 31st Avenue
    Denver, CO 80211
    (303) 866-2825

16. **Electrical and Plumbing Boards**
    Colorado Department of Regulatory Agencies
    1390 Logan Street, Suite 400
    Denver, CO 80203
    (303) 894-2300

17. **Inspections and Consumer Services**
    Colorado Department of Agriculture
    2331 West 31st Avenue
    Denver, CO 80211
    (303) 866-2853 (Farm product/Feed dealers)
    (303) 866-2825 (Fertilizer applicators)

18. **Liquor Enforcement Division**
    Colorado Department of Revenue
    1375 Sherman Street, Room 600
    Denver, CO 80261
    (303) 866-3741

19. **Public Utilities Commission**
    Colorado Department of Regulatory Agencies
    1580 Logan, Office Level 2
    Denver, CO 80203
    (303) 894-2000

Agency Addresses (continued)

20. **Motor Vehicle Division**
Colorado Department of Revenue
140 West 6th Avenue
Denver, CO 80204
(303) 623-9463

21. **Division of Private Occupational Schools**
Department of Higher Education
1290 Broadway, Suite 804
Denver, CO 80223
(303) 894-2960

22. **Colorado Department of Transportation**
4201 East Arkansas
Denver, CO 80222
(303) 757-9011

23. **Racing Commission**
Colorado Department of Regulatory Agencies
1560 Broadway, Suite 1540
Denver, CO 80202
(303) 894-2990

24. **Real Estate Commission**
Colorado Department of Regulatory Agencies
1776 Logan Street, 4th Floor
Denver, CO 80203
(303) 894-2166

25. **Parks and Recreation Division**
Colorado Department of Natural Resources
6315 South University Boulevard
Littleton, CO 80121
(303) 798-2493

26. **Financial Services Division**
Colorado Department of Regulatory Agencies
1560 Broadway, Suite 1520
Denver, CO 80202
(303) 894-2336

27. **Division of Weights and Measures**
Colorado Department of Agriculture
700 Kipling Street, #4000
Lakewood, CO 80215
(303) 866-2845

28. **Securities Division**
Colorado Department of Regulatory Agencies
1580 Lincoln Street, Suite 420
Denver, CO 80203
(303) 894-2320

29. **Colorado Department of Education**
200 East Colfax Avenue
Denver, CO 80203
(303) 866-6600

30. **State Engineer**
Division of Water Resources
Colorado Department of Natural Resources
1313 Sherman Street, Room 818
Denver, CO 80203
(303) 866-3581

31. **Division of Wildlife**
Colorado Department of Natural Resources
6060 Broadway
Denver, CO 80216
(303) 297-1192

If you have any questions regarding state business licensing, as well as federal and local licensing, contact the Small Business Hotline.

Small Business Hotline
Office of Regulatory Reform
Colorado Department of Regulatory Agencies
1560 Broadway, Suite 1530
Denver, CO 80202
(303) 592-5920
(800) 333-7798

11.7 State Excise Taxes

The state of Colorado levies excise taxes upon a number of items.

Alcoholic Beverages Taxes

There is an excise tax of $0.08 (eight cents) per gallon on fermented malt beverages (3.2% beer) sold in Colorado.[21] The tax is paid by the manufacturer if the beer is made in Colorado and by the wholesaler if it is produced outside the state and imported.

Other alcoholic beverages sold in Colorado are subject to excise taxes.[22] Malt liquor (beer with more than 3.3% alcohol) is taxed at $0.08 (eight cents) per gallon. Wine is taxed at $0.0833 (8.33 cents) per liter, of which one cent is dedicated to wine development in Colorado, and other liquor is taxed at $0.6026 (60.26 cents) per liter. In all instances, if the manufacturer is in Colorado, it pays the tax, and wholesalers pay tax for alcoholic beverages produced somewhere else and brought into Colorado.

There is an additional excise tax of $0.04 (four cents) per liter on Colorado-produced wine — $0.03 (three cents) before July 1, 1992. That tax increases to $0.05 (five cents) July 1, 1993. Colorado wineries also pay a tax of $5 per ton of grapes. The tax increases to $8 per ton July 1, 1993 and $10 per ton July 1, 1996. All proceeds will be used to promote Colorado wine.

Businesses liable to pay the tax must file a monthly return on the 20th day of each month with the Colorado Department of Revenue.

Colorado Department of Revenue
1375 Sherman Street
Denver, CO 80261
(303) 534-1805

Severance Tax on Minerals

Because minerals extracted from Colorado deplete the state's natural resources, an excise tax is assessed on all minerals removed from Colorado's resources.[23] Colorado law breaks severance tax into five areas: metallic minerals; molybdenum ore; oil, gas, and carbon dioxide; coal; and oil shale. For more information, call:

Colorado Department of Revenue
1375 Sherman Street
Denver, CO 80261
(303) 534-1209

Metallic Minerals

This category includes all minerals except molybdenum, oil and gas, carbon dioxide, coal, oil shale, gravel and stone products, earths, limestone, and dolomite. The tax is assessed on the gross income of mining operations. No tax is assessed on the first $11 million, but mines pay 2.25% tax on all gross income exceeding $11 million.

There is a severance tax of $0.05 (five cents) per ton on all molybdenum ore mined in Colorado. The tax will increase to $0.10 (10 cents) per ton after 1994.

Molybdenum Ore

Severance tax is assessed on all production in this category, except on oil wells that produce 10 barrels or less per day. The rate varies depending on the total gross income:

Oil, Gas, and Carbon Dioxide

Gross Income	Tax Rate
Under $25,000	2%
$25,000 but under $100,000	3%
$100,000 but under $300,000	4%
$300,000 and over	5%

An 87.5% credit may be taken against ad valorem taxes.

Subject to a few exemptions and credits, a severance tax of $0.36 (36 cents) per ton is assessed on all but the first 25,000 tons of coal produced each quarter.

Coal

Severance tax on oil shale becomes effective on commercial oil shale facilities after they have been operative for 180 days. The first 15,000 tons or 10,000 barrels of shale oil per day, whichever is greater, is exempt from the tax.

Oil Shale

The tax is 1% of gross proceeds the first year, 2% of gross annual proceeds the second year, 3% of gross annual proceeds the third year, and 4% of gross annual proceeds the fourth year and each year thereafter.

Colorado has no state property transfer tax, but there is a documentary fee on any conveyance of real property of $0.01 (one cent) for each $100.00.[24] The fee is paid to the county clerk and recorder in the county where the property is located.

Property Transfer Taxes

A $0.20 (20 cents) per gallon tax is assessed on all gasoline to be consumed by motor vehicles.[25] The tax must be paid to the Colorado Department of Revenue by the refiner, if the gasoline is produced in Colorado; by the distributor, if it is produced elsewhere.

Gasoline and Special Fuels Taxes

Tax is due the 25th day of the month after the month the gas was received. If you are an agricultural user or use gasoline to power stationary machinery you are exempt from gasoline tax. Refunds may be requested from the Colorado Department of Revenue.

Colorado also has an excise tax on special fuel.[26] The law defines special fuel as diesel fuel, kerosene, liquefied petroleum gases, and natural gas used to power or propel a motor vehicle on public roads. The tax is

$0.205 (20½ cents) per gallon and is remitted in the same way as gasoline tax. For more information, call:

Colorado Department of Revenue
1375 Sherman Street
Denver, CO 80261
(303) 534-1805

Cigarette and Tobacco Products Taxes

Colorado assesses a $0.20 (20 cents) per pack tax on cigarettes.[27] The tax is paid by wholesalers of cigarettes who must also obtain a license from the Colorado Department of Revenue. Cities and towns receive a percentage of tax collected under this law and are prohibited from establishing a separate local tax on cigarettes. A tax of 20% of the manufacturer's list price is assessed on all tobacco products other than cigarettes.[28] For more information, call:

Colorado Department of Revenue
1375 Sherman Street
Denver, CO 80261
(303) 534-1208

11.8 Planning for Tax Savings in a Business — State Tax Laws

Some states have special provisions in a number of areas that may save money for new businesses, if they plan ahead. Here are the ways Colorado law addresses these concerns.

Dividends Received Deduction

See Section 11.2 for a discussion on dividends received deductions.

Sheltering Profits on Export Sales

Colorado has no program for Domestic International Sales Corporations (DISCs) as discussed in Section 8.4. There are, however, some programs which assist businesses in exporting. Foreign trade zones have been established in Denver and in Colorado Springs. Export financing may be available from the Colorado Housing Finance Authority, while technical assistance and general export information may be obtained from the International Trade Office.

International Trade Office
1625 Broadway, Suite 680
Denver, CO 80202
(303) 892-3850

Unlimited Marital Deduction

Colorado has no inheritance or estate tax.

State Jobs Tax Credit

Colorado allows the following income tax credits for new business facilities established within an enterprise zone after September 15, 1986:

- New Business Facility Jobs Tax Credit ($500 per new employee);
- New Business Facility Agricultural Processing Tax Credit ($500 per new employee);
- Credit for Employer-Sponsored Health Insurance ($200 per new employee); and
- Triple Investment Tax Credit.

The Division of Employment and Training administers federal job tax credits in the state.

Division of Employment and Training
Colorado Department of Labor and Employment
600 Grant Street, Suite 900
Denver, CO 80203
(303) 837-3918

A sole proprietor who hires a spouse as an employee is not required to pay state unemployment tax on the spouse's wages.

Hiring a Spouse as an Employee

11.9 Miscellaneous Business Pointers

This section briefly outlines several helpful programs and general information you may find useful when starting your business.

Losses on certain small business stock — Section 1244 stock — are deductible as ordinary losses. Any amount not absorbed in the year of the loss becomes part of the stockholder's net operating loss carryover and carryback. Ordinary losses are reported on Part II of *Form 4797*.

Section 1244 Stock

Specific business loan programs are operated by Colorado state government as well as several private organizations. A brief discussion of some of these programs are outlined below.

Business Loan Programs

The Quality Investment Capital program (QIC), funded by the state treasurer, is administered by the Colorado Housing and Finance Authority (CHFA). It provides fixed-rate financing for small business loans guaranteed by the U.S. Small Business Administration for equipment, buildings, and working capital. For more information, contact:

Quality Investment Capital Program

Quality Investment Capital Program
Colorado Housing and Finance Authority
1981 Blake Street
Denver, CO 80202
(303) 297-CHFA
(800) 877-CHFA (in Colorado)

Revolving Loan Funds

Direct loans for businesses that will create jobs for low- and moderate-income individuals in communities of 50,000 population or less are available through state and regional revolving loan funds. For more information, contact:

Office of Business Development
1625 Broadway, Suite 1710
Denver, CO 80202
(303) 892-3840

Colorado Statewide Development Corporation

The Colorado Statewide Development Corporation provides money for working capital, equipment inventory, and real estate. This program is available to businesses in cities with fewer than 50,000 people. For more information, contact:

Colorado Department of Local Affairs
1313 Sherman Street, Suite 518
Denver, CO 80203
(303) 866-2771

Export Financing

Export financing may be available if you qualify for export insurance and cannot get bank financing. For more information, contact the Colorado Housing Finance Authority.

Small Business Administration

The Small Business Administration (SBA) has a list of Small Business Investment Companies (SBICs) it backs that furnish equity, capital, and long range planning to small businesses.

A number of local areas have also developed local development companies to encourage business development. For more information, contact the SBA or contact your local economic development agency or chamber of commerce.

U.S. Small Business Administration
721 19th Street
Denver, CO 80202
(303) 844-2607

Venture Capital Firms

Some people or companies invest in businesses which have the potential for high rates of return. These firms are most likely to invest in high technology or scientific businesses or in companies with newly patented processes or products. For a listing of local and nationwide venture capital companies, contact:

Small Business Hotline
(800) 333-7798

Family and Friends

Do not ignore the most obvious source. You may have family members or friends willing to loan you money or become investors in your company. Make sure you consider all your options.

Colorado's Consumer Credit Code prescribes maximum charges for all people who extend credit and applies to sales, leases, and loans.[29] These requirements, however, do not apply to the extension of credit to government agencies, insurance sales, public utility tariffs or common carrier rates, charges for late payments or discounts for early payments, or to rates charged by pawn brokers or credit unions.

Under the code, as it relates to consumer credit sales, the credit service charge may not exceed whichever is greater:

- 25% per year on that part of unpaid balances for financed amounts less than $630;
- 20% per year for financed amounts between $630 to $2,100; or
- 15% per year on financed amounts of more than $2,100 or 21% per year on unpaid balances.

In addition to the credit service charge, a person extending credit may charge official fees, taxes, and charges for insurance or other benefits to the buyer. For revolving charge accounts, a charge may be made for each billing cycle, which is a percentage of an amount no greater than the adjusted balance; however, if the cycle is monthly, the charge may not exceed 1.75% percent of the adjusted balance.

Supervised loans are subject to the following restrictions:

- 36% per year on unpaid balances of less than $630;
- 21% per year on unpaid balances between $630 and $2,100; and
- 15% per year on balances of over $2,100.

A person may take a security interest in property sold when credit is extended, in goods upon which services are performed, or in land to which goods are attached, maintained, repaired, or improved as a result of the sale of goods and services. This relationship does not occur with leases. The person extending credit, however, cannot take an assignment of earnings for payment or as security. The code also sets, for contracts, a limit of 15% of the unpaid debt after default as reasonable attorney fees.

While the code generally applies to loans, it does not apply to a loan primarily secured by an interest in land or by a mobile home. The state sets a limit on loan finance charges of 12% per year if it does not exceed 1% of the average daily balance of the debt or of the unpaid balance of the debt. The creditor may also charge for official fees and taxes, insurance, annual charges, and other benefits.

A lender cannot make multiple agreements, such as between a husband and a wife, to obtain a higher loan finance charge. A borrower may rescind transactions until midnight of the third business day following the transition of the delivery of disclosures.

If there is no agreement as to an interest rate, 8% per year compounded annually is the maximum interest allowable on any bill, bond, promissory

Usury Laws

note, or other instrument. Greater interest rates may be contracted but not to exceed 45% annually.

Finally, Colorado law does not allow federal pre-emption in mortgages, business and agricultural loans, small business loans or credit loans under the Federal Deposit Insurance Act, National Housing Act, or Federal Credit Union Act.

11.10 State Sources of Help and Information

Do-It-Yourself Incorporation

As stated in Section 11.2, those choosing to incorporate must file articles of incorporation with the secretary of state. Sample articles of incorporation have been developed by, and may be obtained from, the secretary of state's office or the Small Business Hotline.

The authors are unaware of any do-it-yourself incorporation books for the state of Colorado.

Payroll Tax Information

Colorado withholding tables are available from the Taxpayer Service Division at no cost.

Taxpayer Service Division
Colorado Department of Revenue
1375 Sherman Street, Room 186 (by mail)   1560 Broadway, #1530 (in person)
Denver, CO 80261   Denver, CO 80202
(303) 534-1208
(800) 332-2085 (in Colorado)

Unemployment Information

The Colorado *Employer's Handbook,* which explains unemployment procedures and requirements, can be obtained from the Division of Employment and Training at no cost.

Division of Employment and Training
Colorado Department of Labor and Employment
639 East 18th Avenue, 1st Floor
Denver, CO 80203
(303) 839-4922

Statistical Information

If you need statistical information on employment and payrolls, and the number and employment size of businesses by industry, contact the regional census bureau. At the date of this publication, this office provided the booklet, *County Business Patterns.* For more information, contact:

Regional Census Center
Bureau of the Census
U.S. Department of Commerce
6900 West Jefferson Avenue
Lakewood, CO 80235-2307
(303) 969-7750

A number of state agencies can provide you with assistance or information or both.

State Agency Assistance

Office of Regulatory Reform (ORR) — Through the Small Business Hotline, ORR, in conjunction with the Governor's Small Business Office, provides one-stop license and permit assistance on governmental requirements for going into business, as well as management and financial assistance. For more information, call or write to:

Office of Regulatory Reform
Colorado Department of Regulatory Agencies
1560 Broadway, Suite 1530
Denver, CO 80202
(303) 592-5920
(800) 333-7798 (Small business hotline)

Taxpayer Service Division — The Taxpayer Service Division answers all tax-related questions and offers several useful publications to taxpayers, such as the *Colorado Withholding Tables* and *Colorado Sales and Use Tax General Information and Instruction Booklet.*

Taxpayer Service Division
Colorado Department of Revenue
1375 Sherman Street (by mail)   1560 Broadway, #1530 (in person)
Denver, CO 80261   Denver, CO 80202
(303) 534-1208
(800) 332-2085 (in Colorado)

Office of Business Development (OBD) — The Office of Business Development provides technical assistance on location, redevelopment, exporting, and other business needs. The OBD also loans money to businesses in rural areas through revolving loan funds. For details, contact:

Office of Business Development
1625 Broadway, Suite 1710
Denver, CO 80202
(303) 892-3840

Colorado Division of Labor, Labor Standards Unit — This office, through its taped message system, will answer questions regarding state labor laws affecting employers, including wage-hour regulations, child labor, minimum wage, and discrimination laws.

Division of Labor – Labor Standards Unit
1120 Lincoln Street
Denver, CO 80203
(303) 894-7541

Colorado Department of State — The Colorado Department of State provides licensing and general information on the different types of business, such as sole proprietorships, partnerships, and corporations.

For more information, contact:

Colorado Department of State
1560 Broadway, Suite 200
Denver, CO 80202
(303) 894-2200 (Administration)
(303) 894-2251 (Corporations)
(303) 894-2680 (Licensing and Enforcement)
(303) 894-2200 (Uniform Commercial Code)

Minority Business Office — The Minority Business Office provides general and technical assistance primarily to minority business enterprises by facilitating their participation in the state government procurement contracting process. For details, contact:

Minority Business Office
1625 Broadway, Suite 1710
Denver, CO 80202
(303) 892-3840

Job Service — Job Service has 24 offices around Colorado to assist in hiring and training at no cost to the job applicant or to the employer. For more information, contact your local Job Service Center or the Division of Employment and Training.

Division of Employment and Training
Colorado Department of Labor and Employment
600 Grant Street, Suite 900
Denver, CO 80203
(303) 837-3926

Governor's Job Training Office (GJTO) — The GJTO provides training opportunities to employers and employees. For more information, contact:

Job Training Office
720 South Colorado Boulevard, Suite 550
Denver, CO 80222
(303) 758-5020

Greater Denver Chamber of Commerce — This organization provides referral for inquiries on small business related data and issues and collects information on labor and employment statistics. Its Information Source also provides relocation and job search information packets, as well as directories on Colorado businesses and manufacturers.

For more information, contact:

Greater Denver Chamber of Commerce
1445 Market Street
Denver, CO 80202
(303) 534-8500
(303) 620-8073 (Information Source)

Universities, Colleges, and Junior Colleges — Institutions of higher education offer a variety of services to business. Contact the institution in your area for more information.

Public Schools — School districts in Colorado offer a variety of programs. To see if such programs are available in your area, contact your local school district.

Trade and business journals can assist you in keeping up-to-date on business-related activities and events in Colorado. Daily newspapers are also helpful since they cover current state and local news and information, which may affect your business. For your convenience, several state business and trade journals are listed below should you be interested in learning more about or subscribing to any of these publications.

State Business Publications

CBM: Colorado Business Magazine
5951 South Middlefield Road, Suite 204
Littleton, CO 80123-6600
(303) 798-1274

Denver Business
100 Garfield Street
Denver, CO 80206-5550
(303) 322-6400

The Denver Business Journal
2401 15th Street, Suite 350
Denver, CO 80202-1168
(303) 433-0033

Colorado Beverage Analyst
2403 Champa Street
Denver, CO 80205-2621
(303) 296-1600

Colorado Engineer
University of Colorado
P.O. Box 421
Boulder, CO 80309
(303) 492-8635

Colorado Homes & Lifestyles
2550 31st Street, Suite 154
Denver, CO 80216-4845
(303) 455-1944

Colorado Medicine
P.O. Box 17550
Denver, CO 80217-0550
(303) 779-5455

Colorado Municipalities
1660 Lincoln Street, Suite 2100
Denver, CO 80264-2101
(303) 831-6411

The Colorado Pharmacist
770 Grant, Suite 244
Denver, CO 80203-3517
(303) 861-0328

Colorado Rancher & Farmer
2765 S. Colorado Boulevard
Denver, CO 80222-6616
(303) 756-1526

There are number of Small Business Development Centers (SBDCs) located throughout the state which would be of possible assistance to you. These centers, usually located on college and university campuses, provide start-up information as well as sponsor business-oriented seminars. Please review the addresses listed below for the SBDC office nearest you.

Small Business Development Centers

Colorado Small Business Development Center
Office of Business Development
1625 Broadway, Suite 1710
Denver, CO 80202
(303) 892-3809
(303) 894-2427

SBDC: Adams State College
Alamosa, CO 81102
(719) 589-7372

SBDC: Arapahoe Community College
South Metro Denver Chamber of Commerce
1101 West Mineral Avenue, Suite 160
Littleton, CO 80120
(303) 795-0142

SBDC: Burlington
480 15th Street
Burlington, CO 80807-1624
(719) 346-9311

SBDC: Colorado Innovation Foundation
1625 Broadway, Suite 1710
Denver, CO 80202
(303) 892-3840

SBDC: Colorado Mountain College
1310 Westhaven Drive
Vail, CO 81657
(303) 476-4040
(800) 621-1647

SBDC: Colorado Northwestern Community College
500 Kennedy Drive
Rangeley, CO 81648-3598
(303) 675-2261

SBDC: Community College of Aurora
791 Chambers Road, Suite 302
Aurora, CO 80011
(303) 360-4745

SBDC: Community College of Denver
600 Grant Street, Suite 505
Denver, CO 80203
(303) 894-2422

SBDC: Delta/Grand Junction
1765 U.S. Highway 50
Delta, CO 81416
(303) 874- 8772

SBDC: Grand Junction
304 West Main Street
Grand Junction, CO 81505
(303) 248-7314

SBDC: Fort Lewis College
Reed Library, Room 125
Durango, CO 81301-3999
(303) 247-7188

SBDC: Fort Range Community College
3645 West 112th Avenue
Westminister, CO 80030
(303) 466-8811

SBDC: Lamar Community College
2400 South Main
Lamar, CO 81052
(719) 336-2248

SBDC: University of Front Range Community College
4616 South Shields
P.C. Box 2397
Fort Collins, CO 80526
(303) 226-0881

SBDC: Morgan Community College
300 Main Street
Fort Morgan, CO 80701
(303) 867-3351

SBDC: Pikes Peak Community College
102 Cascade Street, 6th Floor
P.O. Drawer B
Colorado Springs, CO 80901
(719) 471-4836

SBDC: Pueblo Community College
900 West Orman Avenue
Pueblo, CO 81104
(719) 549-3324

SBDC: Trinidad State Junior College
600 Prospect Street
Davis Science Building
Trinidad, CO 81082
(719) 846-5645

Footnotes

1. COLO. REV. STAT. § 7-61-103.
2. COLO. REV. STAT. § 7-2-101 *et seq.*
3. COLO. REV. STAT. § 7-22-107.
4. COLO. REV. STAT. § 7-21-101.
5. COLO. REV. STAT. § 7-9-108.
6. COLO. REV. STAT. § 4-6-101 *et seq.*
7. COLO. REV. STAT. § 39-26-106.
8. COLO. REV. STAT. § 24-32-1307.
9. COLO. REV. STAT. § 39-26-201 *et seq.*
10. COLO. REV. STAT. § 39-1-101 *et seq.*
11. COLO. REV. STAT. § 7-71-101 *et seq.*
12. COLO. REV. STAT. § 24-35-301 *et seq.*
13. COLO. REV. STAT. § 39-22-103.5.
14. COLO. REV. STAT. § 39-22-604.
15. COLO. REV. STAT. § 8-70-103.
16. COLO. REV. STAT. § 8-43-101 *et seq.*
17. COLO. REV. STAT. § 8-6-101 *et seq.*
18. COLO. CODE REGS. § 1103-3.
19. COLO. REV. STAT. § 8-12-101 *et seq.*
20. COLO. CONST. art. 2, § 24-34-401 *et seq.*
21. COLO. REV. STAT. § 12-46-111.
22. COLO. REV. STAT. § 12-47-127.
23. COLO. REV. STAT. § 39-29-101 *et seq.*
24. COLO. REV. STAT. § 39-13-102.
25. COLO. REV. STAT. § 39-27-101 *et seq.*
26. COLO. REV. STAT. § 39-27-201 *et seq.*
27. COLO. REV. STAT. § 39-28-101 *et seq.*
28. COLO. REV. STAT. § 39-28.5-101 *et seq.*
29. COLO. REV. STAT. § 5-6-102.

Notes

Index

(continued)

(continued)

Appendix

Checklist of Tax and Other Major Requirements for Nearly All Small Businesses

Requirement	None	1–4	5–10	11–14	15–19	20–99	100+	Chapter–Section Reference
Federal estimated taxes	√	√	√	√	√	√	√	Sec. 4.3, 11.4
Federal income tax returns	√	√	√	√	√	√	√	Sec. 4.12
Form SS-4, Application for Federal I.D. Number:								
Sole Proprietorships		√	√	√	√	√	√	Sec. 5.2
Partnerships	√	√	√	√	√	√	√	Sec. 5.2
Corporations	√	√	√	√	√	√	√	Sec. 5.2
Form 1099 returns	√	√	√	√	√	√	√	Sec. 4.7
Federal payroll tax returns		√	√	√	√	√	√	Sec. 5.2, 5.3
Provide and file W-2's to employees at year-end		√	√	√	√	√	√	Sec. 5.2
ERISA compliance:								
For unfunded or insured employees' welfare plan:								
Provide a Summary Plan Description to employees		√	√	√	√	√	√	Sec. 5.5
File a Summary Plan Description							√	Sec. 5.5
File *Form 5500, Annual Report*							√	Sec. 5.5
Provide a Summary Annual Report to employees							√	Sec. 5.5
File and provide to employees a Summary of Material Plan Modifications							√	Sec. 5.5
File a Terminal Report, if plan terminated							√	Sec. 5.5
For funded employee welfare plan:								
File and provide all items described in ERISA list		√	√	√	√	√	√	Sec. 5.5
For employees' pension or profit-sharing plan:								
Provide a Summary Plan Description to employees and file with U.S. Department of Labor		√	√	√	√	√	√	Sec. 5.5
File *Form 5500, Annual Report*							√	Sec. 5.5
File *Form 5500-C* or *Form 5500-R*		√	√	√	√	√	√	Sec. 5.5
Provide to employees and file a Summary of Material Modifications		√	√	√	√	√	√	Sec. 5.5
File a Terminal Report, if plan terminated		√	√	√	√	√	√	Sec. 5.5
Provide a Summary Annual Report to employees		√	√	√	√	√	√	Sec. 5.5
Bonding requirement for plan officials		√	√	√	√	√	√	Sec. 5.5
Federal Wage and Hour Laws and Regulations — coverage depends on nature of business and employee types not covered		√	√	√	√	√	√	Sec. 5.7
Federal Fair Employment Laws:								
Anti-discrimination laws regarding race, color, religion, sex, etc.					√	√	√	Sec. 5.8
Equal Pay Act for women		√	√	√	√	√	√	Sec. 5.8
Anti-discrimination laws regarding age						√	√	Sec. 5.8
Anti-discrimination laws regarding federal contracts		√	√	√	√	√	√	Sec. 5.8

Requirement	Number of Employees of Business							Chapter–Section Reference
	None	1–4	5–10	11–14	15–19	20–99	100+	
Federal Fair Employment Laws: (continued)								
File *Form EEO-1*							√	Sec. 5.8
Post notice regarding discrimination: racial, sexual, etc.					√	√	√	Sec. 5.8
Post notice regarding age anti-discrimination laws						√	√	Sec. 5.8
Post other anti-discrimination notices by certain federal contractors		√	√	√	√	√	√	Sec. 5.8
Immigration Laws:								
Complete INS *Form I-9* for each new hire		√	√	√	√	√	√	Sec. 5.9
OSHA Job Safety Regulations:								
Health and safety		√	√	√	√	√	√	Sec. 5.6
Post *Job Safety and Health Notice*		√	√	√	√	√	√	Sec. 5.6
Post *Employee Rights Notice* regarding OSHA		√	√	√	√	√	√	Sec. 5.6
Record industrial injuries and illnesses				√	√	√	√	Sec. 5.6
Report job fatalities or multiple injuries to OSHA		√	√	√	√	√	√	Sec. 5.6
Federal and State Child Labor Laws		√	√	√	√	√	√	Sec. 5.7, 11.5
Local business licenses	√	√	√	√	√	√	√	Sec. 4.3, 11.4
Sales and use tax permit and returns, if selling tangible personal property	√	√	√	√	√	√	√	Sec. 11.4
Fictitious business name statement, if using fictitious business name	√	√	√	√	√	√	√	Sec. 11.4
State estimated taxes	√	√	√	√	√	√	√	Sec. 11.4
State income taxes	√	√	√	√	√	√	√	Sec. 11.2, 11.4
State Wage and Hour Laws and Regulations — most employees are covered, yet some types are not		√	√	√	√	√	√	Sec. 11.5
Workers' compensation insurance		√	√	√	√	√	√	Sec. 11.5
State Fair Employment Laws: General prohibition of discrimination		√	√	√	√	√	√	Sec. 11.5

Checklist of Official Government Posters and Notices Required to be Displayed by Businesses

Type of Poster or Notice	When required	Where to obtain
Local business license	Required of practically all businesses operating in a particular locality	Local city hall or county courthouse
Sales tax permit	Must be displayed at each place of business where tangible personal property is sold	Local office
OSHA poster regarding Job Safety and Health	Required to be posted by all employers	U.S. Department of Labor Occupational Safety and Health Administration
OSHA poster regarding rights of employees under OSHA	Required to be posted by all employers	U.S. Department of Labor Occupational Safety and Health Administration
U.S. Fair Labor Standards Act Wage-Hour poster, *Attention Employees, (WH Publication 1088)*	Required to be posted by employers with employees whose wages and working conditions are subject to the U.S. Fair Labor Standards Act	U.S. Department of Labor Employment Standards Administration (Wage-Hour Division offices)
Federal Equal Employment Opportunity poster	Required to be posted by all employers with 15 or more employees, 20 weeks of the year, or with federal contracts or subcontracts or $10,000 or more	Federal Equal Employment Opportunity Commission offices
Federal Age Discrimination poster	Require to be posted by all employers with 20 or more employees 20 weeks a year	U.S. Department of Labor (Wage-Hour Division offices)
Federal Rehabilitation Act poster regarding hiring of handicapped persons	Required to be posted by employers with federal contracts or subcontracts of $2,500 or more	Assistant Secretary for Employment Standards, U.S. Department of Labor Washington, D.C.
Poster regarding hiring of Vietnam-era veterans	Required to be posted by employers with federal contracts or subcontracts of $10,000 or more	The government contracting officer on the federal contract

Notes

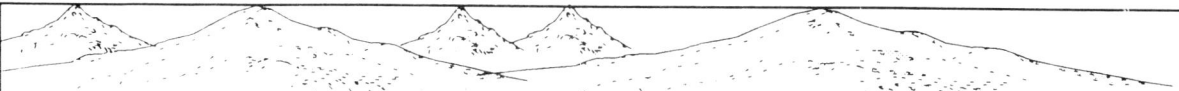

Colorado Employer Registration

✓ TO ESTABLISH WAGE WITHHOLDING FOR STATE INCOME TAXES AND, IF APPLICABLE, REGISTER A TRADENAME AND/OR APPLY FOR STATE SALES TAX LICENSE

✓ TO ESTABLISH COLORADO UNEMPLOYMENT INSURANCE ACCOUNTS

INSTRUCTIONS:

1. Detach this instructional sheet.
2. Complete ALL information requested on the front and back of the *Colorado Employer Registration* form. Please type or print legibly.
3. Your completed registration form may be mailed to: **Colorado Department of Revenue**
   Or processed over the counter at the locations **1375 Sherman Street**
   listed below: **Denver, Colorado 80261**

NEW BUSINESS ASSISTANCE CENTER
1560 Broadway Street, Suite 1530
Denver, Colorado 80202
(303) 592-5920 / 1-800-333-7798

DURANGO DISTRICT OFFICE
1474 Main Street, P.O. Box 277
Durango, Colorado 81301
(303) 259-4342

GLENWOOD SPRINGS DISTRICT OFFICE
406 S. Hyland Park Drive, Suite C
Glenwood Springs, Colorado 81601
(303) 945-1222 / 1-800-221-6042

GREELEY DISTRICT OFFICE
800 East Eighth Avenue, Suite 224
Greeley, Colorado 80631
(303) 352-1165

COLORADO SPRINGS DISTRICT OFFICE
2762 Airport Road
Colorado Springs, Colorado 80910
(719) 632-8812

FORT COLLINS DISTRICT OFFICE
300 East Foothills Parkway
Fort Collins, Colorado 80525
(303) 223-1097

GRAND JUNCTION DISTRICT OFFICE
222 S. Sixth Street, Room 208
Grand Junction, Colorado 81501
(303) 248-7140

PUEBLO DISTRICT OFFICE
720 N. Main Street, Suite 402
Pueblo, Colorado 81003
(719) 542-2920

INSTRUCTIONS FOR THE FRONT PAGE OF THE REGISTRATION FORM

IS YOUR BUSINESS LIABLE FOR ANY OF THE FOLLOWING TAXES? IF SO, MARK THE APPROPRIATE BOX(ES) ON THE FRONT OF THE REGISTRATION FORM.

STATE AND LOCAL SALES TAXES: State sales tax of 3 % must be collected by all retail businesses located in Colorado. City and/or county sales taxes must also be collected if your business is located in a city or county that has a sales tax administered by the state. Call the Department of Revenue for further information or to request the publication Colorado Sales/Use Tax Rates (DRP 1002).

RTD/CD: Regional Transportation District (RTD) tax of 0.6 % and the Scientific and Cultural Facilities (CD) tax of 0.1 % must be collected if your retail business is located in the metro-area RTD/CD District (see DRP 1002).

COUNTY LODGING TAX: Certain counties levy an additional tax on the rental of rooms and accommodations (see DRP 1002).

TOURISM PROMOTION FUND TAX: A statewide tax of 0.2 % is charged to businesses engaged in lodging, food and drink services, skiing, short-term automobile rentals, tour buses, and admissions to tourist attractions (see DRP 1807).

RETAILER'S USE TAX: A use tax of 3 % must be collected by vendors who have no business location in the state, but do business in Colorado. An additional 0.7 % RTD/CD tax must be collected, if applicable (see FYI S-5).

OIL AND GAS WITHHOLDING: Every producer of crude oil, natural gas, or oil shale shall withhold 2 % from the amount owed to any person owning a working interest, a royalty interest, a production payment or any interest in carbon dioxide or oil or gas production in Colorado. No withholding is required from payments made to Colorado or the U.S. Government (see FYI G-4).

WAGE WITHHOLDING TAX: Employers are required to withhold state income tax from wages of Colorado employees.

ADDITIONAL INSTRUCTIONS ON THE BACK OF THIS SHEET

WHAT TYPE OF LICENSE DO YOU NEED?

SALES TAX (regular retail): If you sell tangible personal property at a business location in Colorado, you must have a regular state retail sales tax license.

WHOLESALERS: A wholesaler is a person selling to retail merchants, jobbers, dealers or other wholesalers for the purpose of resale.

WAGE WITHHOLDING: If you pay wages to Colorado employees and are required to withhold federal income taxes, you must also withhold state income taxes.

MULTIPLE EVENTS: This license is available if you engage in retail sales at more than one special event in any two-year licensing period. There is no fee for those retailers with a regular state sales tax license.

SINGLE EVENT: A single event license is available for each sales event where you make retail sales if the event is at a location other than your business (if any). There is not fee for a business with a regular state sales tax license.

A temporary sales tax license may be obtained when the application and appropriate fees are presented at one of the locations listed on the reverse side of this page.

The Department of Revenue offers sales and withholding tax classes. Withholding tax classes are conducted every second and fourth Wednesday of the month. Sales tax classes are conducted every Friday morning and the second Thursday afternoon of the month. Interested taxpayers should call (303) 534-1208 or 800-332-2085 for time and location of classes.

For further information, or to order publications, call 534-1208 (metro area) or 800-332-2085 (statewide).

FEE SCHEDULE

FEES: The correct amount of fees must be entered on the front of the registration form.

DEPOSITS: Retail sales tax license applicants must pay a $50 deposit in addition to the regular license fee. However, if the application is for an additional location of a business which already has a sales tax license, the $50 deposit is not required.

The $50 deposit is required only with regular sales tax accounts. The deposit will automatically be refunded when payment(s) of state sales tax has reached or exceeded $50. **DO NOT CLAIM THE REFUND OF THE $50 ON YOUR SALES TAX RETURN!**

If your account is closed for any reason before you have collected and paid $50 in state sales tax, only the amount of Colorado sales tax you have paid will be refunded.

All licenses, except single event licenses, are valid through December 31, 1991.

	SALES START-UP DATE			
	1/1/90	7/1/90	1/1/91	7/1/91
	to	to	to	to
TYPE OF LICENSE	6/30/90	12/31/90	6/30/91	12/31/91
Sales Tax - regular (retail)	$16.00	$12.00	$8.00	$4.00
PLUS deposit	--	$50.00		--
Wholesalers	$16.00	$12.00	$8.00	$4.00
State approved charitable org.	$8.00	$8.00	$8.00	$8.00
Single Event	$8.00	$8.00	$8.00	$8.00
Multilple Event	$16.00	$12.00	$8.00	$4.00
Retailer's Use	0	0	0	0
Withholding/severance withholding	0	0	0	0
Tourism Promotion	0	0	0	0
County Lodging	0	0	0	0
Trade Name Registration *	$6.00	(initial registration)		
*(if applicable)				

INSTRUCTIONS FOR THE BACK PAGE OF THE REGISTRATION FORM:

Answers to questions in Items 16 and 17 help to determine the date of becoming subject to paying unemployment insurance tax. In answering the first two questions in Item 17, the following example may be helpful. *A domestic household employer hires an employee on February 5; $1000 in wages in a calendar quarter is paid by September 30. The date of meeting the requirement in Item 17 is September 30; the date of first hire is February 5.*

If you have questions regarding unemployment insurance, please contact: U.I. Liability Unit, Colorado Department of Labor and Employment
639 East 18th Avenue, Denver, Colorado 80203
(303) 839-4922.

Any unemployment tax payments should be made on a **SEPARATE** check, payable to Colorado State Treasurer.

CR 001
1375 SHERMAN STREET
DENVER, CO 80261

Colorado Employer Registration

FOR NEW APPLICATIONS ONLY

DO NOT WRITE IN THIS SPACE

Registration Number:

FOR OFFICE USE ONLY		
ACCOUNT TYPE _____ SIC CODE _____ ORGANIZATIONAL CODE _____ LIABILITY CODE _____		
LIABILITY DATE __ / __ / __ QUALIFYING DATE __ / __ / __ STATUS CODE _____		
INACTIVE DATE __ / __ / __ UITR-1S _____ SIGNATURE _____		
TECH SIGNATURE _____ DATE __ / __ / __		

Routing:
DATE   IN   OUT
Revenue _____ _____
Labor _____ _____

1. Check any additional reasons for submitting this form:

[X] Wage Withholding
[X] Unemployment Insurance
[ ] Trade Name Registration
[ ] State Sales Tax License
[ ] Other (Explain _____)

SAMPLE

2. Indicate Type of Ownership:

[ ] Individual   [ ] Association   [ ] Government
[ ] Limited Partnership [ ] Trust   [ ] Non-Profit 501C(3)
[ ] General Partnership [ ] Estate   [ ] Other Non-Profit
[ ] Corporate   [ ] 'S' Corporation   [ ] Other
[ ] Limited Liability Company

3. ★ Information marked with a star (★) will become public record if a trade name is registered

Taxpayer Name (Owner, Partner or Corporation) (Last, First, Middle)
★

Trade Name/Doing Business As (If Applicable)
★

I declare, under penalty of perjury in the second degree, that the statements made on this application are true and complete, to the best of my knowledge.

Signature: (If registering Trade Name)   Date:

4. Street Address of Principal Place of Business in Colorado ★ | City ★ | State ★ | Zip ★

County | City Limits in which business is located (If Applicable) | Telephone ( )

Mailing Address (If different from above) (Include Unit Number) | City | State | Zip

County | Telephone ( ) | Fed. Employer ID No. (If unavailable, Social Sec No.)

5. Brief description of business/What do you sell?:
★ | Dealer's License Number (If selling motor vehicles)

6. If Owners are Corporations, List Corporate Name and Corporate Address:

Name ★	Address ★
★	★

7. Complete for Owner, Partners or Corporate Officers:

Name	Residential Address	Home Phone Number	Title	Social Security Number

8. Bank Name | Bank Address | Bank Account Number

9. If you acquired the business in whole or in part, complete the following:

Prior Owner's Name and Address				Date of Acquisition	Prior Owner's UI Tax Account Number
Street	City	State	Zip	Type of Acquisition [ ] Total [ ] Partial	If Partial, Employees Transferred? [ ] Yes [ ] No

List total number of employees in each of the prior owner's four (4) pay periods preceding transfer date | 1. | 2. | 3. | 4.

10. Payroll Location (List Address and Phone Number)

Filing Frequency: If withholding collected is
[ ] UNDER $400/MONTH, FILE QUARTERLY
[ ] $400/MONTH OR MORE, FILE MONTHLY
[ ] $399/YEAR OR LESS, FILE ANNUALLY

First day of Payroll (Month/Day/Year)

11. Check all taxes to be paid:
[ ] SALES (STATE AND LOCAL)   [ ] OIL & GAS WITHHOLDING   [ ] TOURISM PROMOTION
[ ] WAGE WITHHOLDING   [ ] RETAILER'S USE (NO COLORADO LOCATION)   [ ] COUNTY LODGING

12. If Seasonal, mark each business month
[ ] JAN [ ] FEB [ ] MAR [ ] APR [ ] MAY [ ] JUN
[ ] JUL [ ] AUG [ ] SEP [ ] OCT [ ] NOV [ ] DEC

If applying for Sales Tax License, complete these sections:

13. Filing Frequency: If sales tax collected is | First day of Business (Month/Day/Year)
[ ] UNDER $300/MONTH, FILE QUARTERLY
[ ] $300/MONTH OR MORE, FILE MONTHLY
[ ] WHOLESALE ONLY, FILE ANNUALLY

14. Indicate which applies to you:
[ ] WHOLESALER [ ] CHARITABLE [ ] SINGLE EVENT (PERIOD COVERED) (Month/Day/Year)
[ ] RETAILER [ ] MULTIPLE EVENT
LOCATION _____

15. See Instructions for Fee Schedule | FEES

Trade Name Registration If Applicable $6.00	$.
Sales Tax Deposit If Applicable $50.00	$.
Sales Tax License See Instructions	$.
Make Check Payable to the *Colorado Department of Revenue* Total	$.

If any monies are due Labor and Employment, pay with separate check to *Colorado State Treasurer.*

Continue on Reverse Side

16. Complete the following as it pertains to your business:

A. Agricultural and Crew Leaders: Have you had 10 or more employees for some portion of a day in each of 20 different calendar weeks, or paid cash wages totaling $20,000 in a calendar year? ☐ YES ☐ NO

B. Domestic Household: Have you paid cash wages totaling $1,000 to one or more household or personal employees in any calendar quarter? ☐ YES ☐ NO

C. Religious, Educational, Charitable: Are you a Non-Profit Corporation having an exemption under 501(C)(3) of the Internal Revenue Code? If YES, did you ever have four employees for some portion of a day in 20 different calendar weeks? If yes, please enclose a copy of the I.R.S. letter of exemption under 501(C)(3). ☐ YES ☐ NO

D. Other: Have you ever paid wages to an employee in the State of Colorado? ☐ YES ☐ NO

17. If you answered YES to any questions in Item 16, on what date did you meet the requirement? _____ , 19 ____
(month/day)

On what date did you first hire an employee in the year you met the requirement? _____ , 19 ____
(month/day)

Have you paid any individual that you consider contract or subcontract labor? If YES, describe occupation. ☐ YES ☐ NO

_____

If your entity is a corporation, are any officers paid wages?
(NOTE: Wages or salaries paid to corporate officers are taxable, including "dividends" paid in lieu of wages to a shareholder who performs services in an "S" Corporation). ☐ YES ☐ NO

If you did not meet any of the requirements in Item 16, do you expect to meet such requirements? ☐ YES ☐ NO
If answer is YES, when? _____ , 19 ____
(month/day)
If answer is NO, do not complete the rest of the form. Sign below and return to the Division.

18. Description of Employment Activity in COLORADO - PLACE CHECK MARK IN BOX OF CATEGORY THAT BEST DESCRIBES YOUR ACTIVITY IN COLORADO. PLEASE FURNISH A MORE DETAILED WRITTEN DESCRIPTION OF YOUR BUSINESS IN ITEM #19 BELOW.

☐ Retail Trade (list major products and who sold to)

☐ Construction (list type; general or subcontractor)

☐ Mining (list products extracted or services performed)

☐ Wholesale (list major products and who sold to)

☐ Finance, Insurance, Real Estate (describe)

☐ Government (what type)

☐ Transportation, Communication and Public Utilities (list type)

☐ Agriculture (list type of crops, animals or ag services provided)

☐ Household Domestic

☐ Service (list services provided)

☐ Manufacturing and Assembly (list products made or assembled and materials used)

☐ Other (describe)

19. Product or Services (If more than one activity, indicate major product or activity)	Percent Revenue

20. WORKSITE INFORMATION
You **MUST** complete the following for **EACH** physical location in COLORADO.
For each additional physical location, copy this section and complete all information.

Worksite Trade Name

Worksite Physical Location (Colorado Residence or Business Address)

City	County	State	Zip Code
Worksite Phone Number		Worksite Contact Person	

How many separate worksites (an economic unit, generally at a single physical location, where business is conducted, services or industrial operations are performed) will be covered under this unemployment insurance account? _____

I declare, under penalty of perjury in the second degree, that the statements made in this application are true and complete to the best of my knowledge.

Signature of Owner, Partner, or Corporate Officer	Title, If Corporate Officer	Date

DR 0590 (07/91)
COLORADO DEPARTMENT OF REVENUE
1375 Sherman Street
Denver CO 80261
(303) 534-1208
(800) 332-2085 (CO only)

TAX APPLICATION AND
TRADE NAME REGISTRATION

REGISTRATION OF A TRADE NAME WITH THIS DEPARTMENT DOES NOT ESTABLISH EXCLUSIVE RIGHTS TO THAT NAME

Who must register: Every person, general partnership, or other business organization doing business under any name other than the personal name of its owner or owners must register with the Department of Revenue. (Corporations, limited liability companies and limited partnerships register trade names with the Secretary of State.)

★ If trade name registration with the Department of Revenue is required, the information marked with a star will become public record.
SEE REVERSE SIDE FOR ADDITIONAL INFORMATION AND INSTRUCTIONS

DO NOT WRITE IN THIS SPACE
REGISTRATION/ACCOUNT NUMBER

PURPOSE

REASON FOR FILING THIS APPLICATION

- ☐ Original Application
- ☐ Change in Partners
- ☐ Change in type of ownership

Do you have another business in Colorado? ☐ Yes ☐ No

IF YES, Registration Account # _____

Do you want this number assigned to new location? ☐ Yes ☐ No

OWNERSHIP

- ★☐ Individual
- ☐ Limited Partnership
- ☐ General Partnership
- ☐ Associate
- ☐ Corporation Incorporation Date: _____
- ☐ Limited Liability Company
- ☐ Other

Did you buy this business from someone else? ☐ Yes ☐ No

BUSINESS INFORMATION

Taxpayer Name (owner, partners or other business organization) (last, first, middle)
★

Trade Name/Doing Business As (if applicable)
★

Street Address of Principal Place of Business in Colorado ★	City ★	State ★	Zip ★
County	If business is within limits of a city, what city?	Telephone ( )	
Mailing Address (if different from above) (include unit #)	City	State	Zip
County	Telephone ( )	Federal Employer I.D. # (if unavailable, S.S.#)	
Brief Description of Business/What do you sell?		Dealer's License # (if selling motor vehicles)	

SAMPLE

OWNERSHIP

(1) Owner/Partner Name (last, first, middle) If Corporation, give Corporation name ★	Social Security # (Fed. Emp. # if applicable)
Address (residence or P.O. Box, street, city, state, zip) ★	Telephone ( )
(2) Owner/Partner Name (last, first, middle) If Corporation, give Corporation name ★	Social Security # (Fed. Emp. # if applicable)
Address (residence or P.O. Box, street, city, state, zip) ★	Telephone ( )

If there are other partners, list on separate sheet using the same format.

☐ If Seasonal, mark each business month

☐ JAN ☐ FEB ☐ MAR ☐ APR ☐ MAY ☐ JUN
☐ JUL ☐ AUG ☐ SEP ☐ OCT ☐ NOV ☐ DEC

Check all taxes to be paid (see reverse side)
- ☐ State and Local Sales
- ☐ RTD/CD
- ☐ County Lodging
- ☐ Retailer's Use
- ☐ Wage Withholding
- ☐ Oil & Gas Withholding
- ☐ Tourism Promotion Fund

Do you rent items for 30 days or less? ☐ Yes ☐ No

SALES

FILING FREQUENCY: If sales tax collected is
- ☐ Under $300/month, file quarterly
- ☐ $300/month or more, file monthly
- ☐ Wholesale only, file annually

First Day of Business (MO/DAY/YR)

Indicate which applies to you
- ☐ Wholesaler
- ☐ Retailer
- ☐ Charitable
- ☐ Multiple Event

☐ Single Event - Period Covered (MO/DAY/YR) _____

Location _____

PERIOD TO BE COVERED		FEES	
FROM: MO/YR	TO: MO/YR		
		(89-09) Trade Name Registration (9)	$
		(84-16) Sales Tax Deposit (8)	$
		(83-09) Sales Tax License (9)	$

WITHHOLDING

FILING FREQUENCY: If withholding tax collected is
- ☐ Under $400/month, file quarterly
- ☐ $400/month or more, file monthly
- ☐ $399/year or less, file annually

First Day of Payroll (MO/DAY/YR)

Make check payable to the Colorado Department of Revenue

TOTAL $

I declare under penalty of perjury in the second degree that the statements made in this application are true and complete to the best of my knowledge. (Signature required below)

Signature of Owner, Partner or Corporate Officer ★	Title	Date ★

IS YOUR BUSINESS LIABLE FOR ANY OF THE FOLLOWING TAXES? IF SO, MARK THE APPROPRIATE BOX ON THE FRONT OF THE FORM.

STATE AND LOCAL SALES TAXES: State sales tax of 3% must be collected by all businesses located in Colorado. City and/or county sales taxes must also be collected if your business is located in a city or county that has a sales tax administered by the state. Call the Department of Revenue for further information or request the publication *Colorado Sales Tax Use Rates* (DRP 1002).

RTD/CD: Regional Transportation District (RTD) tax of .6% and the Scientific and Cultural Facilities (CD) tax of .1% must be collected if your business is located in the RTD/CD District (see DRP 1002).

COUNTY LODGING TAX: Certain counties levy a tax on the rental of rooms and accommodations (see DRP 1002)

TOURISM PROMOTION FUND TAX: A statewide tax of .2% is charged to businesses engaged in lodging, food and drink services, skiing, short-term automobile rentals, tour buses, and admissions to attractions (see DRP 1807).

RETAILER'S USE TAX: A use tax must be collected by vendors who have no business location in the state, but do business in the state. State 3% and RTD/CD .7% tax, if applicable, must be collected (see FYI S-5).

OIL AND GAS WITHHOLDING: Every producer of crude oil, natural gas, or oil shale shall withhold 2% from the amount owed to any person owning a working interest, a royalty interest, a production payment or any other interest in carbon dioxide or oil and gas production in Colorado. No withholding is required from payments made to Colorado or the U.S. Government. (See FYI G-4)

WAGE WITHHOLDING TAX: Is for businesses withholding state income tax from wages.

WHAT TYPE OF LICENSE DO YOU NEED?
SALES TAX (regular retail): If you sell tangible personal property at a business location in Colorado, you must have a regular retail sales tax license.

MULTIPLE EVENTS: This license is available if you engage in retail sales at more than one special event in any two-year period. There is no fee for businesses with a regular sales tax license.

SINGLE EVENT: A single events license is available for each sales event where you make retail sales if the event is at a location other than your business (if any). There is no fee for a business with a regular sales tax license.

WHOLESALERS: A wholesaler is a person selling to retail merchants, jobbers, dealers or other wholesalers for the purpose of resale.

WAGE WITHHOLDING: If you pay wages to Colorado employees and are required to withhold federal taxes, you must also withhold state taxes.

DRP and FYI Publications may be ordered by calling 534-1208 or (800) 332-2085

FEE SCHEDULE

TYPE OF LICENSE	SALES START UP DATE			
	7/1/91 to 12/31/91	1/1/92 to 12/31/93	7/1/92 to 12/31/93	1/1/93 to 12/31/93
Sales Tax— regular (retail)	4.00	16.00	12.00	8.00
PLUS deposit	----- $50.00 -----			
Wholesalers	4.00	16.00	12.00	8.00
State approved charitable org	8.00	8.00	8.00	8.00
Single Event	8.00	8.00	8.00	8.00
Multiple Event	4.00	16.00	12.00	8.00
Retailer's Use	0	0	0	0
Withholding/Severance Withholding	0	0	0	0
Tourism Promotion	0	0	0	0
County Lodging	0	0	0	0
Trade Name Registration (if applic.)	$ 6.00	(initial registration)		

FEES: The correct amount of fees must be entered on the front of this form.

DEPOSITS:
Retail Sales Tax License Applicants must pay a $50 deposit in addition to the regular fee of $16 (or prorated portion thereof). However, if the application is for an additional location of a business that already has a sales tax license, the $50 deposit is not required.

The $50 deposit is required only with regular sales tax accounts, the deposit will automatically be refunded when payment(s) of state sales tax has reached or exceeded $50. DO NOT CLAIM THE REFUND FOR THE $50 ON YOUR SALES TAX RETURN!

If your account is closed for any reason before you have collected and paid $50 in state sales tax, only the amount of Colorado tax you have paid will be refunded.

A temporary sales tax license may be obtained when this application and appropriate fees are presented at one of the locations listed below:

NEW BUSINESS ASSISTANCE SERVICE CENTER
1560 Broadway, Suite 1530
Denver CO 80202
(303) 592-5920/800-333-7798

COLORADO SPRINGS DISTRICT OFFICE
2762 Airport Road
Colorado Springs, CO 80910
(719) 632-8812

DURANGO DISTRICT OFFICE
1474 Main Street, P.O. Box 277
Durango, CO 81301
(303) 259-4342

FORT COLLINS DISTRICT OFFICE
300 E Foothills Pky
Fort Collins, CO 80525
(303) 223-1097

GLENWOOD SPRINGS DISTRICT OFFICE
406 S. Hyland Park Drive, Suite C
Glenwood Springs, CO 81601
(303) 945-1222 /800-221-6042

GRAND JUNCTION DISTRICT OFFICE
222 S. Sixth Street, Room 208
Grand Junction, CO 81501
(303) 248-7140

GREELEY DISTRICT OFFICE
800 Eighth Avenue, Suite 224
Greeley, CO 80631
(303) 352-1165

PUEBLO DISTRICT OFFICE
720 N. Main St., Suite 402
Pueblo, CO 81003
(719) 542-2920

The Department of Revenue offers Sales and Withholding tax classes. Interested taxpayers should call 534-1208 for time and place.
Withholding Tax Class: Every 2nd and 4th Wednesday of the month.
Sales Tax Class: Every Friday (AM) and the 2nd Thursday (PM) of the month.

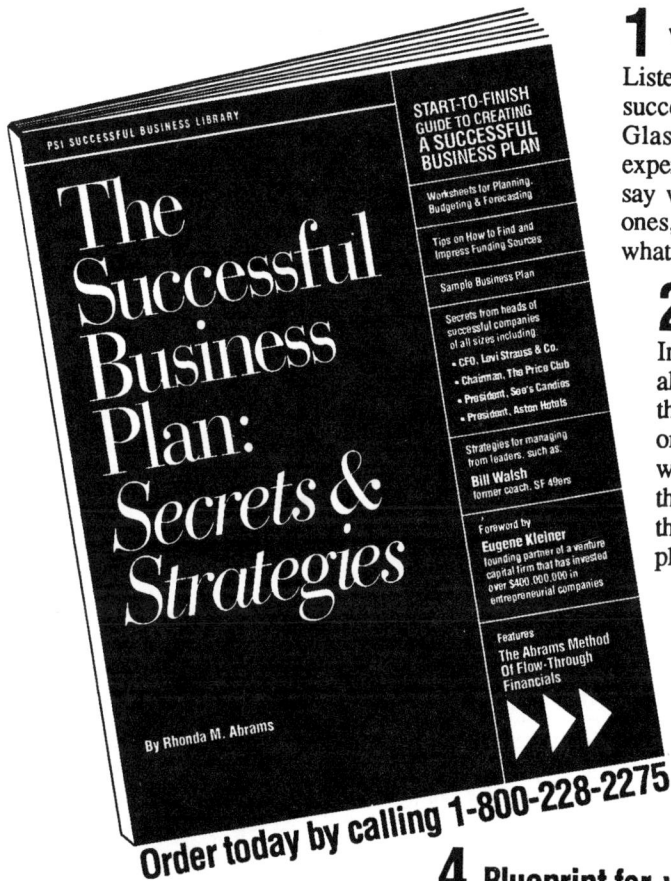

Gain the power of increased knowledge — Oasis is your source.

Acquiring Outside Capital

Financing Your Small Business

Book

Essential techniques to successfully identify, approach, attract, and manage sources of financing. Shows how to gain the full benefits of debt financing while minimizing its risks. Outlines all types of financing and walks you step by step through the process, from evaluating short-term credit options, through negotiating a long-term loan, to deciding whether to go public.

The Loan Package

Book

Preparatory package for a business loan proposal. Worksheets help analyze cash needs and articulate business focus. Includes sample forms for balance sheets, income statements, projections, and budget reports. Screening sheets rank potential lenders to shorten the time involved in getting the loan.

Venture Capital Proposal Package

Book

Structures a proposal to secure venture capital. Checklists gather material for required sections: market analyses, income projections, financial statements, management team, strategic marketing plan, etc. Gives tips on understanding, finding, and screening potential investors.

Financial Templates

Software for IBM-PC & Macintosh

Software speeds business calculations including those in PSI's workbooks, *The Loan Package, Venture Capital Proposal Package, Negotiating the Purchase or Sale of a Business, The Successful Business Plan: Secrets & Strategies.* Includes 40 financial templates including various projections, statements, ratios, histories, amortizations, and cash flows. *Requires Lotus 1-2-3, Microsoft Excel 2.0 or higher, Supercalc 5, or Lotus compatible spreadsheet and 512 RAM plus hard disk or two floppy drives.*

Managing Employees

A Company Policy and Personnel Workbook

Book

Saves costly consultant or staff hours in creating company personnel policies. Provides model policies on topics such as employee safety, leave of absence, flextime, smoking, substance abuse, sexual harassment, performance improvement, grievance procedure. For each subject, practical and legal ramifications are explained, then a choice of alternate policies presented.

A Company Policy and Personnel Workbook

Software for IBM-PC & Macintosh

The policies in *A Company Policy and Personnel Workbook* are on disk so the company's name, specific information, and any desired changes or rewrites can be incorporated using your own word processor to tailor the model policies to suit your company's specific needs before printing out a complete manual for distribution to employees. *Requires a word processor and hard disk and floppy drive.*

People Investment: How to Make Your Hiring Decisions Pay Off for Everyone

Book — available September 1992

Makes the hiring process easier for small business owners. Clarifies the processes of determining personnel needs; establishing job descriptions that satisfy legal requirements; and advertising for, selecting, and keeping good people. Over 40 worksheets help forecast staffing needs, define each job, recruit employees, and train staff.

Managing People: A Practical Guide

Book

Focuses on developing the art of working with people to maximize the productivity and satisfaction of both manager and employees. Discussions, exercises, and self-tests boost skills in communicating, delegating, motivating, developing teams, goal-setting, adapting to change, and coping with stress.

Safety Law Compliance Manual for California Businesses

Book plus optional binder for your company's safety program

Now every California employer must have an Injury and Illness Prevention Program that meets the specific requirements of Senate Bill 198. Already thousands of citations have been issued to companies who did not comply with all seven components of the complicated new law. Avoid fines by using this guide to set up a program that will meet Cal/OSHA standards. Includes forms.

Also available — Company Illness and Injury Prevention Program Binder — Pre-organized and ready-to-use with forms, tabs, logs and sample documents. Saves your company time, work, and worry.

Mail Order

Mail Order Legal Manual

Book

For companies that use the mail to market their products or services, as well as for mail order businesses, this book clarifies complex regulations so penalties can be avoided. Gives state-by-state legal requirements, plus information on Federal Trade Commission guidelines and rules covering delivery dates, advertising, sales taxes, unfair trade practices, and consumer protection.

Why hesitate? If any product you order doesn't meet your needs, just return it for full refund or credit. 800-228-2275.

Proven tools and ideas to expand your business.

Marketing & Public Relations

EXECARDS®
Business Communication Tools

EXECARDS, the original business-to-business message cards, help build and maintain personal business relationships with customers and prospects. Distinctive in size and quality, EXECARDS get through even when other mail is tossed. An effective alternative to telephone tag. Time-saving EXECARDS come in a variety of handsome styles and messages. Excellent for thanking clients, following up between orders, prospecting, and announcing new products, services, or special offers. *Please call for complete catalog.*

How To Develop & Market Creative Business Ideas
Book

Step-by-step manual guides the inventor through all stages of new product development. Discusses patenting your invention, trademarks, copyrights, and how to construct your prototype. Gives information on financing, distribution, test marketing, and finding licensees. Plus, lists many useful sources for prototype resources, trade shows, funding, and more.

Marketing Your Products and Services Successfully
Book

Helps small businesses understand marketing concepts, then plan and follow through with the actions that will result in increased sales. Covers all aspects from identifying the target market, through market research, establishing pricing, creating a marketing plan, evaluating media alternatives, to launching a campaign. Discusses customer maintenance techniques and international marketing.

Customer Profile and Retrieval (CPR)
Software for IBM-PC & compatibles

Stores details of past activities plus future reminders on customers, clients, contacts, vendors, and employees, then gives instant access to that information when needed. "Tickler" fields keep reminders of dates for recontacts. "Type" fields categorize names for sorting as the user defines. "Other data" fields store information such as purchase and credit history, telephone call records, or interests.

Has massive storage capabilities. Holds up to 255 lines of comments for each name, plus unlimited time and date stamped notes. Features perpetual calendar, and automatic telephone dialing. Built-in word processing and merge gives the ability to pull in the information already keyed into the fields into form or individual letters. Prints mail labels, rotary file cards, and phone directories. *Requires a hard disk, 640K RAM and 80 column display. (Autodial feature requires modem.)*

Publicity and Public Relations Guide for Businesses
Book

Overview of how to promote a business by using advertising, publicity, and public relations. Especially for business owners and managers who choose to have promotional activities carried out by in-house staff rather than outside specialists. Includes worksheets for a public relations plan, news releases, editorial article, and a communications schedule.

Cost-Effective Market Analysis
Book

Workbook explains how a small business can conduct its own market research. Shows how to set objectives, determine which techniques to use, create a schedule, and then monitor expenses. Encompasses primary research (trade shows, telephone interviews, mail surveys), plus secondary research (using available information in print).

International Business

Export Now
Book

Prepares a business to enter the export market. Clearly explains the basics, then articulates specific requirements for export licensing, preparation of documents, payment methods, packaging, and shipping. Includes advice on evaluating foreign representatives, planning international marketing strategies, and discovering official U.S. policy for various countries and regions. Lists sources.

EXECARDS®
International Communication Cards

EXECARDS offer unique cards you can send to businesspeople of many nationalities to help build and maintain lasting relationships. One distinguished EXECARD choice is a richly textured and embossed white card of substantial quality that expresses thank you in thirteen languages; Japanese, Russian, French, Chinese, Arabic, German, Swahili, Italian, Polish, Spanish, Hebrew, and Swedish, as well as English. Another handsome option is an ivory card with thank you embossed in Russian and English. To each, you can add a personal note or order a custom printed message. *Please call for more information.*

Give yourself & your business every chance to succeed. Order the business tools you need today. Call 800-228-2275.

Unique cards get you noticed. Books & software save you time.

Business Communications

Proposal Development: How to Respond and Win the Bid

Book

Orchestrates a successful proposal from preliminary planning to clinching the deal. Shows by explanation and example how to: determine what to include; create text, illustrations, tables, exhibits, and appendices; how to format (using either traditional methods or desktop publishing); meet the special requirements of government proposals; set up and follow a schedule.

Write Your Own Business Contracts

Book

Explains the "do's" and "don'ts" of contract writing so any person in business can do the preparatory work in drafting contracts before hiring an attorney for final review. Gives a working knowledge of the various types of business agreements, plus tips on how to prepare for the unexpected.

Complete Book of Business Forms

Book

Over 200 reproducible forms for all types of business needs: personnel, employment, finance, production flow, operations, sales, marketing, order entry, and general administration. Time-saving, uniform, coordinated way to record and locate important business information.

EXECARDS®

Communication Tools

EXECARDS, business-to-business message cards, are an effective vehicle for maintaining personal contacts in this era of rushed, highly-technical communications. A card takes only seconds and a few cents to send, but can memorably tell customers, clients, prospects, or co-workers that their relationship is valued. Many styles and messages to choose from for thanking, acknowledging, inviting, reminding, prospecting, following up, etc. *Please call for complete catalog.*

PlanningTools™

Paper pads, 3-hole punched

Handsome PlanningTools help organize thoughts and record notes, actions, plans, and deadlines, so important information and responsibilities do not get lost or forgotten. Specific PlanningTools organize different needs, such as Calendar Notes, Progress/Activity Record, Project Plan/Record, Week's Priority Planner, Make-A-Month Calendar, and Milestone Chart. *Please call for catalog.*

Customer Profile & Retrieval (CPR)

Software for IBM-PC & compatibles

Easy computer database management program streamlines the process of communicating with clients, customers, vendors, contacts, and employees. While talking to your contact on the phone (or at any time), all notes of past activities and conversations can be viewed instantly, and new notes can be added at that time. *Please see description under "Marketing & Public Relations" section on previous page.*

Business Relocation

Company Relocation Handbook: Making the Right Move

Book

Comprehensive guide to moving a business. Begins with defining objectives for moving and evaluating whether relocating will actually solve more problems than it creates. Worksheets compare prospective locations, using rating scales for physical plant, equipment, personnel, and geographic considerations. Sets up a schedule for dealing with logistics.

Retirement Planning

Retirement & Estate Planning Handbook

Book

Do-it-yourself workbook for setting up a retirement plan that can easily be maintained and followed. Covers establishing net worth, retirement goals, budgets, and a plan for asset acquisition, preservation, and growth. Discusses realistic expectations for Social Security, Medicare, and health care alternatives. Features special sections for business owners.

Career Recordkeeping

Career Builder

Book

This workbook collects all of an individual's career-related data in one place for quick access. From educational details, through work history, health records, reference lists, correspondence awards, passports, etc., to personal insurance policies, real estate, securities and bank accounts, this manual keeps it all organized. Gives tips on successful resumés.

Need it tomorrow? In most cases that's possible if you order before noon, PST. Just give us a call at 800-228-2275.

Step-by-step techniques for generating more profit.

Financial Management

Financial Management Techniques for Small Business

Book

Clearly reveals the essential ingredients of sound financial management in detail. By monitoring trends in your financial activities, you will be able to uncover potential problems before they become crises. You'll understand why you can be making a profit and still not have the cash to meet expenses, and you'll learn the steps to change your business' cash behavior to get more return for your effort.

Risk Analysis: How to Reduce Insurance Costs

Book

Straightforward advice on shopping for insurance, understanding types of coverage, comparing proposals and premium rates. Worksheets help identify and weigh the risks a particular business is likely to face, then determine if any of those might be safely self-insured or eliminated. Request for proposal form helps businesses avoid over-paying for protection.

Debt Collection: Strategies for the Small Business

Book

Practical tips on how to turn receivables into cash. Worksheets and checklists help businesses establish credit policies, track accounts, and flag when it is necessary to bring in a collection agency, attorney, or go to court. This book advises how to deal with disputes, negotiate settlements, win in small claims court, and collect on judgments. Gives examples of telephone collection techniques and collection letters.

Negotiating the Purchase or Sale of a Business

Book

Prepares a business buyer or seller for negotiations that will achieve win-win results. Shows how to determine the real worth of a business, including intangible assets such as "goodwill." Over 36 checklists and worksheets on topics such as tax impact on buyers and sellers, escrow checklist, cash flow projections, evaluating potential buyers, financing options, and many others.

Financial Accounting Guide for Small Business

Book

Makes understanding the economics of business simple. Explains the basic accounting principles that relate to any business. Step-by-step instructions for generating accounting statements and interpreting them, spotting errors, and recognizing warning signs. Discusses how banks and other creditors view financial statements.

Controlling Your Company's Freight Costs

Book

Shows how to increase company profits by trimming freight costs. Provides tips for comparing alternative methods and shippers, then negotiating contracts to receive the most favorable discounts. Tells how to package shipments for safe transport. Discusses freight insurance and dealing with claims for loss or damage. Appendices include directory of U.S. ports, shipper's guide, and sample bill of lading.

Accounting Software Analysis

Book

Presents successful step-by-step procedure for choosing the most appropriate software to handle the accounting for your business. Evaluation forms and worksheets create a custom software "shopping list" to match against features of various products, so facts, not sales hype, can determine the best fit for your company.

Financial Templates
Software for IBM-PC & Macintosh

Calculates and graphs many business "what-if" scenarios and financial reports. Forty financial templates such as income statements, cash flow, and balance sheet comparisons, break-even analyses, product contribution comparisons, market share, net present value, sales model, *pro formas*, loan payment projections, etc. *Requires 512K RAM hard disk or two floppy drives, plus Lotus 1-2-3 or compatible spreadsheet program.*

Yes, we accept credit cards — VISA, MasterCard, American Express, Discover, or your personal or business check.

The Successful Business Plan: Secrets & Strategies

Book

Start-to-finish guide to creating a successful business plan. Includes tips from venture capitalists, bankers, and successful CEOs. Features worksheets for ease in planning and budgeting with the Abrams Method of Flow-Through Financials. Gives a sample business plan, plus specialized help for retailers, service companies, manufacturers, and in-house corporate plans. Also tells how to find funding sources.

Starting and Operating a Business In... series
Book available for each state in the United States, plus District of Columbia

One-stop resource to current federal and state laws and regulations that affect businesses. Clear "human language" explanations of complex issues, plus samples of government forms, and sources for additional help or information. Helps seasoned business owners keep up with changing legislation, and guides new entrepreneurs step-by-step to start and run the business. Includes many checklists and worksheets to organize ideas, create action plans, and project financial scenarios.

Starting and Operating a Business: U.S. Edition
Set of eleven binders

The complete encyclopedia of how to do business in the U.S. Describes laws and regulations for each state, plus Washington, D.C., as well as the federal government. Includes lists of sources of help, plus post cards for requesting materials from government agencies. This set is valuable for businesses with locations or marketing activities in several states, plus franchisors, attorneys, and other consultants.

The Essential Corporation Handbook

Book

This comprehensive reference for small business corporations in all 50 states and Washington, D.C. explains the legal requirements for maintaining a corporation in good standing. Features many sample corporate documents which are annotated by the author to show what to look for and what to look out for. Tells how to avoid personal liability as an officer, director, or shareholder.

Surviving and Prospering in a Business Partnership

Book

From evaluation of potential partners, through the drafting of agreements, to day-to-day management of working relationships, this book helps avoid classic partnership catastrophes. Discusses how to set up the partnership to reduce the financial and emotional consequences of unanticipated disputes, dishonesty, divorce, disability, or death of a partner.

California Corporation Formation Package and Minute Book Book and software
for IBM & Mac

Provides forms required for incorporating and maintaining closely held corporations, including: articles of incorporation; bylaws; stock certificates, stock transfer record sheets, bill of sale agreement; minutes form; plus many others. Addresses questions on fees, timing, notices, regulations, election of directors and other critical factors. Software has minutes, bylaws, and articles of incorporation already for you to edit and customize (using your own word processor).

Franchise Bible: A Comprehensive Guide

Book

Complete guide to franchising for prospective franchisees or for business owners considering franchising their business. Includes actual sample documents, such as a complete offering circular, plus worksheets for evaluating franchise companies, locations, and organizing information before seeing an attorney. This book is helpful for lawyers as well as their clients.

How To Develop & Market Creative Business Ideas

Book

Step-by-step manual guides the inventor through all stages of new product development. Discusses patenting your invention, trademarks, copyrights, and how to construct your prototype. Gives information on financing, distribution, test marketing, and finding licensees. Plus, lists many useful sources for prototype resources, trade shows, funding, and more.

The Small Business Expert
Software for IBM-PC & compatibles

Generates comprehensive custom checklist of the state and federal laws and regulations based on your type and size of business. Allows comparison of doing business in each of the 50 states. Built-in worksheets create outlines for personnel policies, marketing feasibility studies, and a business plan draft. *Requires 256K RAM and hard disk.*

To order these business tools, use the enclosed order form, FAX 503-476-1479 or call us toll-free at 800-228-2275

PSI Successful Business Library / Tools for Business Success Order Form (Please fill out other side also)

BOOKS FROM THE OASIS PRESS® Please check the edition (binder or paperback) of your choice

TITLE	BINDER	PAPERBACK	QUANTITY	COST
Accounting Software Analysis	☐ $ 39.95			
California Corporation Formation Package and Minute Book	☐ $ 39.95	☐ $ 29.95		
Career Builder	☐ $ 34.95	☐ $ 12.95		
A Company Policy and Personnel Workbook	☐ $ 49.95	☐ $ 29.95		
Company Relocation Handbook	☐ $ 49.95	☐ $ 19.95		
Complete Book of Business Forms	☐ $ 49.95	☐ $ 19.95		
Controlling Your Company's Freight Costs	☐ $ 39.95			
Cost-Effective Market Analysis	☐ $ 39.95			
Debt Collection: Strategies for the Small Business	☐ $ 39.95	☐ $ 17.95		
The Essential Corporation Handbook		☐ $ 19.95		
Export Now	☐ $ 39.95	☐ $ 19.95		
Financial Accounting Guide For Small Business	☐ $ 39.95			
Financial Management Techniques For Small Business	☐ $ 39.95	☐ $ 19.95		
Financing Your Small Business		☐ $ 19.95		
Franchise Bible: A Comprehensive Guide	☐ $ 49.95	☐ $ 19.95		
How to Develop & Market Creative Business Ideas		☐ $ 14.95		
The Loan Package	☐ $ 39.95			
Mail Order Legal Manual	☐ $ 45.00			
Managing People: A Practical Guide	☐ $ 49.95	☐ $ 19.95		
Marketing Your Products and Services Successfully	☐ $ 39.95	☐ $ 18.95		
Negotiating the Purchase or Sale of a Business	☐ $ 39.95	☐ $ 18.95		
People Investment: How to Make Your Hiring Decisions Pay Off for Everyone	☐ $ 49.95	☐ $ 19.95		
Proposal Development: How to Respond and Win the Bid (HARDBACK BOOK)	☐ $ 39.95			
Publicity & Public Relations Guide For Businesses	☐ $ 39.95			
Retirement & Estate Planning Handbook	☐ $ 49.95	☐ $ 19.95		
Risk Analysis: How To Reduce Insurance Costs	☐ $ 39.95	☐ $ 18.95		
Safety Law Compliance Manual for California Businesses		☐ $ 24.95		
Company Illness & Injury Prevention Program Binder (OR GET **KIT** WITH BOOK AND BINDER $49.95)	☐ $ 34.95	☐ $ 49.95 BOOK & BINDER KIT		
Starting and Operating A Business in... BOOK INCLUDES FEDERAL SECTION PLUS ONE STATE SECTION —	☐ $ 29.95	☐ $ 21.95		
PLEASE SPECIFY WHICH STATE(S) YOU WANT:				
STATE SECTION ONLY (BINDER NOT INCLUDED) — SPECIFY STATES:	☐ $ 8.95			
U.S. EDITION (FEDERAL SECTION — 50 STATES AND WASHINGTON, D.C. IN 11-BINDER SET)	☐ $295.00			
Successful Business Plan: Secrets & Strategies (GET THE BINDER...IT'S A BUSINESS PLAN KIT)	☐ $ 49.95	☐ $ 21.95		
Surviving and Prospering in a Business Partnership	☐ $ 39.95	☐ $ 19.95		
Venture Capital Proposal Package	☐ $ 39.95			
Write Your Own Business Contracts (HARDBACK BOOK)	☐ $ 39.95	☐ $ 19.95		

BOOK TOTAL (Please enter on other side also for grand total)

SOFTWARE Please check whether you use Macintosh or 5-1/4" or 3-1/2" Disk for IBM-PC & Compatibles

TITLE	5-1/4" IBM Disk	3-1/2" IBM Disk	MAC	PRICE	QUANTITY	COST
California Corporation Formation Package Software	☐	☐	☐	☐ $ 69.95		
★ California Corporation Formation Binderbook & Software	☐	☐	☐	☐ $ 89.95		
Company Policy & Personnel Software	☐	☐	☐	☐ $ 99.95		
★ Company Policy Binderbook & Software	☐	☐	☐	☐ $129.95		
Customer Profile & Retrieval: Professional	☐	☐		☐ $149.95		
Financial Templates	☐	☐	☐	☐ $ 69.95		
The Small Business Expert	☐	☐		☐ $ 59.95		

SOFTWARE TOTAL (Please enter on other side also for grand total)

Please add above totals on other side to complete your order.

SO 4/15/92

PSI Successful Business Library / Tools for Business Success Order Form (please see other side also)
Call, Mail or Fax to: PSI Research, 300 North Valley Drive, Grants Pass, OR 97526 USA
Order Phone USA (800) 228-2275   Inquiries and International Orders (503) 479-9464   FAX (503) 476-1479

Sold to: PLEASE GIVE STREET ADDRESS NOT P.O. BOX FOR SHIPPING

Name _____

Title _____

Company _____

Street Address _____

City/State/Zip _____

Daytime Telephone _____

Ship to: (if different) **PLEASE GIVE STREET ADDRESS NOT P.O. BOX FOR SHIPPING**

Name _____

Title _____

Company _____

Street Address _____

City/State/Zip _____

Daytime Telephone _____

Payment Information:

☐ Check enclosed payable to PSI Research (When you enclose a check, UPS ground shipping is free within the Continental U.S.A.)

Charge - ☐ VISA ☐ MASTERCARD ☐ AMEX ☐ DISCOVER   Card Number: _____ Expires ____

Signature: _____   Name on card:_____

EXECARDS — The Proven & Chosen Method of Personal Business Communications

ITEM	PRICE EACH	QUANTITY	COST
EXECARDS Thank You Assortment (12 assorted thank you cards)	$ 12.95		
EXECARDS Recognition Assortment (12 assorted appreciation cards)	$ 12.95		
EXECARDS Marketing Assortment (12 assorted marketing cards)	$ 12.95		
EXECARDS TOTAL (Please enter below also for grand total)			$

Many additional options available, including custom imprinting of your company's name, logo or message. Please request a complete catalog.

PLANNING TOOLS — Action Tracking Note Pads

ITEM		NUMBER OF PADS
Calendar Note Pad	☐ 1992	
	☐ 92/93	
	☐ 1993	
☐ Progress/Activity		
☐ Make-A-Month		
☐ Milestone Chart		
☐ Project Plan/Record		
☐ Week's Priority Planner		
Total number of pads		
Multiply by unit price:	x	
PLANNING TOOLS TOTAL	$	

UNIT PRICE FOR ANY COMBINATION OF PLANNING TOOLS

1-9 pads	$3.95 each
10-49 pads	$3.49 each
50 or more pads	$2.98 each

YOUR GRAND TOTAL

BOOK TOTAL (from other side)	$
SOFTWARE TOTAL (from other side)	$
EXECARDS TOTAL	$
PLANNING TOOLS TOTAL	$
TOTAL ORDER	$

Rush service is available. Please call us for details.

Please send me:

_____ EXECARDS Catalog

_____ Oasis Press Software Information

_____ Oasis Press Book Information

SO 4/15/92

Use this form to register for advance notification of updates, new books and software releases, plus special customer discounts!

Please answer these questions to let us know how our products are working for you, and what we could do to serve you better.

Title of book or software purchased from us:_____

It is a:
- ☐ Binder book
- ☐ Paperback book
- ☐ Book/software combination
- ☐ Software only

Rate this product's overall quality of information:
- ☐ Excellent
- ☐ Good
- ☐ Fair
- ☐ Poor

Rate the quality of printed materials:
- ☐ Excellent
- ☐ Good
- ☐ Fair
- ☐ Poor

Rate the format:
- ☐ Excellent
- ☐ Good
- ☐ Fair
- ☐ Poor

Did the product provide what you needed?
- ☐ Yes ☐ No

If not, what should be added?_____
_____
_____
_____
_____

This product is:
- ☐ Clear and easy to follow
- ☐ Too complicated
- ☐ Too elementary

Were the worksheets (if any) easy to use?
- ☐ Yes ☐ No ☐ N/A

Should we include:
- ☐ More worksheets
- ☐ Fewer worksheets
- ☐ No worksheets

How do you feel about the price?
- ☐ Lower than expected
- ☐ About right
- ☐ Too expensive

How many employees are in your company?
- ☐ Under 10 employees
- ☐ 10 – 50 employees
- ☐ 51 – 99 employees
- ☐ 100 – 250 employees
- ☐ Over 250 employees

How many people in the city your company is in?
- ☐ 50,000 – 100,000
- ☐ 100,000 – 500,000
- ☐ 500,000 – 1,000,000
- ☐ Over 1,000,000
- ☐ Rural (under 50,000)

What is your type of business?
- ☐ Retail
- ☐ Service
- ☐ Government
- ☐ Manufacturing
- ☐ Distributor
- ☐ Education

What types of products or services do you sell?
_____
_____
_____
_____

What is your position in the company?
(please check one)
- ☐ Owner
- ☐ Administration
- ☐ Sales/marketing
- ☐ Finance
- ☐ Human resources
- ☐ Production
- ☐ Operations
- ☐ Computer/MIS

How did you learn about this product?
- ☐ Recommended by a friend
- ☐ Used in a seminar or class
- ☐ Have used other PSI products
- ☐ Received a mailing
- ☐ Saw in bookstore
- ☐ Saw in library
- ☐ Saw review in:
  - ☐ Newspaper
  - ☐ Magazine
  - ☐ TV/Radio

Where did you buy this product?
- ☐ Catalog
- ☐ Bookstore
- ☐ Office supply
- ☐ Consultant
- ☐ Other_____

Would you purchase other business tools from us?
- ☐ Yes ☐ No

If so, which products interest you?
- ☐ EXECARDS® Communication Tools
- ☐ Books for business
- ☐ Software

Would you recommend this product to a friend?
- ☐ Yes ☐ No

If you'd like us to send associates or friends a catalog, just list names and addresses on back.

Do you use a personal computer for business?
- ☐ Yes ☐ No

If yes, which?
- ☐ IBM/compatible
- ☐ Macintosh

Check all the ways you use computers:
- ☐ Word processing
- ☐ Accounting
- ☐ Spreadsheet
- ☐ Inventory
- ☐ Order processing
- ☐ Design/graphics
- ☐ General data base
- ☐ Customer information
- ☐ Scheduling

May we call you to follow up on your comments?
- ☐ Yes ☐ No

May we add your name to our mailing list?
- ☐ Yes ☐ No

If there is anything you think we should do to improve this product, please describe:_____
_____
_____
_____

Thank you for your patience in answering the above questions.
Just fill in your name and address here, fold (see back) and mail.

Name_____
Title_____
Company_____
Phone_____
Address_____
City/State/Zip_____

PSI Research creates this family of fine products to help you more easily and effectively manage your business activities:

The Oasis Press®
PSI Successful Business Library

PSI Successful Business Software
EXECARDS® Communication Tools

If you have friends or associates who might appreciate receiving our catalogs, please list here. Thanks!

Name_____   Name_____

Title_____   Title_____

Company_____   Company_____

Phone_____   Phone_____

Address_____   Address_____

City/State/Zip_____   City/State/Zip_____

FOLD HERE FIRST

NO POSTAGE
NECESSARY
IF MAILED
IN THE
UNITED STATES

BUSINESS REPLY MAIL

FIRST CLASS MAIL PERMIT NO. 002 MERLIN, OREGON

POSTAGE WILL BE PAID BY ADDRESSEE

PSI Research
PO BOX 1414
Merlin OR 97532-9900

FOLD HERE SECOND, THEN TAPE TOGETHER

Please cut
along this
vertical line,
fold twice,
tape together
and mail.
Thanks!

Snapshot Market Report

Avoid the mistake of opening a business that has too many competitors or not enough population to support your business. Get instant information about the type of business you want to start or about the one you are already operating.

You get specific information about comparable businesses in your city, county or metropolitan area. You get information to compare your business with other similar businesses in your area. This information will be helpful for your business or marketing plans, discussions with your bankers, or annual comparisons to see how your business is doing relative to other similar businesses.

You get the following information with comparisons between the city and county, county and state, or metropolitan area and state.

- Number of establishments
- Retail sales (000s)
- Average sales per establishment (000s)
- Sales per employee (000s)
- Number of people in the area
- Total income per person
- Average dollar expenditures per person for this type of business
- Population density (persons per square mile)
- Total square miles
- Retail density (persons per store)
- Amount spent from persons outside the area (000s)

Easy procedures to obtain your information for only $25 (by mail) or $30 (by FAX).

1. Identify your business by SIC code. If you don't know the code we can help you determine it.

2. Indicate how you want the comparison made:

City/Town level - This report allows you to look at a particular business category in a city or town where the population is 2,500 or more. The categories that are available is dependent on the total number of businesses in that area. The largest cities generally contain over 330 retail and service categories. The city/town is then compared to the county in which it is located .
County level - This report alow you to compare business category in the county with that of Metroplitan Statistical Area (MSA) or if the county is not in an MSA, the comparison is with the state.
Metro Area level - The report allows you to look at a particular retail category in a Metropolitan area and compare it with the state.

There are some minimums for the number of establishments in a given area for the information to be available. Some businesses will not have information available if the number of businesses is fewer than 10 in an area. Therefore, depending on the business information you are after, you may need to go to a higher level of reporting to get the comparisons you want. For example, your city may have three video stores. If so, data will not be available for the city. Your comparison will be between the county and state or the Metro area and the state.

Call 1-800-228-2275 to place your request.

✂ Cut out these post cards along the dashed lines. Just write in the information on reverse side, add your return address, then apply the proper postage and drop in the mail.

Name

Title

Company

Address

City

State & Zip

Affix
Stamp
Here

Small Business Hotline
1560 Broadway, Suite 1530
Denver, CO 80202

Name

Title

Company

Address

City

State & Zip

Affix
Stamp
Here

Division of Property Taxation
Colorado Department of Local Affairs
1313 Sherman Street, Suite 419
Denver, CO 80203

Name

Title

Company

Address

City

State & Zip

Affix
Stamp
Here

Labor Standards Unit
Colorado Division of Labor
1120 Lincoln, Room 1302
Denver, CO 80203-2140

Name

Title

Company

Address

City

State & Zip

Affix
Stamp
Here

Taxpayer Service Division
Colorado Department of Revenue
1375 Sherman Street, Room 186
Denver, CO 80261

Attn: Small Business Hotline

Please send me:

☐ *Colorado Business Start-up Kit*

☐ *Articles of Incorporation (forms)*

☐ *Loan Programs for Small Business*

Name _____

Title _____

Company _____

Address _____

City _____ State _____ Zip _____

Post card provided by The Oasis Press, 300 North Valley Drive, Grants Pass, OR 97526   5/92

Attn: Labor Standards Unit

Please send me:

☐ A copy of the Colorado Youth Employment Act

☐ A copy of the Colorado Wage Law

☐ A copy of the Colorado Wage Order (Minimum Wage) and poster

☐ Posters required to be displayed by employers

Name _____

Title _____

Company _____

Address _____

City _____ State _____ Zip _____

Post card provided by The Oasis Press, 300 North Valley Drive, Grants Pass, OR 97526   5/92

Attn: Division of Property Taxation

Please send me:

☐ *Understanding Property Taxes*

☐ *Property Valuation and Taxation for Business and Industry*

Name _____

Title _____

Company _____

Address _____

City _____ State _____ Zip _____

Post card provided by The Oasis Press, 300 North Valley Drive, Grants Pass, OR 97526   5/92

Attn: Taxpayer Service Division

Please send me:

☐ A list of Colorado Department of Revenue publications

☐ *Colorado Withholding Tables*

☐ *Colorado Sales and Use Tax General Information and Instruction Booklet*

Name _____

Title _____

Company _____

Address _____

City _____ State _____ Zip _____

Post card provided by The Oasis Press, 300 North Valley Drive, Grants Pass, OR 97526   5/92

✂ Cut out these post cards along the dashed lines. Just write in the information on reverse side, add your return address, then apply the proper postage and drop in the mail.

Name
Title
Company
Address
City
State & Zip

Affix
Stamp
Here

Attn: Communications Dept. – CWS4
Pacific Bell Directory
101 Spear Street, Room 429
San Francisco, CA 94105

Name
Title
Company
Address
City
State & Zip

Affix
Stamp
Here

U.S. Small Business Administration
Office of Business Development
Sixth Floor
409 3rd Street, SW
Washington, DC 20416

Name
Title
Company
Address
City
State & Zip

Affix
Stamp
Here

U.S. Department of Labor
ESA/Office of Public Affairs
Room C 4325
200 Constitution Avenue, NW
Washington, DC 20210

Name
Title
Company
Address
City
State & Zip

Affix
Stamp
Here

U.S. Department of Labor
OSHA Publications Office
200 Constitution Avenue, NW
Washington, DC 20210

Attn: Communications Dept. – CWS4

Please send me:

☐ A complimentary copy of *Small Business Success*

Name _____

Title _____

Company _____

Address _____

City _____ State _____ Zip _____

Post card provided by The Oasis Press, 300 North Valley Drive, Grants Pass, OR 97526 6/93

Attn: U.S. Small Business Administration

Please send me:

☐ A list of the Business Development publications you offer (SBA 115A)

Name _____

Title _____

Company _____

Address _____

City _____ State _____ Zip _____

Post card provided by The Oasis Press, 300 North Valley Drive, Grants Pass, OR 97526 6/93

Attn: U.S. Department of Labor – ESA/OPA

Please send me:

☐ Your most current version of *Your Rights Under the Fair Labor Standards Act* (WH Publication 1088)

Name _____

Title _____

Company _____

Address _____

City _____ State _____ Zip _____

Post card provided by The Oasis Press, 300 North Valley Drive, Grants Pass, OR 97526 6/93

Attn: U.S. Department of Labor – OSHA

Please send me:

☐ A list of free OSHA publications available from the OSHA Publications Office.

☐ A list of OSHA publications available from the Government Printing Office for a small fee.

Name _____

Title _____

Company _____

Address _____

City _____ State _____ Zip _____

Post card provided by The Oasis Press, 300 North Valley Drive, Grants Pass, OR 97526 6/93

✂ Cut out these post cards along the dashed lines. Just write in the information on reverse side, add your return address, then apply the proper postage and drop in the mail.

Name
Title
Company
Address
City
State & Zip

Corporate Agents, Inc.
1013 Centre Road
P.O. Box 1281
Wilmington, DE 19899

Name
Title
Company
Address
City
State & Zip

The Oasis Press
300 North Valley Drive
Grants Pass, OR 97526

Name
Title
Company
Address
City
State & Zip

Equal Employment Opportunity Commission
2401 E Street
Washington, DC 20507

Name
Title
Company
Address
City
State & Zip

PSI Research
300 North Valley Drive
Grants Pass, OR 97526